SECRET IDENTITIES

An Unofficial and Unauthorised
Guide to *Alias*

SECRET IDENTITIES

An Unofficial and Unauthorised Guide to *Alias*

Mark Clapham and
Lance Parkin

Virgin BOOKS

This edition first published in 2003 by
Virgin Books Ltd
Thames Wharf Studios
Rainville Road
London
W6 9HA

A catalogue record for this book is available from the British Library.

ISBN 0 7535 0896 6

Typeset by TW Typesetting, Plymouth, Devon
Printed and bound by CPI Antony Rowe, Eastbourne

Contents

Introduction

There's nothing worse, nothing more disappointing, than someone or something turning out to be *less* than it appears or promises to be. Conversely, there's nothing more charming than something that comes along, and surprises you with a depth you wouldn't have guessed was there.

That's *Alias*, a television programme that proves to be far more than it initially appears.

On the surface, *Alias* is a female-led action show of the kind that is increasingly common these days, from *Buffy The Vampire Slayer* through to *Dark Angel*. It's visual roots are in glossy European cinema, from *La Femme Nikita* to *Run Lola Run*. The mixture of espionage action and conspiracy theories has precursors in everything from *Mission: Impossible* to *The X-Files*. The lead character is Sydney Bristow, a young woman leading a double life, flying around the world and trying to bring down a criminal organisation from within.

So far, so exciting, visually arresting and impressive. Which in most cases would be more than enough to keep audiences happy. However, look closer, and you'll find that *Alias* has more to it than at first seems. Indeed, the more you look, the more you see. On the most basic level, an attractive female secret agent runs (and kicks) her way around the world in a succession of amusing and low-cut disguises. The publicity for the show concentrates on the charms and talents of Jennifer Garner, the star of the show. There's plenty to go on there – after just a season, Garner was famous in America and was winning awards and roles in films so often that other TV stars must have weeped with envy. Garner's previous highest-profile project was, unbelievably now, either as Kate Beckinsale's plain friend in *Pearl Harbor* or as one of the twins in *Dude, Where's My Car?*

Jennifer Garner is a huge asset, but she heads a stellar cast. The main regular characters are all established character actors from the movies; the supporting cast are all talented stand-up or sitcom names and, when they say 'Guest Star', they mean it – the guest actors are all big movie stars.

The show is beautifully acted, directed and designed. But what distinguishes it is the writing. A lot of US drama nowadays is witty and fast-paced. *Alias*, though, in addition, has such intricately plotted and structured scripts that it leaves most other contemporary shows in the dust. While many genre shows with complex stories have found themselves mired in their own continuity or looking remarkably like they are being made up as they go along, *Alias* has seemingly throwaway lines of dialogue that prove to have huge relevance several episodes later, hidden agendas that slowly emerge and minor points that suddenly become blindingly clear.

All the characters have such nuances and complexities that, even at the end of the show's second successful season, we're only now beginning to scratch the surface. The factions within the world of the show fight, not just over political power and high technology, but also to obtain control of secrets lost since the Renaissance, secrets that have a distinctly occult edge.

Some episodes have so many plot developments and twists that a lesser show would take a whole season to cover the same ground. Regular characters die, switch allegiance, are involved in action sequences that blow most movies out of the water; there's a comedy sequence, some heartrending character moment . . . and then the opening credits kick in. Halfway through the second season we get the episode that, by rights, should be the very last episode of the very last season. In the space of an hour, everything we know is blown up and replaced with something, almost impossibly, that's even more exciting.

It's way beyond the double-bluff (one of the regular characters is at the very least a *quintuple* agent). Clues to the big picture abound, and *Alias* rewards close, attentive viewing. And, when you've analysed every line of dialogue, you can decode the clues and piece together the other information. You spot that just about every episode has the number 47 popping up somewhere. You start realising that just about every password, codeword or seemingly insignificant piece of information adds up to something – an anagram, a numerical pattern, a hidden message. And then you realise that if you've got the right code you can email the characters from the show *and they email you back*.

It's no exaggeration to say that, whatever level of interest you have, however hard you look at the show, there's something there waiting for you to see it.

Which is why we're here. *Alias* is a complex show with many subtleties, and we've been there, paying attention and taking notes, from the very first episode to the very latest. We've reviewed, analysed and assessed what we've seen; argued and discussed and dissected every detail of the show.

These are our findings: an unofficial guide to one of the best television shows of the last few years, a show that encompasses kick-ass action, a compelling, astonishing story and characters we can love, hate, or sometimes both at the same time.

Every episode has some form of twist or surprise development. While episodes of *Alias* can withstand repeated viewings and don't rely on shock tactics, it's best to use this book as an aide-mémoire – you'll want to see this stuff, not just read about it.

This is Sydney Bristow's story. Look closer, and you'll find more there than you would have ever thought possible.

The Manual: How To Use This Book

In these pages you'll find guides to the first 44 episodes of *Alias*, all of the first two seasons, along with articles on the *Alias* spin-off books and the webgame.

The main body of the book is the episode guide – each episode has its own entry, providing production information and analysis under a series of categories. We'll add additional categories as we see fit, and some categories change as the plots develop through the episodes. But to begin with, each entry runs something like this:

Title

Production Code

1st US Transmission Date
1st UK Transmission Date

Writer(s)
Director
Guest Cast

Briefing: A brief run through the episode's plotline.
OMG: As in 'Oh My God!' An ad hoc category for any moments that made us go 'wow!' There are a lot of these – cool revelations, shocking cliffhangers and just really big special effects scenes.
Mission: Activities at SD-6, including Sydney's main missions.
Countermission: As above, but for the CIA.
Destination: A list of the locations featured in the episode. Sydney visits some exotic locales, most of which are named on screen in the series' signature captions. You'll notice that the camera moves through highlighted letters in each location card: these are called 'push-throughs', and the letters will be underlined here.

Timescale: Notes on timings within episodes: how long it is since certain events occurred, what day it is, what time of year.
Transcripts: Notable quotes from the episode.
The characters' development through the series, along with their relationship to the series' complex plotlines and conspiracies, is covered in separate sections for each one. The main characters, and the actors who play them, are described in the **Profiles** section of this book. New characters come and go throughout the series.
Intelligence: The main plot points in the episode, including major revelations within the ongoing narrative of the series.
Office Politics: The political wranglings within both SD-6 and the CIA.
Home Front: Sydney's attempts at a normal life include her flatmate, Francie, and her friend Will. She's also studying to be a teacher. This category covers these normal, healthy activities – and the way they fall apart due to Syd's double life.
Lies: Who is deceiving who?
Breaking the Code: Clues hidden within the episodes. This section will also list the 'push-through' letters from each episode.
Plot Devices: Superspy gadgets, pseudo-science jargon and other cool stuff thrown in to keep the plot bouncing along.
Action: Notable stunts and action scenes.
Undercover: Aliases, disguises, accents – everything the characters do to impersonate someone else and complete their missions.
Reality Checks: A real-world context for some of the wacky stuff in the series – there are references to real legislation, organisations and politics in the show, and we'll go into some of these in detail and suggest how credible we think these references really are.
Reference Points: In parallel to **Reality Checks**, references to other fictional works – films, books etc. – within the series.
Background Checks: Information on guest stars and production staff of note: who they are, where you've seen them or their work, and how well they fit into the show.

Music: *Alias* boasts a soundtrack featuring some notable tracks from an eclectic range of acts, which we'll list in this section. The series also has a distinct techno-style score, including a tendency to play the central theme in a wide variety of musical styles depending on the featured location. We'll note the various musical tricks used here to build a mood.

The Big Picture: There's a big uber-story behind *Alias*, involving lost Renaissance inventions and worldwide conspiracies. This section tracks these developments.

Debrief: A final (brief) opinion on the episode in question, subjectively summing up its relative merits.

Profiles

Jennifer Garner (Sydney Bristow)

A young woman still terribly affected by the death of her mother during childhood, Sydney Bristow works for SD-6, a covert branch of the CIA. None of her friends know what she does for a living and, as she is about to find out, neither does Sydney.

Sydney is a breakout role for Jennifer Garner, who appeared as Hannah Bibb in several episodes of the JJ Abrams-created drama series *Felicity*. Garner's other pre-*Alias* roles include the movies *Pearl Harbor* and *Dude, Where's My Car?* Since playing Sydney, being twice nominated for an Emmy (2002 and 2003) and winning a Golden Globe in 2002 for the role, Garner has gone on to bigger things in film, including an appearance in Steven Spielberg's *Catch Me If You Can* and the female lead of Elektra in comic-book film *Daredevil*, a role for which she received the Best Breakthrough Female award at the 2003 MTV Movie Awards. Roles on Garner's cinematic slate at the time of writing include age-swap comedy *13 Going On 30* and an *Elektra* spin-off movie.

Ron Rifkin (Arvin Sloane)

Head of SD-6, a supposed covert branch of the CIA, Arvin Sloane is ruthless in his response to threats against SD-6's secrecy.

Ron Rifkin's long career as an actor includes a memorable run of episodes in the second season of *ER*, as well as film roles in *Wolf*, *The Sum of All Fears*, *Dragonfly*, *The Majestic* and *L.A. Confidential*.

Michael Vartan (Michael Vaughn)

Michael Vaughn is an agent with the CIA, albeit one not trained for field duties.

French-born Michael Vartan appeared in the movies *Never Been Kissed*, *Dead Man's Curve* and *One Hour Photo*, and made a notable guest appearance in *Ally McBeal*.

Bradley Cooper (Will Tippin)

Will is a journalist on newspaper the *LA Register*. He's a friend of Sydney's, but has deeper feelings for her.

Bradley Cooper trained at the legendary Actor's Studio in New York (he can be spotted in the audience in at least one of the *In The Actor's Studio* broadcasts), and was in *Sex and the City* before moving to LA and appearing in *Alias*. His film work includes the recent horror movie *My Little Eye*.

Merrin Dungey (Francie Calfo)

Francie is Sydney's best friend, and has no idea what Sydney does for a living. Francie works in catering, but has ambitions to be her own boss.

Merrin Dungey had recurring roles in the TV shows *Grosse Pointe* and *Malcolm In The Middle*, as well as making appearances in the movies *Deep Impact* and *Edtv*.

Carl Lumbly (Marcus Dixon)

Dixon is a family man and SD-6 agent, who is Sydney's partner on most of her missions.

Jamaican-born, US-raised actor Carl Lumbly starred as a scientist-turned-superhero in *M.A.N.T.I.S.*, and provides the voice of the similarly heroic Martian Manhunter in the *Justice League* cartoon.

Kevin Weisman (Marshall Flinkman)

Marshall is the 'Q' figure at SD-6, a nerdy optechs expert who creates all the gadgets Sydney uses on her missions. He lives with his mother.

A founding member of the Buffalo Nights Theater Company, Kevin Weisman has previously appeared in *Buffy the Vampire Slayer* under heavy make-up as a minion, as well as in the films *Gone In 60 Seconds* and *The Rock*.

Victor Garber (Jack Bristow)

Jack is Sydney's estranged father. Their relationship is overshadowed by the death of Sydney's mother, and Jack is a distant figure who seems to be only interested in his job at Jennings Aerospace.

Victor Garber played Jesus in *Godspell*, both on the Toronto stage and in the 1973 movie. He spent two decades on Broadway, originating roles in two Stephen Sondheim musicals, *Sweeney Todd, the Demon Barber of Fleet Street* and *Assassins*, as well as receiving Tony nominations for *Deathtrap*, *Little Me*, *Lend Me A Tenor* and *Damn Yankees*. On film, he memorably played the designer of the eponymous ship in James Cameron's *Titanic*, as well as roles in *Legally Blonde*, *The First Wives Club* and *Sleepless in Seattle*. He received two Emmy nominations for the role of Jack in *Alias*.

Greg Grunberg (Eric Weiss)

CIA Agent Eric Weiss is Michael Vaughn's colleague and best friend.

While not strictly a member of the leading cast, Greg Grunberg is credited here for one simple reason – he isn't credited on screen. A star of the WB Network's *Felicity* (former home to both JJ Abrams and Jennifer Garner), Grunberg was allowed to play for another network providing he didn't receive an on screen credit. In an interview with *TV Guide Online* in 2001, Grunberg described the role of Weiss as a 'cool cameo' – albeit a cameo that reoccurs in most episodes of the first season! As well as *Alias* and *Felicity*, Grunberg has also appeared in *Austin Powers in Goldmember*, *Hollow Man* and *BASEketball*.

JJ Abrams (series creator, writer, director, composer)

Renaissance man Jeffrey 'JJ' Abrams created the television series *Felicity* as well as writing the movies *Regarding Henry*, *Forever Young*, *Armageddon*, *Taking Care Of Business* (aka *Filofax*) and *Joyride* (aka *Roadkill*). His role on *Alias* is that of creator, executive producer, frequent writer and sometime director. He also composed *Alias*'s compulsive, frequently reinterpreted techno theme music. In 2002 Abrams became the latest writer attached to Warner Bros.' cinematic revival of *Superman*, courting Internet controversy with some of his radical plans for the Man of Steel.

Michael Giacchino (composer)

While JJ Abrams provides the series' theme, Michael Giacchino gives each episode its often lavish score. His previous work includes scoring several video games, including the best-selling *Medal of Honor* World War II games.

List of Episodes

Season One

1. Truth Be Told
2. So It Begins . . .
3. Parity
4. A Broken Heart
5. Doppelganger
6. Reckoning
7. Color-Blind
8. Time Will Tell
9. Mea Culpa
10. Spirit
11. The Confession
12. The Box (Part One)
13. The Box (Part Two)
14. The Coup
15. Page 47
16. The Prophecy
17. Q and A
18. Masquerade
19. Snowman
20. The Solution
21. Rendezvous
22. Almost Thirty Years

Season Two

23. The Enemy Walks In
24. Trust Me
25. Cipher
26. Dead Drop
27. The Indicator
28. Salvation
29. The Counteragent
30. Passage I
31. Passage II
32. The Abduction
33. A Higher Echelon
34. The Getaway
35. Phase One
36. Double Agent
37. A Free Agent
38. Firebomb
39. A Dark Turn
40. Truth Takes Time
41. Endgame
42. Countdown
43. Second Double
44. The Telling

Season One

Regular Cast:

Jennifer Garner (Sydney Bristow)
Ron Rifkin (Arvin Sloane)
Michael Vartan (Michael Vaughn)
Bradley Cooper (Will Tippin)
Merrin Dungey (Francie Calfo)
Carl Lumbly (Marcus Dixon)
Kevin Weisman (Marshall Flinkman)
Victor Garber (Jack Bristow)

Created by JJ Abrams

1
Truth Be Told

Production #535J

1st US Transmission Date: 30 September 2001
1st UK Transmission Date: 23 January 2002

Writer: JJ Abrams
Director: JJ Abrams
Guest Cast: Edward Atterton (Danny Hecht), Jay Gerber (Professor Mizzy), Angus Scrimm (McCullough), William Wellman Jr. (Priest), Ric Young (Suit and Glasses), Lorenzo Callender (Messenger), Greg Collins (Kenny), Vicki Davis (Intern), Ming Lo (Agent), Raymond Ma (Taiwanese Businessman), Miguel Najera (Agent Gonzales), Greta Sesheta (CIA Receptionist), Philip Tan (Taiwanese Security Officer), Emily Wachtel (Beth (Airline Counter)), Nancy Wetzel (Amy Tippin)

Briefing: Sydney Bristow's friends think that she works for a bank, Credit Dauphine. Credit Dauphine is in fact a cover for SD-6, which Sydney thinks are a covert branch of the CIA. When Sydney gets engaged to Danny Hecht, she tells him about SD-6 but, while Sydney is on a mission in Taipei, SD-6 head Arvin Sloane finds out what Danny knows, and has him killed. Sydney refuses to return to SD-6, but they want her for another mission in Taipei. SD-6 attempt to kill Sydney, but she's saved by her father, Jack, another SD-6 agent, who tells her the truth – that SD-6 are not part of the CIA, but a criminal organisation. Jack gives Sydney the chance to leave the country, but instead she goes to Taipei to complete the mission SD-6 want to send her on, where she is captured and tortured. Sydney nonetheless escapes and completes her mission. Having proven her loyalty to Sloane and averted the death threats, Sydney turns herself in to the CIA, and becomes a double agent. She finds that she's not alone – her father is also a CIA double agent.

Mission: To their employees, SD-6 are a covert branch of the CIA. To the public they're Credit Dauphine, a bank with international clients. In fact, they're a branch of the Alliance of Twelve, a group of internationally based intelligence agents who became mercenaries and freelancers a decade before. High-level agents such as SD-6 director Arvin Sloane and Jack Bristow are aware of SD-6's true nature, but lower-level agents think they work for the real CIA.

Sydney is sent to Taipei to locate the lab where a plan by late scientist Oscar Mueller is being kept. The lab is in the Cultural Affairs Building, an FTL cover station in Taipei. Sydney completes the mission, but the murder of Danny Hecht causes her to leave SD-6.

Three months later, FTL have constructed the Mueller device, and SD-6 want Sydney to retrieve it. She succeeds, destroys the lab and then dumps the device on Sloane's desk.

Countermission: Sydney turns herself in to the CIA as a 'walk-in'. The Agency need to authenticate her very long statement about SD-6, but want her to be a double agent, alongside their other agent in SD-6, Jack Bristow.

Destination: Los Angeles, Taipei (Taiwan). Jack wants to send Sydney to Switzerland for safety, but she doesn't go.

Timescale: Sydney and Dixon fly out to Taipei on a Monday, and the Cultural Ambassador's reception is on Tuesday, when they undertake their reconnaissance mission. Sydney is given a month off by SD-6, but has taken three by the time Dixon finds her at college. After delivering the Mueller device to Sloane, Sydney takes another week off work.

Transcripts: Dixon (on SD-6's secrecy): 'If there's one rule you don't break, that's the rule you don't break.'

Sydney (to Jack): 'Who are you to come to me, and act like a father? If you want to help me, stay away from me.'

Sydney Bristow: Sydney is a grade student who is studying to become a teacher. She fitted a profile and was recruited to SD-6 while she was at college, having been approached to take tests. Sydney took the job, and applied for agent training, then advanced within the ranks to the CIA-equivalent rank within SD-6 of Operations Officer. She maintains a double life but, when her fiance Danny begins to talk about having children, Sydney feels the need to share her secret with him, unable to keep lying.

When Danny is killed by SD-6's Security Section, Sydney goes directly to SD-6 to confront Sloane. She survives interrogation by McCullough, then takes leave of absence from SD-6 for three months, refusing to return. She finds the involvement of her estranged father in SD-6 unbelievable, even to the extent of checking whether he's someone else wearing a mask.

Sydney's motivations stem from the death of her mother. Distanced from her father, Sydney lacked a purpose in life, which she found through working for SD-6. While Danny provides a new purpose, she still can't give up her job, but his death changes that, and she becomes a full-time student until SD-6 try to kill her. By the end of the episode Sydney has a new purpose – to bring down SD-6 from within, as a double agent for the CIA.

Jack Bristow: Sydney's estranged father Jack ostensibly works in the sale of aeroplane parts. He is a very prickly man, and verbally tears Danny apart when he phones to ask him for Sydney's hand in marriage. Jack works for SD-6, undercover at the aerospace firm, and claims loyalty to Sloane, telling him he understands when Sloane orders Danny killed. At Danny's funeral, Jack watches Sydney from a distance, unable to interact with her life. Later, he saves her life, and tries to get her to leave the country. When he tells Sydney that he's the other double agent within SD-6, he thanks her for leaving his name out of her CIA report.

Through all of this Jack seems distant from Sydney's everyday life, and when they are brought together by their joint mission infiltrating SD-6, Jack seems reluctant. Jack has always been a disappointment to Sydney as a father, and it remains to be seen whether he can bridge the gap between father and daughter.

Arvin Sloane: Sloane is head of SD-6, and briefs Sydney on her missions. When he sends Sydney and Dixon to Taipei, he genuinely seems to care for their welfare, but while they're away he orders that Danny Hecht be murdered because he is aware of SD-6. Sloane tells Sydney that, by breaching the Codes of Conduct, she not only caused Danny's death but put the lives of everyone at SD-6 at risk.

Michael Vaughn: Michael Vaughn is a young agent within the CIA of a similar age to Sydney, who is assigned by his Director, Devlin, to handle Sydney as a double agent for the CIA within SD-6. He works with Agent Weiss (Greg Grunberg – uncredited), and has a photograph of himself with a young blonde woman on his desk – a photo he turns away when he sees Sydney looking at it. Vaughn claims to instantly trust Syd because of an instinct he has, although she is not as sure about him.

Will Tippin: Will is a friend of Sydney's, a journalist who runs with her at a track. He lives with his sister Amy, who sets him up on blind dates. (At Danny's funeral Amy looks just like Sydney does when she borrows Amy's passport and hair dye (see **Undercover**).) Will seems to have an unrequited crush on Sydney, judging by his bad reaction to her announcement of her engagement.

Marcus Dixon: Dixon is Sydney's partner at SD-6. A family man, he's close enough to Sydney to notice she has a glow about her after getting engaged. When Sydney has been away from SD-6 for three months, it's Dixon they send to talk her back. Unlike Sydney, Dixon knows that he can never tell his wife of twelve years, Diane, about what he does. At the reception in Taipei, Dixon fakes a collapse to cause a distraction.

Marshall Flinkman: Marshall is SD-6's technical expert, providing gadgets for Sydney's missions. His briefings are full of stutters and digressions, and he likes prime numbers.

Francie Calfo: Sydney's best friend, Francie, works in catering. She doesn't think much of Jack, telling Sydney that her father only ever disappoints her. When Sydney gets engaged, Francie thinks her late mother would have been happy.

'Suit and Glasses': An interrogator working for FTL, the Taiwanese torturer referred to in the credits only as 'Suit and Glasses' also seems to have some wider security role related to the Mueller experiment, standing guard at the party during Sydney's first trip to Taipei. He finds Sydney attractive, flattered by her attentions early on, and complimenting her while torturing her three months later. His speciality in torment is dental work, using painkillers – then threatening to let them wear off.

Office Politics: Potential threats to SD-6 are handled by Security Section, and within that section McCullough tests the probity of suspect agents.

Home Front: Sydney has a normal life away from her work for SD-6. She has a boyfriend in Danny, close friends in Will and Francie who she can spend time with, and her studies. The death of Danny takes one of these pillars away from her, while the revelations about her father's involvement with SD-6 and the CIA prove to Sydney that her life was never entirely normal. The loss of 'real life' is a thread that will run through the series, and provide a goal that Sydney is constantly trying to attain . . .

Lies: Sloane is deceiving SD-6's agents about their status and the agents themselves are obliged to lie to everyone they know to keep SD-6's existence a secret.

Plot Devices: Marshall provides Sydney with an RF scrambler (disguised as a cigarette lighter) to knock out video cameras in a 420-yard radius for four minutes, and a camera (disguised as a lipstick) that takes three-dimensional images. Sydney has a lockpick inserted in the heel of

her shoe. In Taipei for the second time, Syd steals a car, so presumably she can break into one and hotwire it.
Action: The car chase with Jack is particularly impressive. Sydney fights her way out of the lab in Taipei, destroying it in a gas explosion in the process.
Undercover: On their mission to Taipei, Sydney and Dixon pose as representatives of Modero Plastics. At the reception Sydney wears a long, shocking pink sleeveless dress, and adopts a thick southern American accent. On her second trip to Taipei Sydney has no backing from SD-6, and so disguises herself as Amy Tippin, with pink hair and union jack T-shirt. She uses constant chatter to make herself seem less threatening.
Reference Points: Vaughn compares the length of Sydney's statement on SD-6 to the works of Tolstoy, author of the very long *War and Peace*. Sydney's missions owe a lot to *La Femme Nikita* and *Run Lola Run*.
Background Checks: Ric Young played Mao Tse-Tung in Oliver Stone's *Nixon*, as well as roles in *Indiana Jones and the Temple of Doom* and *The Last Emperor*. Angus Scrimm is the big bad guy in the *Phantasm* series of cult horror films.
Injuries: Sydney is bruised during the assassination attempt, and loses teeth in Taipei.
Music: Danny proposes by singing The Foundations' 'Build Me Up Buttercup' to Sydney, in memory of a loud man present at their first date. A 'stealth' version of the theme plays as Sydney steals the Mueller device. Songs featured are 'You're A God' and 'Give You Back' by Vertical Horizon, 'Never Grow Old' by The Cranberries, 'Under The Gun' by Supreme Beings of Leisure, 'Trouble' by Cat Stevens, 'Here Comes The Flood' by Peter Gabriel, 'Sofisticated' by the Stereo MCs and 'No Man's Woman' by Sinead O'Connor.
Intelligence: Sydney discovers the truth about SD-6, and becomes a double agent for the CIA. She discovers her father is also a double agent.
The Big Picture: Oscar Mueller, a recently deceased scientist and supposed modern-day alchemist, wrote his notes in ancient languages. After Mueller's death various

multi-nationals and agencies are competing to locate his notes. The Mueller device is a short mechanism, perhaps a foot long, with a curved end. When activated, a red sphere floats above the curve and, when the power is cut off, the sphere disappears with a burst of water. Whatever the device is, it is of intense interest to corporations, governments and agencies worldwide . . .

Debrief: 'I guess we'll just have to learn to trust each other.' *Alias* is a difficult concept to get to grips with, a blend of comic-book conceits (superspies with gadgets, the villainous Alliance), and brutally realistic consequences (Sydney's torture by 'Suit and Glasses', the death of Danny), all delivered in an earnest, straight-faced style without a hint of knowing camp. It's a testament to this episode that it goes most of the way towards making us accept this seemingly ludicrous combination. The episode's success can be credited to excellence in all departments: JJ Abrams's script knows exactly what it is doing, building and layering the *Alias* world with believable characters and flashes of unreal style; the special effects and action are glossy and exciting; the music complements the action perfectly; and the performances anchor the action, with Garner an instant star as Sydney, a young woman trying desperately to lead her life with integrity in very trying circumstances. It's Garner and the rest of the cast who perhaps deserve the most plaudits for making *Alias* work – what could have been ludicrous is anchored by the reality that Garner, Garber, Rifkin and company bring to their roles. The characters feel real, and as such the *Alias* world feels real too.

2
So It Begins . . .

Production #E631

1st US Transmission Date: 7 October 2001
1st UK Transmission Date: 30 January 2002

Writer: JJ Abrams
Director: Ken Olin
Guest Cast: Evan Dexter Parke (Charlie), Aharon Ipale (Hassan), Alex Kuz (Shcherbakov), Ravil Isyanov (Karpachev), Sarah Shahi (Jenny), Ammar Daroiseh (Supplier), Azdine Melliti (Bodyguard #1), John Storey (CIA Officer), Xavier J Nathan (French Officer), Gregory Phelan (Student), Seema Rahmani (Sara)

Briefing: Sydney provides Vaughn with information on various branches of SD-6, their contacts and suppliers. On her return to SD-6, Sydney is sent to Moscow to retrieve information relating to nuclear arsenals in the Cold War, which she has copied to the CIA. The documents relate to a nuclear weapon buried on US soil. Sydney finds the device, and SD-6 sell it on to arms dealer Anini Hassan. Sydney travels to Cairo to neutralise the bomb. She removes the core, but Hassan holds a gun to her head . . .

Vaughn is removed as Sydney's CIA handler. Will begins to investigate Danny's death.

OMG: Vaughn rolls out a huge map of the SD-6 organisation, showing how little Sydney knows about the scale of the Alliance.

Mission: Sydney and Dixon are sent to Moscow to stop the sale of stolen, twenty-year-old information relating to Soviet–American nuclear arsenals to Navor, a military attaché from the Sudan. The sellers are Russian mafia, and Dixon impersonates Navor, while Sydney raids Navor's hotel room for the money for the purchase. But Sydney finds there was never any money – Navor intended to steal the files from the Russians. Sydney swaps the disks with the information for two beermats – but she and Dixon still end up having to fight the Russians before escaping.

The documents relate to the 'Doomsday 6' operation, which saw six nuclear weapons buried in the USA. Although in 1989, after the Cold War ended, the six weapons were disarmed, the stolen intelligence reveals that a seventh nuclear weapon was buried. Sydney is sent to Buckingham, Virginia, to meet Milovich Ivanov, since Sloane believes he knows where the seventh weapon is. Sydney finds that Ivanov's address is a graveyard, where

he is buried. Sydney digs up the grave, and opens the coffin to find a nuclear weapon, which begins to count down. Marshall tells her over the phone how to deactivate it.
Countermission: The CIA arrange to give Sydney countermissions to undertake while on her SD-6 assignments. The arrangements are made through dead-drops (parcels and papers left in waste bins) and phone calls disguised as wrong numbers (using the name 'Joey's Pizza'). As Vaughn explains, SD-6 are far greater than the Los Angeles office disguised as Credit Dauphine – which is why the CIA have never raided it. The CIA want to close down the whole operation, not just one branch. One way Vaughn has of setting up meetings with Sydney uses a fake blood-donation van parked on Sydney's campus.

Sydney's first countermission is to give the stolen information to an agent at the airport in LA, so that they can be copied before being passed back to her to give to SD-6. Sydney drops the disks into a bucket Vaughn is carrying as she leaves customs, allowing him to copy the disks. Vaughn drops the disks back into her bag as Sydney and Dixon are about to get into a car. When they find out about the nuclear weapon, the CIA want to send in a team to capture Ivanov. Vaughn persuades them that Sydney's cover will be blown if they do that, and to delay the operation by five hours.

After Sydney calls Marshall to disarm the nuclear weapon, SD-6 take it. Vaughn is unhappy that a nuclear weapon fell into enemy hands, and that it's already been sold to Hassan. Sydney contacts Jack to arrange for him to cover for her at SD-6 while she goes to Cairo to steal the nuclear weapon back.
Destination: Moscow, Los Angeles, Virginia, Cairo.

Also Paris (three years ago), Memphis (Egypt, six months ago).
Timescale: SD-6 sent Sydney to steal something for Leonard Dreyfuss three years ago, and to buy arms from Hassan six months ago. Her meeting with Vaughn is one week after the events of episode **1**, 'Truth Be Told', with her first day back at SD-6 (after the week's leave she takes

when delivering the Mueller device) the next day. Her second day at work sees her in Moscow.

Transcripts: Sydney: 'I am sitting here for one reason only, and that is to destroy SD-6. After I am out, I want no more of this spy crap.'

Sydney Bristow: Sydney wants to get her CIA mission done quickly, and leave. She believes she can deliver SD-6 on a plate to the CIA, destroying the whole organisation in less than two months, and thinks Vaughn is wasting her time with his plans for counter-missions. When Vaughn compares a plan of what Sydney knows about SD-6 to a sprawling map of the organisation as a whole, she realises that the job will take a little longer than expected . . .

Sydney has had many questions since finding out the truth about her father, the main one being whether he knew that Danny was going to be killed. After she hears his answer, she never wants to speak to him again but, when she finds out Jack tried to save Danny, she thanks him. Sydney pleads emotional distress to stop Will from investigating Danny's death.

The first thing Sydney does when returning from a mission is put her engagement ring back on. She has friends in the Middle East, but Hassan is not one of them.

Jack Bristow: To help their work for the CIA, Jack has asked to be able to tell Sydney the truth about his work for SD-6. Jack admits to Sydney that he knew that Sloane was going to have Danny killed. Sydney slaps him, but later she works out that it was Jack who booked Danny on a flight to Singapore that night, intending for her and Danny to escape. He was too late. Jack covers for Sydney with SD-6 while she goes to Cairo, telling Sloane that she's having difficulty adjusting to what her father does.

Arvin Sloane: Sloane shows concern for Sydney's well-being when she returns to work. Sloane seems suspicious of Jack when he talks about Sydney, suggesting a rivalry between their father-figure roles with her.

Michael Vaughn: Sydney has little time or patience with Vaughn to begin with, and he shows restraint in slowly explaining to her the extent of what she is dealing with –

even though she's already dismissed him as both too young and probably sexist. When Vaughn is visibly worried while Sydney is on her mission, his friend Weiss reminds him that his girlfriend's name is Alice. Vaughn stands up to his superiors to protect Sydney's cover and Weiss nicknames him 'balls of steel'. But, when Vaughn has successfully argued Sydney's importance, Devlin orders that a more senior officer be assigned to Sydney – removing Vaughn from her case. The job Vaughn is transferred to is a presentation on non-proliferation – ironic for an agent who has just lost a nuclear weapon!

Will Tippin: Sydney and Will have known each other for three years, although he says it feels like longer. He still hasn't had a satisfactory explanation from Sydney for her taking his sister's passport and running off. He believes that it has something to do with Danny's death, and won't accept her insistence that he drop it. Sydney begs him not to investigate Danny's death. Nevertheless he does, and finds that, on the night he was killed, Danny was booked on a flight from LAX in Los Angeles to Singapore.

Will's latest story for the newspaper is about a pregnant woman who has a craving to eat newspaper. He receives a report of a cat being run over. He's not happy about working on this quality of story. Jenny, a twenty-year-old intern, wants to date him, but he insists he's too old.

Marcus Dixon: Sydney and Dixon know Navor from a previous mission, after which Dixon is surprised Navor can walk.

Marshall Flinkman: Marshall tells Sydney he's not much of a social person (hardly a surprise). He's sorry about Danny, and glad to have Sydney back at work. Some nights Marshall's mind is racing so much he has to use his own knock-out device to go to sleep. He once accidentally touched the device at work, banging his head on the desk.

Francie Calfo: Francie has a boyfriend, Charlie, who receives a job offer.

Office Politics: SD-6 rely on Dreyfuss in Geneva for funding, and get firearms from Hassan's group in Memphis, Egypt. There's also a geneticist in Kuala Lumpur,

Malaysia, but we hear little about him. At the CIA, Vaughn is taken off Sydney's case as he's considered too junior.

Home Front: Sydney becomes Francie's housemate.

Lies: Will investigates Danny's death. Sydney lies to him about why she had to borrow his sister's identity, see **1**, 'Truth Be Told', and lies to him about her reasons for not wanting him to investigate Danny's death – in reality, she's concerned for his safety if he looks into an SD-6 killing.

Breaking the Code: Location letters: S, A, N and I. Ivanov's address is 1936 Lake.

Plot Devices: In the Paris mission three years previously, Sydney used a blocking device to disrupt the security camera in the elevator – presumably a precursor to Marshall's RF blocker, see **1**, 'Truth Be Told'. She then used a mechanism to pull her up the elevator cable to the top of the lift shaft. For the Moscow mission, Marshall gives them a device that knocks someone out cold with one touch – Sydney uses this on one of Navor's bodyguards. Her lock pick is hidden in the arms of her spectacles, and she uses it to open Navor's briefcase.

Action: In flashback, Sydney escapes in Paris by sliding up an elevator-support cable, beating up a few guards on the way out. In Moscow she kicks one of Navor's guards around the hotel room. When the Russians become suspicious and pull a gun on Dixon, he and Sydney have to beat them up and run.

Undercover: During Sydney's mission at the start of the episode, she wears all-black burgling gear with a long, black, straight-fringed wig. In Moscow she has long blonde hair and wears a maid's costume under a severe long black coat. Underneath the maid's costume she is wearing a metallic blue plastic dress, along with a black choker with a small diamond square in the centre. Dixon is disguised as Navor in full Sudanese outfit and adopts the appropriate accent. Sydney wears a burkha in Cairo because, if Hassan recognises her, her cover at SD-6 will be blown.

Reality Checks: The Aquarium is indeed the headquarters of the GRU ('Glavnoye Razvedyvatelnoye Upravlenie' –

'Main Intelligence Administration', the Russian military intelligence), based at an airfield near Moscow.
Background Checks: Evan Dexter Parke appeared in *The Cider House Rules* as well as Tim Burton's ill-fated reimagining of *Planet of the Apes*. Aharon Ipale played the Pharoah in both *The Mummy* and *The Mummy Returns*. Sarah Shahi appeared in the movie *Old School*. Ken Olin is a co-executive producer as well as regular director on *Alias* – he is also an actor with credits including *thirtysomething*.
Trivia: The episode begins with Sydney's first-person narration of the series' basic premise, accompanied by clips from **1**, 'Truth Be Told'.
Music: 'Looking for a Friend' by Roland Gift and 'This Woman's Work' by Kate Bush.
Intelligence: Sydney completes her first countermission. Jack denies any involvement in Danny's death and Will begins to investigate it.
The Big Picture: The extent of SD-6's arms dealing is unveiled – not only do they buy arms from Hassan, but they also sell him a stolen nuclear device.
Debrief: 'This is not about cutting off the arm of the monster, this is about killing the monster.' The series' second episode keeps up the pace of the first, while filling out Sydney's world through flashbacks to various SD-6 missions. Exposition also plays a part, and Vaughn's unrolling of his map of SD-6 is a key *Alias* moment – we thought we knew what was going on, but the truth is bigger than we imagined . . .

3
Parity

Production #E632

1st US Transmission Date: 14 October 2001
1st UK Transmission Date: 6 February 2002

Writers: Alex Kurtzman and Roberto Orci
Director: Mikael Salomon

Guest Cast: Evan Dexter Parke (Charlie), Gina Torres (Anna Espinosa), Aharon Ipale (Hassan), Keone Young (Professor Choy), Elaine Kagan (June Litvack), Mark Rolston (Lambert), Greg Grunberg (Weiss), Carole Gutierezz (Laura Stenson), Duane Journey (Sniper Team Leader), Luis Medina (Eduardo Benegas), Randy Mulkey (Navy SEAL), Russell Alexander Orazco (MC), Alfonso Paz (Lead Security Officer), Tony Sears (SD-6 Agent), Anthony Vatsula (Doorman)

Briefing: Sydney distracts Hassan by throwing the plutonium core in the air, which knocks him out, and she catches it on the way down. She then escapes from Cairo. Sydney is sent to Madrid to steal a sketch by Milo Rambaldi, and has an encounter with her K-Directorate nemesis, Anna Espinosa (see **Anna Espinosa**), before escaping with the sketch. Marshall is unable to unlock the box containing the sketch, so Sloane brings in Jack to plan a way to get the box open. A meeting is arranged where Sydney and Anna both open the box to see what is inside, and both factions get the intelligence. When the box is opened, they are both shocked by what they see . . .
OMG: Sydney and Anna attacking the vault from different directions.
Mission: SD-6 are still examining the Mueller device. Sloane has found out that Mueller did not design it; in fact, he was an academic who appropriated the design from the work of Milo Rambaldi. Rambaldi's work has become a priority for SD-6. Two Rambaldi sketches had the halves of a binary machine code sequence written on the back – SD-6 have one, and the other is held by Eduardo Benegas, who keeps it in a vault. Sydney and Dixon are sent to Madrid to get the code, using a fundraising event as their cover. As Sydney is breaking in with her hi-tech devices, K-Directorate agent Anna Espinosa is getting into the vault by crawling through the air conditioning and cutting in with a blowtorch. Anna gets the box containing the sketch, but as she is climbing up on to the roof to get to her helicopter, Sydney shoots through the box's shoulder strap, and it falls to the ground where she grabs it.

SD-6 cannot open the box, and Anna has the key. Jack arranges a meeting between Sydney and Anna in Berlin, so that they can open the box together and both get the code.

The meeting is in a stadium, with snipers from both sides set up in the stalls and the two agents meeting in the field.
Countermission: The CIA share SD-6's interest in Rambaldi, and Sydney's countermission is to complete her mission for Sloane. Sydney says she will make a dead-drop of the code to the CIA in Barcelona. Lambert, her new CIA handler, refers to her as a girl and can't get Danny's name right. For the meeting with Espinosa, Lambert wants Sydney to plant a bug on Anna. Sydney thinks the plan is idiotic, and tells Lambert that if the CIA want anything they should reinstate Vaughn as her handler, promoting him if necessary. They do exactly that.
Destination: Madrid, Berlin.
Transcripts: Sydney: 'I have a thousand questions. They're keeping me awake at night.' Jack: 'Then take something.'
Will (to Sydney, at the 'bank'): 'I need to borrow a million bucks. The Olsen twins went public and I'm looking to invest.'
Sydney Bristow: Sydney is falling behind with her studies, missing the deadline for her paper due to the Cairo mission. She describes her relationship with Jack as awkward, and can't imagine being able to ask him for advice, although she always hoped that one day she would connect with him. Francie encourages her to speak to Jack, and she goes to his workplace. She asks him whether he was involved in her recruitment to SD-6 and whether her mother's death was related to his work. She asks him the same question again when he is brought into SD-6 to work on a strategy.
After drinking too much, Sydney kisses Will, then instantly regrets it and pulls away. Her attitude to Vaughn is improving, to the extent that she gets him reinstated as her handler and refers to him as her guardian angel.
Jack Bristow: Jack is unhappy when Sydney comes to see him outside the aerospace firm he is based at, and refuses to answer her questions. When pressed, Jack confirms that her mother knew he worked for the CIA, and that she died in the car accident, as he told her. He is SD-6's best game theorist, and is brought back to the Los Angeles office to work out a scenario to open the box containing the

Rambaldi sketch. His plan is a symmetrical scenario where both sides get what they want – the code.
Arvin Sloane: Sloane sees himself as a rationalist, but one who cannot deny the evidence of Rambaldi's prophetic abilities.
Michael Vaughn: Vaughn is not convinced by the Agency's interest in Rambaldi. At their meeting, he tells Sydney he will no longer be her handler, see **2**, 'So It Begins . . .'. Vaughn is worried that none of his potential replacements will be competent, and he is concerned about Sydney's safety on her Madrid mission. Weiss thinks that this is because he is becoming too attached to her.
Will Tippin: As a favour to Sydney, Will picks up some of Danny's stuff from his old apartment. While he's there, he realises that there is a traffic camera exactly opposite the window. Will tries to obtain shots from the camera for the night Danny was killed, but all the cameras were out of order. After Sydney kisses him and pulls away, Will goes to get Danny's box of stuff from his car – a hint that he realises why she pulled away.

He is supposed to be writing an article on genetics, a subject he barely understands. He is virtually blind without his glasses.
Marcus Dixon: Dixon finds the idea of Rambaldi ludicrous.
Marshall Flinkman: Marshall waxes lyrical on the history of the numerals one and zero. He has heard of Benegas (see **Mission**) because of the man's huge collection of pornographic art.
Francie Calfo: Francie is worried that Charlie doesn't seem too enthused about his job offer and, when she finds a matchbook in his pocket with a girl's name and number on it, she thinks he's cheating on her. Francie could never forgive Jack, if he were her father. However, she thinks that if Sydney is capable of that forgiveness then she should try talking to her father.
Anna Espinosa: Anna is an agent for rival intelligence agency, K-Directorate, and an old rival of Sydney's. Born in Cuba and raised in Russia, this former Cold-Warrior

shot off the back of the head of one of Sydney's contacts in Yugoslavia to prove that Sydney was out of her league. Anna takes the key to Benegas's box from him while making love – the only way to get past his bodyguards.
Intelligence: Sydney finds out about Milo Rambaldi and his work.
Office Politics: Vaughn is replaced by Lambert as Sydney's handler because of his junior status and the increasing importance of her missions. The Agency promote Vaughn so that he can return to his handling role.
Home Front: Sydney, Will, Francie and Charlie have a drunken evening playing cards.
Lies: Sydney tells Will that her trip is to San Diego. He doesn't tell her that he's still looking into Danny's death. Jack admits to Sloane that the story he told Sydney about her mother's death wasn't the truth.
Breaking the Code: Location letters: D and R.
Plot Devices: In Madrid, Sydney has a vocal transmitter in her necklace, and a sonic-wave emitter disguised as a peseta. The emitter is triggered by a transmitter disguised as a pen, and the sonic wave can break glass to cause a distraction. Marshall provides a remote modem to stick in the alarm system junction box. This week's lock-pick disguise: in a fan.
Action: Dixon disrupts the scrambler signal emitted by a K-Directorate van in Madrid by simply driving his own van into it. Sydney swings down on a length of chain to crash into Anna who responds by attacking her with an iron bar.
Undercover: In Madrid, Sydney attends the fundraiser wearing ginger hair and a long orange dress, cut low at the front. At the same event, Anna is disguised as a waitress.
Reality Checks: Vaughn's description of Rambaldi – as a cross between Da Vinci and Nostradamus – is pretty much spot on. Leonardo Da Vinci (1452–1519) was an artist and inventor and one of the greatest minds of any generation, and between 1513 and 1516 he worked in Rome, undertaking a variety of projects for the Pope. Michel de Nostradame (1503–1566) was a doctor renowned for writing prophecies, which have been interpreted in ways that seem

to reflect actual events. Both men are seen as greatly ahead of their time (albeit in different ways), and both make regular appearances in conspiracy theories and fantasy fiction. As such, Rambaldi is a combination of the most extreme qualities of both men.

Reference Points: The introduction of mystical elements and archaeological treasure hunts harks back to *Raiders of the Lost Ark*, but the female-orientated spin that Sydney and Anna bring to the proceedings is pure *Tomb Raider*.

Background Checks: Gina Torres (Anna) is married to *The Matrix* star Lawrence Fishburne. Her other television roles include leads in *Firefly* and *Cleopatra 2525*. Writers and co-executive producers Alex Kurtzman and Roberto Orci were writers on *Hercules: The Legendary Journeys*, which regularly guest starred Gina Torres. Mikael Saloman is not just a director with credits including *The Agency* and *Hard Rain*, he's also an accomplished cinematographer.

Music: 'The Beginner' by Miranda Lee Richards, 'La Cienega Just Smiled' by Ryan Adams, 'Rings A Bell' by Bill Bonk and 'Go Get It' by Spookie Daily Pride.

The Big Picture: The Mueller device is based on the work of Milo Rambaldi, who died in 1496. Rambaldi was chief architect to Pope Alexander VI, and was excommunicated and executed for suggesting that some day science would allow man to know God. After his death Rambaldi's workshop was destroyed, and for five centuries his designs were lost across the world. Recently, a Russian scientist examining Rambaldi's early work found a design for something that resembled a transistor, revealing that Rambaldi was a prophet. SD-6 have acquired a Rambaldi notebook with designs for a cellular phone.

K-Directorate are a Russian underground organisation, and Anna Espinosa is one of their agents.

Debrief: 'It's just weird, having that feeling that someone you love isn't telling you everything.' As the title indicates, this is an episode about parallels and balances. We're introduced to Sydney's evil counterpart, Anna Espinosa, and the MacGuffin code is split into two sections – as well as being in binary, of course. Just as trust is gained (Sydney's new faith in

Vaughn), so it is lost elsewhere (Jack's poor relationship with Syd, Will's lies, Charlie's potential betrayal). However, in spite of all this thematic cleverness, the main thing this episode will be remembered for is the introduction of a man long dead, whose influence will continue to dominate the series – Milo Rambaldi. Rambaldi's prophetic abilities bring mysticism into what was previously a hard-edged, albeit preposterous, espionage story. This new aspect is very welcome, adding an extra level to the show.

4
A Broken Heart

Production #E633

1st US Transmission Date: 21 October 2001
1st UK Transmission Date: 13 February 2002

Writer: Vanessa Taylor
Director: Harry Winer
Guest Cast: Miguel Sandoval (Anthony Russek), Gina Torres (Anna Espinosa), Evan Dexter Parke (Charlie), Faran Tahir (Bak Ibrahim), Maurice Chasse (Jacqneau), Bernard White (Sawari), Angus Scrimm (McCullough), Sarah Shahi (Jenny), Arabella Holzborg (Sydney's Mom), Hector Aristizabal (Waiter), Sayed Badreya (Vendor), Jeff Chase (Bodyguard), Haley Gilbert (Rachel), Soren Hellerup (Doctor), Subash Kundanmal (Dhiran Patel), Tony Sears (German SD-6 Agent), Alex Veadow (K-Directorate Officer)

Briefing: A security mechanism releases corrosive chemicals on to the document containing the code as Anna and Sydney open the case, but they both memorise the code. Sydney is sent to Spain to retrieve a Rambaldi artefact, then onto Morocco to monitor a meeting in a local marketplace. From that meeting she discovers a bomb is going to be planted on peace prize-winner Dhiran Patel. Sydney goes to São Paulo, and witnesses a bomb being implanted in Patel's body . . .
Mission: SD-6 decipher the code, which leads Sydney to a 500-year-old church in Malaga, Spain. She finds a mysteri-

ous item referred to as a 'golden sun', a glass disc within a stained glass window. Anna gets there too, and she fights Sydney for the sun, but Sydney takes it and leaves Anna handcuffed to a pew.

Zero Defence attacked the United Commerce Organisation (UCO) ministerial conference a year ago, and intend to attack again this year, in São Paulo. Zero Defence leader Luc Jacqneau will be in Morocco to arrange a deal for the São Paulo event. Sydney and Dixon are sent to Morocco to monitor the meeting and stop Jacqneau achieving his aims. Sydney records him and his contact discussing 'Phase Three' of their project but one of the bodyguards at the meeting recognises her from a previous fight in Corsica, and spots SD-6's surveillance. She beats up the bodyguard, and Dixon flees. SD-6's local contact, Makto, is shot dead.

Sloane analyses the recording from Morocco, identifying Jacqneau's contact as Malik Suwari, a demolition expert who has invented the BLU 250 explosive. Dhiran Patel, winner of the Edgar Peace Prize, will be used to send a message to the UCO to disband the organisation – he will be rigged with explosives. Sydney and Dixon are sent to São Paulo to foil the plan. When Patel collapses at a reception, Sydney and Dixon find he's been drugged with a sedative. He is taken away in an ambulance that Sydney follows on a motorbike, and she sees surgeons implant a bomb in him.

Countermission: Vaughn orders Sydney to give the correct Rambaldi code to SD-6 against her wishes. The CIA consider it worse for K-Directorate to get critical information before SD-6 than for SD-6 to have it.

The CIA don't know why SD-6 are interested in UCO, and didn't know that Jacqneau would be there, thinking he was going to Bahrain. Sydney's countermission is to dead-drop her account of the meeting for the CIA to pick up.

Destination: Los Angeles, Malaga, Spain; Los Angeles, Morocco, Los Angeles, São Paulo.

Timescale: Sydney and Dixon arrive in São Paulo on a Wednesday. Her dinner with Jack is planned for Thursday night.

Transcripts: Sydney: 'I think spying on your boyfriend is generally regarded as a bad relationship precedent.'

Vaughn (to Sydney): 'When you're at your absolute lowest, at your most depressed, just remember that you can always . . . you know . . . you've got my number.'

Sydney Bristow: Sydney is beginning to feel that Anna is less of an enemy, because of their mutual desire to take down SD-6. She feels weird about having kissed Will. After seeing Charlie with another woman, Sydney asks Will to keep an eye on Francie while she's away, and advises Francie to talk to Charlie and see if there is an explanation. When Francie says she will kill Charlie if he's cheating on her, Sydney quietly says she should never say that. As Sydney touches Makto's corpse, the scene echoes her finding Danny, and the experience is visibly traumatic for her.

Sydney compliments Jack on his strategy for Berlin, and invites him to meet her for dinner but he doesn't show up, disappointing her again. She is devastated, and calls Vaughn to cry on his shoulder over Jack, the death of her friend in Morocco and the difficulties of her life with SD-6. She feels like she's falling apart and, when her beeper rings, she throws it into the sea.

Jack Bristow: Jack comes into SD-6 for a routine psychiatric evaluation with McCullough. He's hypnotised during the session, and under hypnosis he sees Sydney's mother holding her as a baby. The mother becomes Sydney, who says that it is only a matter of time before she learns the truth, and this image breaks Jack out of his hypnotic state.

Jack briefly forces a polite smile when Sydney compliments him on Berlin. He calls her to cancel dinner, claiming he's at work, when in fact he's parked outside the restaurant.

Arvin Sloane: Sloane's wife, Emily, is feeling a little ill (a minor fact, but one that will become significant later).

Michael Vaughn: Vaughn looks crumpled and slightly distressed when he meets Sydney, who thinks he's had an argument with his wife, but he corrects her emphatically, seeming slightly alarmed that she thought he was married, but admits that he had a huge fight with his girlfriend.

Vaughn tells Sydney that when she first walked into his office he thought she was crazy and that her responsibility should be to not let the darkness of what she does darken her, and to call him if she needs him.

Will Tippin: Danny was supposed to be registered at a medical conference in Singapore, but Will has discovered that he wasn't registered at any of them. Jenny the intern says Will sounds different while on the phone to Sydney, and he bluntly tells her not to analyse him. He uses a promise of a date with Jenny to get someone to give him the name of the person booked on the flight to Singapore with Danny – Kate Jones.

Will kisses Sydney again, but she is unresponsive, and he feels like an idiot.

Francie Calfo: Francie's paranoia about Charlie leads to her and Sydney spying on him. She's surprised at how Sydney knows how to follow someone by car without being seen. When they see Charlie meet and hug a young blonde woman, Francie believes the worst and refuses to return his calls, but she agrees to meet him for coffee. He says that Rachel is just a friend, and that they were just hanging out, but Francie walks out on him.

Intelligence: Jack is keeping a secret from Sydney, which he fears she will discover.

Office Politics: Sloane refers to SD-3, one of SD-6's sister agencies. SD-6's contact in Morocco is Makto, an Egyptian commando recruited two years before. Anthony Russek has transferred to SD-6 from Jennings, and sits in on briefings.

Home Front: Much to Sydney's distress, her normal life becomes an espionage exercise as she helps Francie spy on Charlie.

Lies: Sydney claims to be in Chicago while she is in Morocco. When Will is unconsciously fiddling with the tag on her luggage, Sydney intercepts him, realising that the name 'Kate Jones' is emblazoned on the baggage tag.

Breaking the Code: Location letters: N, A, G, O, E and S.

Plot Devices: For Morocco, Sydney has a purse with built-in parabolic microphone and laser transmitter, which has a 300-yard radius and blanks out any background wind noise. In São Paulo, she uses a reed-thin telescope to observe the operation on Patel.

Action: Sydney and Anna hit each other with religious artefacts in the church in Malaga, including a lectern and a long candle holder. In Morocco, Sydney beats a bodyguard around the head with a small table.

Undercover: Sydney and Dixon's aliases in Morocco are Kate Jones and Justin Burnell, travelling with Mindspring Learning Tours. Sydney wears pigtails, a head scarf and a green crochet knit cardigan. In São Paulo, she wears an ornate gold top with gold lamé trousers, and she has straight brunette hair with blonde highlights and slightly bronzed skin.

Reality Checks: The protests against the UCO are clearly modelled on the protests that have occurred at all recent meetings of major trade alliances like the World Trade Organisation.

Background Checks: Miguel Sandoval (Anthony Russek) has appeared in TV series *Murder One*, *The West Wing* and *Kingpin*, as well as movies such as *Jurassic Park*, *Jungle Fever* and *Get Shorty*. Writer and co-producer Vanessa Taylor previously wrote for *Gideon's Crossing*, and has since moved on to *Everwood*. Harry Winer has previously directed *Felicity* and *Hart to Hart*.

Injuries: Sydney forces Anna's hand into a candle to burn it.

Music: At the warehouse in São Paulo, the theme is heard in a bass and reverb heavy variant. The tracks heard are Bill Bonk's 'Halfway Home', Nina Storey's 'If I Were An Angel' and Sarah MacLachlan's 'Angel'.

The Big Picture: Rambaldi's ideas were so advanced that he was considered insane, which is why no one in the present day has heard of him. His sketches include the ID serial numbers of components manufactured in the twenty-first century. He spent the last decade of his life working on a single project. No one knows what that project was – but they all want it.

The golden sun Sydney retrieves was made of a synthetic polymer 500 years ago – before there were such substances.

Debrief: 'I feel like I'm losing my mind, like I don't even know who I am any more.' A more straightforwardly emotional episode than usual, **4**, 'A Broken Heart' sees betrayal and lies eating away at every aspect of Sydney's life. All the cast excel as the characters go through the wringer, especially Victor Garber, as Jack seems visibly torn between the preservation of his secrets and his feelings for his daughter.

5
Doppelganger

Production #E634

1st US Transmission Date: 28 October 2001
1st UK Transmission Date: 20 February 2002

Writer: Daniel Arkin
Director: Ken Olin
Guest Cast: Tom Everett (Paul Kelvin), Norbert Weisser (Schiller), Lori Heuring (Kate Jones), Maurice Chasse (Jacqneau), Kevin E. West (Logan), Yvonne Farrow (Diane Dixon), Robert Bailey Jr. (Dixon's Son), Subash Kundanmal (Dhiran Patel), Pablo Santos (Boy), Kenneth Ivan (UCO Host), Jeff Chase (Bodyguard), Cliunt Lilley (Patel's Bodyguard), Tristin Mays (Dixon's Daughter), Kevin Mitnick (Hacker)

Briefing: In São Paulo, Sydney is captured by Jacqneau's guards, but escapes to team up with Dixon the next day to abduct Patel and remove the bomb. Back in LA, SD-6 want the formula for a vaccine created by reclusive scientist Schiller for the Hensel Corporation. Sydney abducts Schiller, and swaps him for a CIA double, Paul Kelvin; while SD-6 interrogate Kelvin the real Schiller gives his information to the CIA. Sydney and Dixon go to Hensel's laboratory in Badenweiler to steal vaccine inhalers for SD-6 and destroy the building after they leave. Sydney disarms Dixon's explosive so a CIA team can get into the lab, but he has a secondary trigger, and unknowingly kills the CIA team when he detonates the explosive.

Will's investigation leads him to an encounter with 'Kate Jones'. Sydney discovers an FBI agent called Calder may have been investigating Jack.
OMG: The ambulance chase through São Paulo.
Mission: In São Paulo, Sydney is captured by the Russian bodyguard she fought with in **4**, 'A Broken Heart', but she escapes and makes her way back to the conference, where she steals an ambulance while Dixon abducts Patel. In the back of the ambulance Dixon extracts the bomb as Jacqneau catches up with them, and he throws the bomb on to the road, just as Jacqneau hits the remote trigger. Jacqneau's car is blown up by his own explosive.

Hensel Corporation is a German chemical conglomerate with roots in the Third Reich. Jerome Schiller, a leading biotech engineer who has access to Hensel's vaccine to combat biological weapons, wants out and he is prepared to give the vaccine to SD-6 in exchange for safety in the USA. Sydney is sent in to extract Schiller, while Dixon pumps gas into the Hensel building as a distraction. She hacks into the computer to email out the vaccine formula, and takes Schiller to the basement. When 'Schiller' is at SD-6, Sloane wants him to tell them the location of the plant where the prototype is being made for the vaccine inhaler; Sloane has the formula, but there were five long years between formula and prototype, years he wants to skip. When he doesn't get the information, Sloane becomes suspicious.

Once Jack has obtained the information from 'Schiller', Sydney and Dixon are sent to Badenweiler, in the Black Forest, to steal the inhalers and blow up the plant. When Dixon finds his trigger doesn't work, he uses a back-up detonator to destroy the plant.
Countermission: Vaughn is disappointed Sydney never identified the Alliance member who was supposed to be at the conference in São Paulo, but she is pleased to have saved the life of an important man, and is upset at the criticism.

The CIA have been observing Hensel for years, and they are afraid that SD-6 will sell the vaccine to a radical leader, who will then be able to vaccinate his own people and start a biological war. Sydney is introduced to Paul Kelvin, who will impersonate Schiller with SD-6 while the real Schiller is taken elsewhere by the CIA. After taking the real Schiller to the basement of the Hensel building, she swaps him with the CIA for Kelvin before rejoining Dixon. Schiller doesn't believe he's talking to the real CIA – he wants to meet with Sloane, and refuses to give them the password to the website to which he sent the vaccine formula. Meanwhile, Kelvin provides Sloane with a false website, which has enough real information to keep SD-6 busy, while providing the CIA with access to the SD-6 computer system.

Sydney gets the real Schiller to tell her about the location of the prototype, but she can't get that information to Kelvin to give to Sloane. She passes it to Jack, who whispers it to Kelvin while interrogating him. Kelvin then screams out the location as Jack breaks his arm. Once Sloane is satisfied, Kelvin gets to go home and nurse his broken arm, while the real Schiller disappears into the American mid-west with $200,000 of Sloane's money.

Sydney's Badenweiler countermission is to meet with a CIA team while Dixon sets up the explosives, swap the inhalers for CIA duplicates and then disable Dixon's explosives so that the CIA team can do a thorough investigation of Hensel's labs. The mission goes to plan, with the CIA team meeting up with Sydney as the alarms evacuate the security staff. However, although Sydney disengages Dixon's primary trigger for the explosives, he has a secondary detonator and the CIA team are killed in the explosion.

Sydney and Vaughn's meetings now take place in a warehouse, in a wire-caged area, which will remain their main meeting place for some time. To give Sydney her countermission for Badenweiler, Vaughn meets her at the pumps in a petrol station.

Destination: Berlin, Los Angeles, Badenweiler.

Timescale: Halloween is that Wednesday.

Transcripts: Jack (on Sloane): 'He finds me useful in . . . difficult situations.'

Jack (to Kelvin): 'I need to prove you're Schiller and I'm SD-6. Paul, I have to hurt you.'

Sydney Bristow: Sydney gets a copy of the CIA file on Jack from Vaughn and, although she has a paper to finish, she spends her time in the university library reading the file. There are pages missing from the file that seem to be related to something called Case 332L and an FBI Agent called Calder. If the FBI were involved, they would have to have been investigating Jack. Sydney wants to bring Dixon in as a double agent for the CIA, as her countermission involves making the switch with him nearby.

Sydney wants Francie to stop referring to Sydney's kiss with Will as humiliating.

Jack Bristow: Jack tells Sydney that he's overseeing six cases, is very busy and therefore they shouldn't make any plans until things calm down. He is a personal friend of Paul Kelvin, but he's also a man Sloane uses in interrogations, and he beats the living hell out of Kelvin in the interrogation room, breaking his arm. This is a terrifying new side of Jack, one where he does unspeakable things in the course of his life as a double agent. The most frightening thing is that the main reason Jack is so desperate is that he needs to convince Sloane of the information he's being given from the interrogation to maintain his own and Sydney's position at SD-6 – this is what Jack does to *protect* his daughter.

Arvin Sloane: Sloane becomes suspicious of the false Schiller, and questions Dixon over the change of plans during the Berlin operation – which allowed Sydney to make the switch. Sloane is almost apologetic to Sydney when he gets the location of the prototype, and believes Kelvin is the real Schiller.

Michael Vaughn: Vaughn sticks his neck out for Sydney, copying Jack's file to give to her in the hope it will answer her questions. It's his idea to hack into SD-6's computer via the false formula website, a plan that earns him Sydney's respect. Vaughn has looked into Case 332L, but found the records removed.

Will Tippin: Will tells Francie he is searching for Kate Jones as part of his Danny investigation. He gets a phone call from a Kate Jones who claims to be the one he is looking for, finds out that a 'Kate Jones' has been to São Paulo recently and is shocked by the listed social security number. He then finally meets his 'Kate Jones', a young blonde woman who claims to have been having an affair with Danny. She was supposed to go to Hong Kong with him, but he called it off. Will confronts her with one important detail of the story: according to the relevant social security records, Kate Jones died in 1973. She walks out of the meeting, and Will is left wondering who he was talking to.

Will goes to the Halloween party as Richard Nixon. He tells Francie that the mistake he made when he first met Sydney was to wait and not talk to her about how he felt.

Marcus Dixon: Dixon has to punch out Patel to abduct him from the conference, and is mortified at having done that to a peace maker and diplomat who he worships and respects. Dixon unknowingly kills an entire CIA team, a terrible consequence of his continuing ignorance of who SD-6 really are and of Sydney's countermission.

Francie Calfo: Francie works with a professional party planner and, as such, her Halloween preparations are suitably elaborate. She wants to see Charlie again, and invites his nephew to her party as a pretext. She tells Will to stop his investigation into Danny's death, to which he agrees and, in return, he advises Francie to talk to Charlie.

Intelligence: Will is given a fake 'Kate Jones' to investigate. The FBI may have been investigating Jack.

Home Front: Sydney and Francie have a Halloween party.

Lies: When Will bumps into Sydney and Francie as he comes out of the Medical School on campus, he claims to be researching a story on SAT scores (in fact, he's trying to find Kate Jones). When he tells Francie about his investigation and she disapproves, he tells her he's dropped it. Sydney describes her briefing by Sloane as an important meeting with the higher-ups at the Bank. Sloane tells Sydney and Dixon that the prototypes in Badenweiler are being made for a Neo-Nazi group, and that's why the plant must be destroyed.

Breaking the Code: Case 332L has details missing from Jack's file. Location letters: L, O and W.
Plot Devices: Marshall has designed a business card that can be used to hack into the Edsel computers so Schiller can send out the formula.
Action: There's a huge car chase in São Paulo.
Undercover: Sydney's alias in Germany is as a supervisor working for Rhinecom, sent in to work on Edsel's fibre-optics upgrade. Her look is very severe – black thigh-length leather coat, tied-back dark hair and thick dark-rimmed glasses. Sydney's regular travel alias of Kate Jones continues to cause trouble for Will.
Background Checks: Writer Daniel Arkin is a co-producer of *Alias*, and previously wrote for *The X-Files*.
Injuries: Jack breaks Kelvin's arm to make the interrogation convincing.
Music: 'I'm Wrong About Everything' by John Wesley Harding, 'Get Down Massive' by Freestylers and 'Trans Am' by Leroy.
Debrief: 'I don't know how much longer I can do this, sit in these meetings with Sloane, look at him as if I don't despise him.' Any episode which starts with a spectacular car chase and ends with a huge explosion has to be good. Sydney and Jack's position at SD-6 is threatened by Sloane's suspicion of the false Schiller, putting them in severe danger and leading to very desperate measures. SD-6's lies lead Dixon to cause a massacre, while the mystery around Jack deepens. Hectic and exciting.

6
Reckoning

Production #E635

1st US Transmission Date: 18 November 2001
1st UK Transmission Date: 27 February 2002

Writer: Jesse Alexander
Director: Daniel Attias

Guest Cast: John Hannah (Martin Shepard), Nancy Dussault (Mrs Calder), Evan Dexter Parke (Charlie), Lori Heuring (Kate Jones/Eloise Kurtz), Eugene Lazarev (Dr Kreshnik), Sarah Shahi (Jenny), Maurice Godin (Fisher), Daniel Betances (Pearson), Neil Dickson (John Smythe), Haley Gilbert (Rachel), Arabella Holzbog (Laura Bristow), Paul Lieber (Bentley Calder), Cole Peterson (Boy), Tom Waite (Guard #1), Nancy Wetzel (Amy Tippin)

Briefing: In the Black Forest, Dixon drags the traumatised Sydney away as they're pursued by armed security guards. Sydney speaks to Calder's wife, and finds out he died in the same accident as her mother.

Will tracks down Eloise Kurtz (alias Kate Jones), who refuses to talk to him, and later disappears. The next SD-6 mission is in London, where Sydney snatches an FTL decoder. To use it SD-6 need DNA from the body of murdered FTL agent Parkashoff. Sydney is sent to a Romanian asylum to talk to Parkashoff's killer, Martin Shepard. Sydney's SD-6 back-up, Fisher, is killed, leaving her trapped in the madhouse without hope of rescue . . .

Mission: FTL have abandoned a number of their bases, leaving behind musical greeting cards. There is a high-frequency code buried in the music and, when they raided FTL's floating lab, an SD-6 team found plans for an encoding device. Without that device, SD-6 cannot intercept any FTL communications and find out the purpose of FTL's relocation. Only eight decoders exist, and one is in the possession of John Smythe, owner of the Hobbs End Photo Gallery in London. In London, Dixon causes a distraction at an exhibition while Sydney breaks into Smythe's safe and takes the decoder.

The decoder works by taking a cell sample from the user's DNA, creating a code, then using it in the greeting cards. One of the recipients of a card was FTL cell leader Gareth Parkashoff, who was killed by Martin Shepard. SD-6 need a cell sample from Parkashoff's body to use the decoder. Sydney is sent to a mental institution in Bucharest, where Shepard is a patient, to get the location of the body. Agent Fisher is to back up Sydney in the mission, by posing as a doctor and checking her in as a patient. She is admitted to the hospital and tries to talk to Shepard, who attacks her when she quotes the lines of poetry to trigger his condition. Fisher's cover is blown and he is killed, leaving Sydney on her own, exposed as an agent.

Countermission: Sydney plants a CIA listening device disguised as a dead insect (a bug in two ways, as Sydney says) in Smythe's office. There's no time to make a switch with the decoders but, as the CIA still have a tap into SD-6's computers, they can access the decoded information as it is passed around the Alliance affiliate offices. The CIA so far have two per cent of the information on the SD-6 network – they're taking it slowly to avoid detection.

With Vaughn at the funeral of the Badenweiler agents, Jack passes on Sydney's countermission for Bucharest – to give the correct code to SD-6. After Sydney has gone, the CIA find out that the man who runs the hospital, Kreshnik, is with K-Directorate.

Vaughn meets Sydney at a golf range to brief her for London.

Destination: London, Los Angeles, Romania.

Timescale: Charlie's gig is on a Friday, so either Sydney is called into SD-6 after it that night, or she gets to Romania remarkably quickly – because she's already checked into the hospital by the time Will goes to meet Kurtz, a meeting set for the afternoon after the gig.

Transcripts: Sydney: 'I was working with these people. They were . . . terminated.' Francie: 'The economy sucks.'

Sydney (to Jack): 'Every time I think I know just how awful you are, I learn something worse. This time, I'm going to make sure you pay.'

Sydney Bristow: Sydney blames herself for the death of the CIA agents in Badenweiler, and wants to bring Dixon in to the CIA to stop this happening again. She spends some quality time moping over a photo of her mother.

Sydney talks to Helen Calder, the wife of the late FBI agent that Sydney suspects of investigating Jack. Agent Bentley Calder died in a car accident in 1981 – the same accident as Sydney's mother. Sydney's world view is shaken by this revelation. She will do whatever she can to turn Jack in, should he be guilty of being a KGB double agent. She tells him he will pay. She tells Vaughn he could never understand what it's like to lose a parent to the spy game (see **Laura Bristow** and **Michael Vaughn**).

Jack Bristow: Jack tells Sydney that she doesn't have clearance to know the truth about what happened to her mother, but that the conclusions she has jumped to are incorrect. He justifies his adherence to the rules of disclosure by reminding Sydney what happened when she broke them (i.e. Danny's death), and he tells her not to make assumptions based on partial information.

Jack's assignment at Jennings Aerospace is complete, and he has transferred to the SD-6 field office under the cover of being a portfolio manager at Credit Dauphine. He will now take a more active role in the planning and execution of missions.

Laura Bristow (deceased): Sydney has been told that her mother died when a drunk postal worker had crashed into her parents' car, causing Jack to drive off the bridge. The involvement of Agent Calder in the crash links Laura's death directly to Jack's suspected treachery.

Arvin Sloane: Sloane congratulates Sydney on a successful mission in Germany. When he finds out SD-6 may have a mole, Sloane arranges to meet Alliance member Alain Christophe.

Michael Vaughn: Vaughn tries to convince Sydney that there was nothing she could do in Badenweiler to stop the CIA men getting killed. He advises her to be cautious in her investigation into Jack and not to endanger their work of taking down SD-6. He offers to look into it for her and finds that Jack is clean.

Vaughn's father was an Agency man who died when Vaughn was eight years old. Vaughn watched the CIA representative at his father's funeral, and now has to do the same at the funerals for the men who died at Badenweiler, but he breaks CIA protocol by telling one of the dead men's sons that his father was a hero, then hugging him.

Will Tippin: Will finds out via a licence plate that the woman who told him she was Kate Jones is, in fact, Eloise

Kurtz. He tracks her down, and she pepper sprays him in the face to get him to back off, but phones him later saying that she was given $2,000 to say she was having an affair with Danny. He arranges to meet her at 3 p.m. the next day but finds that the flat has been stripped clean.

Jenny the intern is still bugging Will about his relationship with Sydney. Will takes his sister to Charlie's first gig.

Francie Calfo: Francie has a bad night at a Bar Association dinner. She has agreed to meet Charlie and thinks he's going to break up with her. In fact, he has a different revelation – he wants to quit law and be a singer. Rachel is a pianist, and they have a gig together on Friday, where he shows he really can sing.

Marshall Flinkman: Marshall is worried by the fact that the SD-6 computer system seems to be slow and glitchy. He realises there must be some kind of tap and cuts the hardline to stop the worm.

Martin Shepard: Shepard has been programmed to react to a specific phrase – he takes all orders given to him, then forgets what he has done immediately after the phrase is repeated. He therefore has no idea about the murders he has committed. He has recently checked himself into a mental hospital in Bucharest. His trigger phrase is from Donne – 'no man is an island . . .'

Intelligence: The 'Kate Jones' who spoke to Will was paid to play the role. Laura Bristow's death may have been the result of an FBI investigation. Vaughn's father was a CIA man, killed in action.

Breaking the Code: Smythe's alarm code is 3583. Location letters: D, S and A.

Plot Devices: Vaughn's 'bug' was copied by the CIA from a Russian device planted in the US Embassy. It acts as a listening device when hit by a microwave from an orbital satellite and is undetectable. Sydney's green-tinted specs act as real-life X-ray glasses.

Undercover: In London, Sydney wears a long black wig with a straight fringe, and a tight sleeveless green dress. Dixon impersonates a wealthy art dealer, speaking with a

French accent and smoking a large cigar, and Sydney poses as his pampered girlfriend.

In Bucharest, Sydney is admitted as a woman suffering a bipolar breakdown, who believes the government is trying to kill her and who has failed to respond to experimental treatments.

Reality Checks: Vaughn describes a book at Langley, listing agents killed in action – this really exists.

Reference Points: Hobbs End is the name of the London Underground station underneath which an alien spaceship is discovered in the BBC television series, and Hammer film remake, *Quatermass and the Pit*.

Background Checks: Scottish actor John Hannah came to fame in *Four Weddings and a Funeral*. He also starred in *The Mummy* and its sequel, while on British television he played the lead character in both *Rebus* and *McCallum*.

Writer Jesse Alexander is a producer on the show, and also wrote the movie *Eight Legged Freaks*. Daniel Attias has a career in television directing stretching from *Miami Vice* to *CSI: Miami*.

Injuries: Sydney lies on top of a scalding pipe while hiding from Smythe's guards.

Music: Charlie's song has the refrain 'have a little faith in me', and is ironically played over Sydney entering the SD-6 office. The music in Romania is more classical, with heavy use of Hermannesque strings. The songs are 'Going, Going, Gone' by Stars, 'Tornado' by Garbage and 'Be Still My Soul . . .' by Lisbeth Scott.

Debrief: 'What you think you know, you don't know.' The story inches onwards in this episode, which otherwise lacks any real identity of its own. Squeezed between the fallout from Badenweiler and the beginning of Sydney's Romanian nightmare, the London mission is fun but undistinguished. Nonetheless, the revelations and exposition are worthwhile, and the grim ending as Sydney is stranded in the hellish asylum is worth the wait.

7
Color-Blind

Production #E636

1st US Transmission Date: 25 November 2001
1st UK Transmission Date: 6 March 2002

Writers: Alex Kurtzman and Roberto Orci
Director: Jack Bender
Guest Cast: John Hannah (Martin Shepard), Evan Dexter Parke (Charlie), Elaine Kagan (June Litvack), Eugene Lazarev (Dr Kreshnik), Sarah Shahi (Jenny), Mark Galasso (Ed Davis)

Briefing: Sydney runs from the room where she found Fisher's body, and is chased by an orderly. She is captured and tortured by Dr Kreshnik, who works for K-Directorate, and makes a deal to get the information from Shepard and pass it to Kreshnik. Instead, she persuades Shepard to help her escape. While hiding at an SD-6 safehouse, Sydney realises that Shepard killed Danny, but he is a puppet, as damaged by SD-6 as she is. Sydney reveals her CIA mission to Shepard, and he tells her where Parkashoff's body is so that she can use the information to harm SD-6. SD-6 find the body and use the DNA to decode the FTL message – there's a Rambaldi artefact being analysed in England and Sloane wants Sydney to go and get it.

Eloise Kurtz is found shot dead. Jack tells Sydney he was being exonerated by the FBI, but that the investigation may have led to Laura Bristow's death. Sloane believes there is more than one mole within SD-6, and promises to deal with them . . .

OMG: Shepard is seen killing Danny.

Mission: SD-6 know something is wrong when Fisher and Sydney fail to make contact at the agreed time. However, Sloane believes Sydney can look after herself. Sydney gets the information from Shepard – that Parkashoff's body was dumped in marshland on the Texas–Louisiana border, off the I10. She passes this on to Sloane, and tells him that

Shepard committed suicide, throwing himself off a bridge as they crossed into Bulgaria.

SD-6 find Parkashoff's body, take a genetic sample and run it through the decoder to reveal the message, which relates to a Rambaldi artefact in Tunisia. FTL have already obtained the artefact and taken it to Oxford University to be analysed. Sydney is sent to England to retrieve the item.

Countermission: Vaughn meets with Jack to tell him that Sydney may be in danger from K-Directorate. Vaughn wants to send in an extraction team, but Jack advises him not to do anything to jeopardise Sydney's cover at SD-6. When she returns, she tells him that she let Shepard live and escape to try and rebuild his life. Vaughn admits that some people at the CIA want Shepard found – but Sydney insists he's as much a victim as anyone.

Sydney's Oxford countermission is simply to photograph the Rambaldi artefact before handing it over to SD-6.

Destination: Los Angeles, but the bulk of the episode is in the asylum in Bucharest.

Timescale: Sydney gets home on Thanksgiving.

Transcripts: Jack: 'You pulled my file last week. That's my problem, Mr Vaughn. Now, did curiosity just get the better of you, or were you trying to impress my daughter?'

Jack: 'Shepard killed Danny, I presume you know that?' Sydney: 'Well, if I hadn't, thank you for breaking it to me so gently.'

Sydney Bristow: Sydney realises Kreshnik is K-Directorate because his accent is Georgian, the former Soviet Republic being K-Directorate's main area for recruitment. She's sympathetic towards Shepard, someone who, like her, has had his life ruined by unwitting involvement in espionage and slaughter. Sydney offers to tell him what has happened to him in exchange for his help escaping. Shepard's confession to Danny's murder is too much for her, and she runs into the woods in tears. When she returns to the safehouse she tells Shepard all about Danny, how SD-6 ordered him killed and about her double-agent status.

Sydney lies to Sloane about Shepard, but not to Vaughn – she's sick of all the lies she has to deal with. When Jack offers to show her the FBI report on him, she turns down the chance to take it, instead taking his word for it. She invites him to stay for Thanksgiving and, although he declines, she later gives him a tub of leftovers to reheat.

Jack Bristow: When Jack finds Vaughn waiting for him at his favourite Chinese restaurant, he slams him against a wall and puts a gun to the back of his head until he's found out who he is. Jack thinks the younger agent is naïve, and accuses him of rifling through his file to impress Sydney. Jack argues that Sydney wouldn't appreciate her mission undercover at SD-6 being scrapped just because she's in danger – he considers her determination to destroy SD-6 to be the thing that keeps her going.

On Thanksgiving, Jack goes to Sydney's house to give her the FBI report exonerating him of any involvement with the KGB, but says that in some sense he *was* responsible for Laura Bristow's death, in that the accident was the result of the FBI pursuing him. He says that if he could give Sydney her mother back, he would. He declines the opportunity to spend Thanksgiving with his daughter, instead returning to work.

Arvin Sloane: Sloane tells Jack that he has faith in Sydney, and believes in her as if she were his own daughter. Sloane refuses the offer to sit on the inflatable furniture in Marshall's office.

Michael Vaughn: Vaughn arranges with Devlin to meet Jack to try and arrange Sydney's extraction from Bucharest. He believes Sydney's life is more important than her mission. When Jack tells Vaughn he knows about his file being pulled, he wants to know why Jack was checking, and how it relates to Sydney's belief that he worked for the KGB. Vaughn is glad to have Sydney back from her Romanian excursion.

Vaughn spends Thanksgiving with his mother, having broken up with Alice.

Will Tippin: Eloise Kurtz has been found shot dead. Will thinks there's something big going on, and wants to publish the story, but his boss says she can't print an unsupported conspiracy theory and tells him to bring it back to her when the story is more developed. When he does, she reads it and wants to run the story, even though Will has second thoughts. She says that the piece is now a valid story and if he doesn't work on it, someone else will.

Will takes Jenny to Sydney's Thanksgiving dinner. Jenny is so young she was asked for ID while trying to buy wine, and she doesn't look too pleased when Sydney talks about Will wearing a sweater she bought him for Christmas. For his part, Will tells Syd that his relationship with Jenny is strictly professional. Jenny kisses him during the party.

Francie Calfo: Charlie proposes to Francie; she accepts.

Marshall Flinkman: Marshall has an inflatable chair in his office – it's therapeutic. He has driven the virus out of the SD-6 computer system.

Martin Shepard: Shepard doesn't want Sydney's help, and believes he has seen her before somewhere. He considers her to be one of 'them' – the people who know the words in his head. Shepard likes to look after plants, and create pictures with charcoal: bleak landscapes under a yellow sky. Shepard is colour-blind, a symptom of his programming – being a killer is supposed to occur while he's under the influence, so he remains detached from what he does. The training is short-circuiting, and the colour-blindness is a symptom of him remembering his crimes. When Shepard first got the visions he thought they were seizures, until he went to a street where a murder had occurred and recognised the details. He came to Romania to lock himself away in case he really was a murderer. Shepard's colour vision seeps into a flashback to a killing – one where he saw a framed photo of Sydney. When Sydney tells him the whole truth – that he killed her fiancé and that he was probably programmed by McCullough – Shepard tells her where Parkashoff is buried, so that information will help bring down SD-6, for what they did to them both.

Later, Shepard sends Sydney a postcard to thank her for helping him, saying that he can see blue skies again.

Intelligence: Jack and Vaughn meet for the first time. Sydney meets the man who killed Danny – but he never knew he was a killer, so she lets him go. Will encounters a second murder in the course of his investigation.
Home Front: After her Romanian adventure, Sydney is glad to get back to the relative normality of Francie burning a Thanksgiving turkey.
Lies: Sloane tells Marshall that the virus in the SD-6 computer system was a Security Section test, which Marshall passed far faster than anticipated. Sydney lets SD-6 think Shepard is dead.
Breaking the Code: Location letter: S. I10.
Undercover: For the reception in Oxford, Sydney is given an alias as a representative of the Marissa Foundation, on the lookout for grant candidates.
Reference Points: There's more than a hint of *The Manchurian Candidate* (John Frankenheimer, 1962) and other conspiracy lore in this story of brainwashed assassins.
Background Checks: Director Jack Bender has worked on *Boomtown*, *The Sopranos* and *Felicity* as well as the movie *Child's Play 3*, and made the occasional acting appearance.
Trivia: Edward Atterton makes an uncredited cameo in the flashback to Danny's murder.
Injuries: Sydney is submerged in water and electrocuted. There's a fantastically unsubtle cut from that electrocution to meat frying in the Chinese restaurant.
Music: 'The Wait' by the Pretenders, 'Everything's All Right (I Think It's Time)' by Jude and 'Not In This Life' by Natalie Merchant.
Debrief: 'I feel like I've been stolen from myself. I don't know if there was ever a me.' By far the best episode of the series to date, **7**, 'Color-Blind' is cold, harsh, but also the most emotional story so far. The presence of guest star John Hannah adds weight to the role of Shepard, and his flashback to the killing of Danny is chilling and surprising. It's refreshing to see Sydney dealing with a low-tech problem for once, stranded in Romania without any gadgets to help. This low-key tone, more subdued than normal, leads from the drabness of the asylum to a hut in

the woods, where Sydney and Shepard discuss Danny's death in a surprisingly intimate scene. The revelation is shocking and cathartic, but most of all beautifully played by Garner and Hannah.

8
Time Will Tell

Production #E637

1st US Transmission Date: 2 December 2001
1st UK Transmission Date: 13 March 2002

Writer: Jeff Pinkner
Director: Perry Lang
Guest Cast: Tobin Bell (Dryer), Gina Torres (Anna Espinosa), Robert Clendenin (Kostia Bergman), Peter Dennis (Professor Bloom), Keone Young (Professor Choy), Elaine Kagan (June Litvack), Jack Axelrod (Giovanni Donato), Michael Halsey (Professor Hoyt), Sam Ayers (Man on Phone), Del Zamora (Mike)

Briefing: In Oxford, Sydney snatches the device – an old clock – before Anna can get it. Back in LA, she finds herself being tracked by SD-6's Security Section. She takes the clock to Donato, a clockmaker in Positano, who fixes it, before one of Anna's snipers kills him. As SD-6 search for the mole within their ranks, Sydney has to beat a biometric lie detection test to avoid being caught. Marshall fits the golden disc (see **4**, 'A Broken Heart') into the clock, producing a star chart pointing to a position near Mount Aconcagua, near the border of Chile and Argentina. After viewing the results of the test, Dryer tells Sloane he thinks he's found the mole. Dixon and Sydney go to Mount Aconcagua, and Sydney finds Rambaldi's journal in an underground cave. However, Anna catches up with her, and steals the book, kicking Sydney off a ladder from a great height . . .
OMG: Donato's slip of the tongue suggests he knew Rambaldi – and is therefore almost five centuries old!
Mission: In Oxford, Sydney uses a scanner to copy a keycard in Professor Hoyt's pocket to gain access to the

lab. Meanwhile, Anna is chatting up the ageing Professor Bloom, getting him to give her a tour so she can punch him out and steal his card. Dixon alerts the FTL guards that someone is trying to break into the engineering lab, and the guards jump on Anna, while Sydney walks straight past and uses her cloned card to swipe herself into the lab, then pours wine over the mechanism to lock it. Anna follows and shoots through the protective glass, but Sydney gets the device and escapes through the window.

The device Sydney retrieved from the lab in Oxford is a clock, the work of Giovanni Donato, who died in 1503. Donato was Rambaldi's only collaborator, a master clock-maker who made the clock on Rambaldi's commission. There is a gear assembly within the clock that doesn't seem to serve any purpose, and it also has a number on the back, a date on which nothing significant ever happened. The clock doesn't work, and Sydney is sent to meet Donato's descendant in Positano to get him to fix it.

The original Donato made a clock for Rambaldi, in return for Donato living an impossibly long life. When asked about the number on the clock, Donato says that Rambaldi never told him what it meant – suggesting that this Donato is the same one who met Rambaldi. He fixes the clock, and is shot dead by a sniper's bullet meant for Sydney, who runs away with the clock.

Back in Los Angeles, the clock is taken by Sloane as evidence that Rambaldi's inventions were part of a greater whole. When the gold disc from Malaga is placed in the clock, a light is shone through and the clock strikes 12.22, the disc becomes a starchart, a map of the sky above a specific place at a specific time. Along with the date and time listed on the clock – 16 August 1523 at 2.22 a.m. GMT – it acts as a global positioning system, pinpointing a location on the southern slope of Mount Aconcagua, on the Chile–Argentina border. Sydney and Dixon are sent to the location to find what Rambaldi was pinpointing.

In Argentina, Sydney and Dixon dig up a hatch in the ground marked with the Rambaldi symbol. They lift the slab, and Sydney descends a ladder into a deep shaft. In a cavern at the bottom, she discovers a case containing Rambaldi's journal, a leatherbound folder containing loose sheets of parchment. On the ground, Dixon is attacked by K-Directorate agents. Anna finds Sydney, and they fight while trying to climb out of the pit. Sydney is kicked down the shaft, falling into the darkness . . .

Countermission: For her trip to Argentina, Sydney is given a digital camera transmitting to a CIA satellite, so she can send instant images of whatever she finds. She photographs the Rambaldi journal pages.

Destination: Oxford, Positano, Los Angeles, Argentina.

Transcripts: Donato: 'The clock is fixed. Now, it's over.'

Marshall (on Rambaldi): 'That sound? Y'know, that boom? That's my mind blowing.'

Sydney Bristow: Sydney's academic career is suffering again – her papers are late, she's missing classes and she's threatened with a 'D' for her latest paper because it lacks any spirit. Her tutor thinks her heart isn't in her studies. With an investigation underway at SD-6 to try and find the mole, she's under increasing pressure, split between too many commitments, making it hard for her to become unemotional enough to beat the biometric tests. When preparing her, Vaughn asks her whether she's romantically interested in anyone, the biometric monitor beeps a reaction. When she takes the test for real, she thinks she has failed, but refuses to be extracted from SD-6.

Sydney finds codes in the margins of one of her mother's old books. These are revealed after Francie spills lemonade on the book, and Sydney is reading it by lamplight. The books were first editions bought by Jack for Laura, shipped from a bookstore in Prague. Sydney takes this as evidence that her father was a double agent for the KGB, receiving messages via the books.

Sydney's arch rivalry with Anna continues. When she gets into the lab first in Oxford and locks Anna out, she plants a kiss on the inside of the glass door.

Jack Bristow: Jack is the man responsible for assigning recently promoted SD-6 agent Eloise Kurtz to put Will off Sydney's trail by posing as 'Kate Jones' (one of Sydney's regular aliases). Kurtz was recommended to him on McCullough's assessment of her potential as a field agent. Jack wants to save Sydney the pain of losing another friend, and encourages Sloane to let him deal with Will, promising he'll get him off the case – or kill him himself. Jack has the passenger manifests for the flight to Singapore retroactively altered, removing Kate Jones from the list.

Jack is one of only five agents in the SD-6 office who know the truth about SD-6.

Arvin Sloane: Sloane had Eloise Kurtz, the junior agent assigned to distract Will, killed and dumped in Echo Park – 'retired', in SD-6 parlance. He thinks Jack put them all at risk by using an untried field agent to put Will off the scent, and doesn't understand how Will could have got a lead on the Kate Jones alias in the first place. Sloane considers it a possibility that they might have to kill Will.

Michael Vaughn: Vaughn works with Sydney and a biometric scanner, training her to beat the test. He's interested in her story about her father and the books, but insists that she concentrate on the tests, as her life will depend on passing them to SD-6's satisfaction. When she thinks she may have failed the test, Vaughn offers her a way out and a place in witness protection, a chance to save her life should SD-6 turn on her.

Will Tippin: Will's editor, June Litvack, wants a quote from Sydney to use in the Danny Hecht story, which Will tries to stop from running. He has until three o'clock the following day to get a quote and finish the story, or Litvack will get another writer to finish it for him. When Will goes to talk to Sydney, he's thrown by her concerns about her work, and the fact that she's wearing her engagement ring. Will's story is spiked when Litvack finds one of the key pieces of evidence – the passenger manifest for the flight to Singapore – does not refer to Kate Jones. Litvack presumes that Will's cold feet over the story are because he made it up.

Just as Will is about to give up, he receives a call from his mechanic friend Mike, who Will had recommended to Eloise Kurtz. Mike still has Kurtz's car, which she never picked up. Will goes in to examine the car, and finds a brooch, which makes electronic hissing sounds when his mobile is active. He takes it to an expert, who finds that it's a highly advanced bugging device, probably Intelligence issue.

Will must be feeling favourable towards Jenny as he gives her a research credit on the Danny Hecht story, even though she didn't do any of the research. He justifies it to Litvack as a kind lie.

Marcus Dixon: Dixon tells Sydney he's proud of her – of all the people he's worked with, she makes it look the easiest, and he admires her courage for perservering with SD-6 even after what happened to Danny. Dixon says they don't do their jobs for themselves, but for their country.

Intelligence: Jack has been the one deceiving Will, and may be KGB. Sydney finds the Rambaldi book, but Anna takes it.

Office Politics: In SD-6, Carl Dryer uses biometric scanners to perform a deep lie detector text on suspect agents, a test so deep it monitors blood flow within the brain.

Lies: Jack tells Sloane he doesn't know how Will got on to the Kate Jones alias – when he knows full well he was investigating Danny's death and the flight Jack set up to try and save Syd and Danny from SD-6. Sydney tells Will she might have to take a lie detector test at the bank, due to some thefts from petty cash.

Breaking the Code: Location letters: X, I, O and A. The number of the lab is 364. Sydney and Dixon's co-ordinates in Argentina are 32.42 by 70.01.

Plot Devices: In Oxford, Sydney has a scanner in her bag which can read the passcard in Professor Hoyt's pocket in thirty seconds, transmitting the data to Dixon so that he can create a cloned card. Jack has a signal jammer in a pen that blocks out surveillance for sixty seconds.

The clock is incredibly precise for its time – Marshall claims it only loses one second a decade. The bug Will finds in Kurtz's car is so advanced it skips channels too fast for anyone to trace the signal.

Action: Sydney beats up the Security Section man sent to tail her, much to Sloane's displeasure. In Positano, she

runs to the top of Donato's apartment building to escape Anna's thugs, and drops to the ground using an abseiling cable. As the cliffhanger Sydney falls from a great height.
Undercover: In Oxford, Anna poses as a journalist whose family was in the demolition business. Sydney's alias is Molly Zirden, and she has an English accent, shoulder-length red hair and a black dress that falls away at one shoulder.
Reality Checks: Biometric testing is usually just fingerprints, retinal and a face scan. The most advanced stuff has behaviourial aspects, like voice print and typing pattern recognition. The key to it is that there's *already* a pattern in the system. You can't just 'biometrically scan' someone; you compare them to an existing record. So, even if the 'bloodflow to the brain' test was real, it could only be used if Sydney had already been tested.
Reference Points: Will's technical mate asks, 'What's the frequency, Kenneth?', in reference to the REM song.
Background Checks: Jeff Pinkner wrote for *Ally McBeal* and *Profiler* before becoming a writer and producer on *Alias*. Perry Lang has directed episodes of *Millennium*, *ER* and *Gilmore Girls*.
Injuries: Sydney is shot by Anna in Argentina, but her bulletproof vest takes the impact – she's winded, but recovers after a minute.
Music: Ivy's 'Edge Of The Ocean'.
The Big Picture: The magnific order of Rambaldi is represented by the symbol '< ○ >', and was a noble order dedicated to protecting Rambaldi's work, but became corrupted over time. The clockmaker Donato was promised an unnaturally long life by Rambaldi, and he may be the same Donato who is shot dead by one of Anna Espinosa's thugs.
Debrief: 'If this were for real, I'd be dead by now.' A masterpiece of creative thinking and control of tone, **8**, 'Time Will Tell' veers close to pure fantasy without ever tipping over the edge. The moment when Sydney suspects Donato may be old enough to remember the Renaissance is exhilarating, a jolt that leaves the audience feeling that

they're at the edge of some bigger, greater mystery. Meanwhile, the codes in Sydney's book are the strongest evidence to date that Jack may be an out-and-out bad guy, a series-altering revelation, should it prove to be true. A thrilling episode.

9
Mea Culpa

Production #E638

1st US Transmission Date: 9 December 2001
1st UK Transmission Date: 20 March 2002

Writers: Debra J Fisher and Erica Messer
Director: Ken Olin
Guest Cast: Miguel Sandoval (Anthony Russek), Tobin Bell (Dryer), Timothy Landfield (Kretchmer), Christopher Thornton (Neville), David St James (Mr Franco), Jon Curry (Phillips), Yvonne Farrow (Diane Dixon), Timothy Halligan (Dr Mallaska), Richard F Whiten (Officer Pollard), Kaline Carr (Franco's Assistant), David Franco (Guard), Maurice Irvin (Man in the Couple), Cosimo Fusco (Logan Gerace)

Briefing: Sydney finds herself swinging upside down from the ladder, close to the cavern floor. She climbs out and finds Dixon shot and delirious, and contacts the CIA to get Dixon to a hospital in Buenos Aires, from where SD-6 pick them up.

SD-6 are pursuing Hassan's financial interests, and Sydney goes to Tuscany to get the details of his offshore account. Sloane tests Sydney's loyalty, by giving out orders for her assassination on a server that he knows is tapped, seeing if she will be rescued. Jack prevents a CIA extraction, and the assassination order turns out to be fake.

Will uses the bug (**8**, 'Time Will Tell') to make contact with a 'deep throat', a contact who feeds him information. Sydney and Russek go to Geneva to get Hassan's account number. SD-6 monitor a rogue signal in Geneva, and Sydney is snatched by Security Section.

Mission: The Argentina mission is a failure, with the Rambaldi journal in K-Directorate's possession. SD-6 retrieve Sydney and Dixon from Buenos Aires, sending him to the Angel of Mercy hospital – an SD-6-controlled facility. The cover for Dixon's injury is that he was shot in a robbery attempt outside Credit Dauphine.

Hassan's assets in the US have been frozen, so he uses the cover of a bank raid to send men to hack into the computers of one of his banks and transfer his money. SD-6 are not in business with Hassan any more; he's relocating and they suspect he will join with a hostile power. Sloane wants to close Hassan down and steal back his money. Sydney is sent to infiltrate a party thrown by Logan Gerace, Hassan's accountant, in Tuscany, and steal Hassan's offshore account number. She is then to dead-drop the information in a park five miles away. Without an invitation to the party, Sydney parachutes into the grounds of the villa, then walks into the party. She gets the information and makes the drop without incident.

The information from Gerace's computer tells SD-6 the location of Hassan's account, but not the account number – that's held in a safety deposit box in a bank, Omnicore Incorporated in Geneva. Sydney and Russek are sent in to get the codes. Sydney tours the bank vaults, knocking out her guide with a spray. She burns out the lock on the deposit box with a clamp-on laser, then reads the code to Russek (who is monitoring the op from a van).

Dryer is convinced that, Sydney is the mole – her results on the biometric test were too perfect, and her recent mistakes on missions, for example, losing the Rambaldi journal to Anna in **8**, 'Time Will Tell', are incriminating. Sloane is not convinced, and gives orders for Sydney to be assassinated when she makes her dead-drop, putting the request to the SD-6 office in Rome through Server 5. When no one moves to stop the drop and extract her, Sloane considers her to be cleared of any suspicion and tells Dryer to concentrate on finding the real mole. However, when Sydney is in the vault in Geneva, Marshall detects an additional signal – one not belonging to SD-6. Marshall tells Dryer, who passes the report to Sloane. Sydney is seized by SD-6 Security Section.

Countermission: For her mission, Vaughn gave Sydney the satellite phone she uses to call for help in Argentina. Her CIA callsign is 'freelancer'. When Sydney uses the CIA satcom to get help, Dixon hears and deliriously repeats her CIA codename.

The CIA know that SD-6 have no interest in bringing Hassan to justice. After Sydney disarmed the nuclear weapon that SD-6 sold to Hassan, he thought he had been double-crossed, so he took his revenge by taking the money and running. SD-6 want to send a message to their other partners by dealing with Hassan and the CIA want to capture Hassan. They also want SD-6 to have Hassan's money, so they can trace the transactions and get a picture of SD-6's financial activity. Sydney is sent to get a copy of the information from Gerace's computer.

The CIA get Sloane's order to kill Sydney and Vaughn arranges an extraction team for Sydney. Jack stops the extraction, realising it's a test – the intelligence was leaked to the CIA via Server 5, which SD-6 know is being monitored. Only by making the dead-drop without interruption can Sydney prove her loyalty to SD-6. The CIA hold back, and she makes her drop.

The CIA give Syd a new transmitter for Switzerland, one which picks up everything she says. She's to read Hassan's codes out loud – SD-6 will get them as well, but the CIA will tag the accounts and be able to track the money. They do exactly that as Sydney reads the codes to Russek.

Destination: Tuscany, Geneva.

Timescale: Sydney is in Tuscany on a Saturday afternoon, LA time.

Transcripts: Sloane (to Sydney): 'I always thought of you as my daughter, even from the beginning.'

Weiss (after Sydney survives the dead-drop): 'I just lost thirty pounds.'

Francie (to the bug): 'Stop torturing Will Tippin! He's my friend!'

Sydney Bristow: When Sloane says he's always looked out for her, Sydney feels that he was saying goodbye, that he knew she wouldn't return from Tuscany. She finds his paternal attitude creepy, and is surprised that he gave her a chance to escape (and be extracted) in Tuscany should she have been exposed as the mole. Sydney is weary that it's going to take a long time to bring down SD-6. She assures Francie she has no problems with her wedding arrangements despite being engaged before Danny's murder.

Jack Bristow: As soon as Vaughn tells him that they're extracting Sydney, Jack suspects it's a mistake. He goes to Marshall, telling him to check for communiques to SD-4 in Rome, claiming a message he sent never got through. Jack finds that Server 5 (via which Sloane's message was sent) has been isolated by Security Section ever since the recent 'drill'. Jack stops the extraction of Sydney, yet again bashing heads with Vaughn.

Arvin Sloane: Sloane says he thinks Sydney is innocent, and that Dryer's theory is that of a desperate man required to give the Alliance results. However, when Dryer threatens to go straight to the Alliance, he says he will deal with her personally.

Sloane tells Sydney she passed the test. He claims Danny's death was the last thing he wanted and that he begged Security Section not to kill him. When she doesn't believe him, he says he would protect her because of his long history with her – he has known Jack since Langley in 1971, he went to the Bristows' wedding and he saw her as a baby. Although he was out of the country on various operations during her childhood, he kept an eye on her until she was recruited to SD-6 seven years ago. He always knew she was special, even thinking of her as a daughter. He wanted to tell her this before she went to Tuscany.

When Sydney gets back – and Sloane considers her in the clear – he whispers into her ear, congratulating her on a job well done.

Michael Vaughn: Vaughn tells Sydney she'll get through the situation at SD-6. He wants her to contact him as soon as she returns from Tuscany – regardless of whether she completes her mission. Vaughn would rather blow her SD-6 cover by extracting her than take the slightest risk that Jack is wrong. However, Jack overrules him.

Will Tippin: Will's reporter instincts tell him there's something fishy about the cover story for Dixon's shooting. He's still trying to discover more about the bug-brooch he found, taking it to Neville the electrics expert to analyse. Neville finds that the bug is turned on. Will tells it what he's trying to investigate. He's worked out that if the person behind the bug had killed Danny and Kurtz, he would have already killed him for posing a threat. Will asks the bug to call him on his mobile, and he gets a call – but it's just Francie. Later, he shows her the bug, at which point he gets a phone call from a vocodered voice telling him to stop talking about the bug to people, which sobers him up pretty quickly. He gets another call at work, which leads him to a phone box, where the mystery voice asks him how far he's willing to go. He says he's ready to go as far as is needed, then finds an envelope in his car, containing an audio tape of someone being shot . . .

Will was inspired to become a reporter by the Howard Hawks movie *His Girl Friday*, which he claims is one of the best movies ever made. It made being a reporter look fun – but he no longer thinks it is.

Marcus Dixon: Dixon's wife is told that her husband was shot in a robbery. Sydney's use of her CIA callsign in front of Dixon plants evidence in his mind that could expose her to Sloane. Luckily, when Dixon recovers he cannot remember anything since just before he was shot.

Francie Calfo: Francie is looking at wedding dresses, and thinks Sydney isn't there because she's upset she isn't doing the same for her own wedding to Danny. Films Francie says are better than *His Girl Friday*: *The Godfather*, *On The Waterfront*, *Raging Bull* and *The Empire Strikes Back*.

Marshall Flinkman: Marshall has a jar of candy in his office to try and make it more inviting. He offers some to Jack – an entirely wasted attempt at social nicety! When Marshall discovers the anomalous signal from the Geneva operation, he's worried that by reporting it to Dryer he may have got someone into trouble.

Intelligence: The Rambaldi book is in K-Directorate hands. Hassan has gone to ground. Will gets a source feeding him intelligence for his story. Sydney is suspected of being a mole within SD-6.

Office Politics: Dryer has the authorisation to go straight to the Alliance should his findings on the security breach in SD-6 be ignored by Sloane.

Home Front: Sydney and Francie arrange to go shopping for wedding dresses on a Saturday, but Sydney misses the appointment because of her Tuscany mission. Francie is left on her own. Will and Francie spend a slightly drunken night watching *His Girl Friday*, admiring the witty dialogue.

Lies: Everyone outside SD-6 is told that Dixon was shot when he resisted thieves who pulled up in a car outside Credit Dauphine and tried to get the computer codes for the bank from him and Sydney. Sydney's cover for the Tuscany mission is a trip to Boston. When Will gets a call about the bug, he's told to tell Francie it was a wrong number – which he does.

Breaking the Code: Sydney's CIA callsign is 'freelancer'. Will's mobile number is 310 555 0153. Gerace's box number in Geneva is 22364. Hassan's account code is D6135C7E. Location letters: U and V.

Plot Devices: Neville says Will's bug is MEMS – micro electro mechanical systems – technology. For Tuscany, Marshall gives Sydney a mobile phone with a biometric sensor to scan Gerace's fingerprint from any smooth surface, to create a liquid latex copy Sydney can use to open the door to his private quarters. Marshall provides her with a device to extract the information from Gerace's hard drive at 40GB in two minutes – the CIA provide a device to piggyback that one and copy the information for them.

Action: Sydney parachutes into the grounds of Gerace's villa in Tuscany, before pulling off her jumpsuit to reveal her best party clothes.

Undercover: In Tuscany, Sydney goes to the party wearing a short, high-necked, sleeveless black dress and bobbed, straight-fringed dark hair. In Geneva, Sydney's alias is Christiana Stephens of Dryberg Diamonds, who is looking for a bank to recommend to clients for volume storage.

Background Checks: Writers Debra J Fisher and Erica Messer also serve as story editors on the show.
Injuries: Dixon is left hospitalised after being shot by K-Directorate.
Music: 'Out Of Order' by Duncan Sheik, 'Diggin' Your Scene' by Smashmouth and 'Sacred Way' by Munkafust.
Debrief: 'I'm, like, living in a puzzle. I can't figure anything out, I don't know who is doing what, I'm a mess. And whoever's listening can go to hell.' A less action-packed episode with a wider focus beyond Sydney's escapades, **9**, 'Mea Culpa' features a number of ongoing plot strands that inch forwards. It also spends time with the supporting cast, putting Dixon on the critical list, developing Will and ratcheting up the tension between Vaughn and Jack. The 'dead-drop' scene is a real nailbiter, the highlight of a quieter moment in the season.

10
Spirit

Production #E639

1st US Transmission Date: 16 December 2001
1st UK Transmission Date: 27 March 2002

Writers: JJ Abrams and Vanessa Taylor
Director: Jack Bender
Guest Cast: Miguel Sandoval (Anthony Russek), Scott Paulin (Robert Stoller), Aharon Ipale (Hassan), Christopher Thornton (Neville), Scotch Ellis Loring (Gordon), Sarah Shahi (Jenny), James Warwick (Driscoll), Conrad Gamble II (Bodyguard), Erica Inez (Hotel Manager), Kevin McKorkle (Agent), Don Took (Agent Grey), Scott Vance (Security Section Agent #1), Nancy Wetzel (Amy Tippin)

Briefing: Knocked out by security section, Sydney comes to in a holding cell, where she is about to be tortured, but suspicion turns to Russek and she is released. Russek is then interrogated and killed. Sydney is sent to Kenya to find a forger who is creating a new identity for Hassan. She realises Jack set up Russek to set her free. Will meets

David McNeil, a man imprisoned because of SD-6. Jack is sent to Cuba by Sloane to kill Hassan, but is seized and Sydney goes to Cuba to get him back. She, too, is captured and Jack is told to kill her. He raises the gun . . .
OMG: Jack points a gun at Sydney when Hassan tells him to prove his loyalty by shooting her.
Mission: Sloane asks Russek if he had any clue Sydney was the mole, then sends him in to tell her that SD-6 believe they are both moles, and that he will be tortured and killed if she doesn't confess and give up information on her activities. An injured Russek is thrown into the cell with Sydney to make her crack, but she tells the guards she won't talk to Sloane. An interrogator is sent in to deal with her. Marshall finds evidence that Russek is the mole and that he was transmitting to K-Directorate. Russek is subjected to interrogation while Sydney is released.

SD-6 have intercepted signals regarding Hassan coming from Semba Island, a private resort in Kenya used as a bolthole for rich fugitives avoiding extradition. Severin Driscoll is a forger based on the island, and SD-6 believe he has made new identity papers for Hassan. Sydney is sent to Kenya to locate Driscoll and find Hassan's new identity. She talks to Driscoll, then finds and breaks into his suite. She reports to SD-6 that the mission is a failure (see **Countermission**), but Sloane discovers that Hassan is living in Havana as Nebseni Saad. He wants to set an example, and Jack is sent to Cuba to locate Hassan and kill him.
Countermission: Vaughn and Sydney meet at a flower stall, and he confirms that the CIA were not responsible for rescuing her. Russek could be K-Directorate – but they have no evidence he has ever had contact with the Russians. Vaughn tells Sydney that Russek was killed.

Sydney is told to keep Hassan's new identity from SD-6, and pass it to the CIA instead. When she finds details of his new identity, she realises she bumped into him the previous day at the resort. Jack's CIA countermission in Cuba is to tell Hassan that he has been sent to assassinate him, but wants to leave SD-6 and will help him fake his death in exchange for his client list. However, the plan is that a CIA team will snatch him after his death has been faked, and he will never be free again. The mission goes wrong, and Hassan captures Jack. Devlin can't send a CIA team into Cuba, as it would draw too much attention, so Sydney has to go alone. In Havana, she shows a photo of Jack to the locals to find him. Meanwhile, Jack talks to Hassan, telling him SD-6 know his new identity and where he is, and offering the deal. Sydney is captured and dragged before Hassan. As a test of good faith, he tells Jack to kill her.

Destination: Kenya, Havana.

Transcripts: Sydney: 'If you knew what I dealt with every day you might thank me for doing my job so well.' Will: 'What the hell are you talking about?'

Jack (to Vaughn): 'Neither your experience nor your intelligence have earned you the right to question a thing that I do.'

Sydney Bristow: Sydney tries to get her torturer to identify with her, to make it difficult for him to hurt her – she tells him her name, talks about work, says she wondered what he did. Sydney doesn't give in to save Russek's life when she's in the cell, because his erratic blinking shows that he's lying, and not in any real danger. When Russek is fingered as a K-Directorate agent, she can't believe it. When Vaughn tells her about his briefing with Jack for the Cuban mission, she realises he is omitting something from the report.

Sydney gets an antique picture frame from Vaughn for Christmas, and is torn between two photos of herself as a child – one of her with her mother, another with her father. The picture of Jack reminds her of when she asked him whether Father Christmas existed. His flat reply that of course he did was said exactly the same way he said that Russek was a K-Directorate mole. She knew he was lying as a child, and knows he's lying now. She feels guilty because Russek died for what she did, and doesn't believe Jack had the right to sacrifice someone else's life for hers.

Jack Bristow: Jack finds Sydney's desk has been cleared by Security Section and that she is under arrest. He later denies setting up Russek to take the fall, claiming his K-Directorate allegiance came as a shock to him. He says this with a casualness which seems totally forced and therefore deeply suspicious. Jack sympathises with Sloane, saying that, with both Russek and Hassan in one week, Sloane is having a difficult time.

When directly accused by Vaughn, Jack admits that he set up Russek to take the fall for Sydney by hacking into the SD-6 computer and altering the transmission to put him in the frame. Vaughn can judge Jack if he wants – Jack doesn't care. He still has no respect for Vaughn, and thinks he has no right to be investigating him. He also wants him to stop pushing, and to decline any further opportunities to be his handler. As before, see **5**, 'Doppelganger', when Sydney is threatened Jack resorts to violent action to protect her, in this case allowing a man to die.

Arvin Sloane: Sloane, rather regretfully, believes that Sydney will not see a colleague suffer for her crimes. Echoing Jack in **5**, 'Doppelganger', he chillingly tells Russek that they will need to make it seem convincing that he has been interrogated. When he receives evidence that Russek is K-Directorate, he makes the interrogation for real, and Russek is killed. Similarly, Sloane wants Hassan killed to send out a message not to steal from SD-6.

Sloane tells Jack of a time when he was new to the CIA, before they had even met. After a briefing at the White House, he had needed to get some air, overwhelmed by the perfect moment of where his life was, and he walked to the Jefferson Memorial, his favourite. He claims that even on that night he was aware that there was darkness ahead, that it would all go wrong. Since then, the CIA have betrayed him, and his wife has been diagnosed with lymphoma. He comforts himself whenever things go wrong, by reminding himself that he knew it was coming.

Michael Vaughn: Vaughn buys Sydney a Christmas present, which he picked up in an antique store. After briefing Jack for Cuba, he tells him he compared the CIA logs of the SD-6 transmissions, and the transmission which damned Russek didn't match the one SD-6 had earlier logged. This is a lie – Vaughn simply had a hunch and his bluff gains Jack's confession, if not his respect.

When Sydney feels guilty about Russek, Vaughn tells her not to feel any pity, as he was an early SD-6 member who knew exactly who he was working for, and tells her to ask herself what she would have done in Jack's shoes.

Will Tippin: Will takes the tape of the shooting to Neville, who says the shots are 9 mm, a close-range hit probably putting two shots in the chest and one in the head. Will says this is exactly how Kurtz was killed, and that the recording was made from the transmissions from the brooch. As the recording is cleaned up, he hears Kurtz being asked if she told him about SD-6. The only reference to SD-6 Will can find is in a court case, *The People vs David McNeil*, and he approaches Stoller, the man who defended McNeil, a computer programmer who created a company. When he didn't want to sell to a larger company, a government investigation stitched him up for larceny, and he was locked up for sixteen years. His wife killed herself – though her husband didn't believe it was suicide – and he wanted to make sure nothing happened to his daughter. Will goes to visit him in Lompoc Federal Penitentiary and tells him that he's interested in SD-6. McNeil says he knows nothing, then tells Will to stay away.

Will wants Sydney to quit her job, which he thinks makes unnatural demands on her, and is baffled by her insistence that it's so important. When she comes around to apologise for snapping at him, she finds that Will has Jenny staying. Will later tells Francie that the relationship doesn't mean anything. Will needles Sydney about her present from Vaughn, saying that he probably likes her.

Marcus Dixon: Dixon is still recovering from being shot.

Francie Calfo: Francie refers to Jenny as a cheerleader.

Intelligence: Will hears the name SD-6 for the first time, and meets David McNeil. Russek takes the fall as the mole within SD-6, leaving Sydney in the clear.

Home Front: Sydney, Will, Francie and Amy play a wordgame one evening, which is interrupted by Sydney

being called into SD-6. Sydney wants to spend some time away with her friends over the next week or so, perhaps going out to Lake Arrowhead with them.
Lies: Jack lied to Sydney as a child about whether there was a Santa Claus. He lies about framing Russek, but is tricked into admitting it by a bluff from Vaughn.
Breaking the Code: In Kenya, Sydney is next door to suite 47, while Driscoll is permanently based in suite 350. Location letters: N and V.
Plot Devices: For Kenya, Marshall provides Sydney with sunglasses that contain telephoto lenses and take pictures, but are also appropriately stylish. He also supplies her with a mobile phone that unscrambles key card readers, allowing her to break into any room on Semba Island.
Undercover: Sydney's alias for Semba Island is Victoria King, daughter of industrialist Martin King. She wears tumbling long blonde hair, a short white safari dress buckled at the front and a large black and white sunhat. By the pool she wears a black bikini.
Reality Checks: Semba Island just off the coast of Kenya.
Trivia: Jack names Isaac Lohan and Juli Schroeder as two people SD-6 eliminated.
Injuries: Russek gets knocked about to make his interrogation convincing, then is tortured for real. Jack and Sydney both take a beating in Cuba.
Music: 'Love Grows (Where My Rosemary Goes)' by Freedy Johnston, 'Domino' by Thunderball and 'Santa's Dilemma' by Klyph.
Debrief: 'Threat to colleagues is a fundamental interrogation technique.' One of the more James Bond-esque episodes, **10**, 'Spirit' merrily skips to a Kenyan Island, then later to sunny Cuba. It's great to see Jack as a superspy, saving Sydney then street fighting in Havana. This is a critical episode in the Jack/Sydney relationship, with him going to an extreme to protect his daughter, and her being revolted by the extent of his actions. Elsewhere, frequent *Alias* director Ken Olin steps in front of the camera to bring integrity to the role of David McNeil, SD-6 victim.

11
The Confession

Production #E640

1st US Transmission Date: 6 January 2002
1st UK Transmission Date: 3 April 2002

Writers: JJ Abrams and Daniel Arkin
Director: Harry Winer
Guest Cast: Aharon Ipale (Hassan), James Handy (Devlin), Francesco Quinn (Minos Sakkoulas), Joanne Young (Mychella), Vincent Lappas (Techie), J. Anthony McCarthy (Bouncer), Matthew James Williamson (Bodyguard)

Briefing: Jack blinks at Sydney, giving her a morse code message. He tells Hassan that shooting her would prove nothing. At his signal, Sydney and Jack fight their way out of the stand-off, before they successfully abduct Hassan, fake his death and pass him to the CIA. One of Hassan's underlings, Sakkoulas, is planning to sell something called 'the package', and SD-6 send Sydney and Dixon to find out what it is. Although SD-6 get that information, Hassan tells the CIA where to find the package in Crete. Sydney passes a note to Jack asking him to tell Sloane where the silo is, so that she will be sent to Crete.

The Cyrillic codes Sydney found in the books owned by her mother – presents from Jack – have been analysed by NSA. Vaughn reports that they are KGB orders for the elimination of a dozen CIA agents, who died 25 years before. There is still a mystery over who murdered the CIA officers, and Vaughn is certain Jack is guilty. Sydney doesn't want to report Jack, uncertain of his involvement. Vaughn tapes his conversation with Sydney and, when Sydney argues that they need Jack to bring down SD-6, Vaughn produces the tape – but he can't bring himself to use it against her. He tells her that the situation is personal for him too – his father was one of the agents killed. Vaughn has set up a meeting with Devlin to report Jack, and wants Sydney with him.

Sydney and Vaughn have their meeting with Devlin; Jack is present, sitting alongside Devlin. He wants to talk in public so that Sydney will believe him, in front of the CIA men who know. He confirms the orders to kill in the books, but the agent to carry out those orders was not Jack – it was Sydney's mother.

OMG: Laura Bristow was a KGB killer!

Mission: Jack tells Sloane that his mission was a success, and that Hassan is dead. He even has the photos to prove it. Sloane is delighted.

Sloane tells his agents that Hassan has been mysteriously murdered. With Hassan dead, Minos Sakkoulas has been trying to contact his clients and take over the business. He is planning to sell a 'package', probably a new device Hassan was having constructed. Sydney and Dixon are sent to Greece, to Sakkoulas's cover, Club Panthera, where a meeting is set up with potential buyers. Their mission is to break into Sakkoulas's office and get the specifications for the package. In Greece, Sydney heads into the club, while Dixon takes out the security man and uses the club's own cameras to locate Sakkoulas. Sydney slinks her way into the private side room where Sakkoulas is sitting, and stands seductively, meeting his gaze. With the club lighting interfering with the retinal scan, Sydney needs to get closer, sliding up to Sakkoulas and letting him take her into a back room while she gets a lock on his retinas. Once Dixon has the print, Sydney finds herself kept back to wait for Sakkoulas to complete his meeting, and she has to fight a guard to get out. Dixon is already putting on the contacts to get the plans himself while Sydney escapes. He successfully gets into the office and downloads the information, while Sydney is recaptured by Sakkoulas's guards. Sakkoulas sleazes over her, and she and Dixon have to fight their way through him and his men.

Jack provides Sloane with information – apparently from his contacts in the Middle East – leading SD-6 to Hassan's weapons silo on Crete, where the package is being kept. Sydney is sent in.

Countermission: Jack successfully gets the client list from Hassan and fakes his death. Jack and Sydney deliver him to the CIA, and he is moved to a CIA safehouse in Los

Angeles, where Vaughn interrogates him about the package. He wants his wife and son retrieved and protected from his enemies before he talks, but the CIA refuse to co-operate and Hassan refuses to talk.

Sydney's countermission in Greece is to record the specs for the CIA. She is given unclassified weapon designs to photograph for SD-6's benefit. However, with her being waylaid while getting Sakkoulas's retinal prints, Dixon gets to the office first and completes the mission for SD-6, denying Sydney her countermission.

With no deal available, Hassan tells Vaughn that the package, and other weapons, are stored in a silo on Crete. Sydney wants to go on a CIA mission to Crete, but Vaughn thinks it's too dangerous to send her anywhere without SD-6's knowledge, especially so soon after Cuba. She asks that they feed the information to Sloane via Jack, so that she can go to Crete with SD-6's knowledge. On Crete, she goes into the silo, which Hassan says has minimal security, partly because of its innocuous disguise. Following Hassan's instructions, Sydney finds a keypad and enters the vault. She finds the package – an electromagnetic (EM) refractor – but the vault locks her in. Hassan has set her up – the wrong code activated an anti-intruder device: the room will be filled with gasolene, and a minute later a light will be struck. Hassan wants a signed declaration from Devlin that his family will be taken into the Witness Protection Programme. While Weiss types the statement, Vaughn runs to get Devlin, who rushes down to the Ops Room to sign the statement, and Hassan gives them the correct code. Sydney punches it in and the system deactivates. The security system has summoned Sakkoulas, who, unable to use his gun in the gas-filled room, fights Sydney with a knife. His knife goes into an electric socket and Sydney flees as a short circuit causes an explosion, killing him.

Destination: Athens, Los Angeles, Crete, Los Angeles.

Timescale: The Athens mission is on a Thursday, the meeting with Devlin to report Jack the following Monday.

Transcripts: Jack (to Sydney): 'There are . . . there are so many things which I should probably do, I mean, as a father . . . things I should ask, and say . . .'

Sydney (to Vaughn): 'We need him right now. We will never destroy SD-6 without my father.'

Vaughn: 'You made a connection with your father for the first time in your life, and turning him in would mean sacrificing that, I understand.'

Sydney Bristow: Sydney has never been very good at morse code, and takes a couple of tries to get Jack's blinked message. She wants to know why he never told her the truth about SD-6. She thanks Vaughn for helping her to get to Cuba, and tells him he was right about the things people do when a loved one is in trouble – she realises that, in Jack's position, she would have sacrificed Russek too. Having seen Jack in action in Cuba, she is impressed with his abilities as an agent and is, therefore, reluctant to turn him in for his possible KGB involvement, saying that the orders were 25 years ago, and they can't be sure of the extent of his involvement. Although she agrees with Vaughn that they have to do the right thing, she asks for a little time to acclimatise herself to what she has to do. When she comes back to Vaughn with more reasons not to report Jack, he tells her about his father. Sydney's response is to tearfully visit Will. She can't tell him what's wrong, but stays with him in a close hug to feel better.

Sydney is disgusted by Sakkoulas licking her face, and even more disgusted that, because of him, she failed her CIA mission.

Jack Bristow: In Cuba, Jack describes his gunshot wound as being of no concern – it certainly doesn't slow him down. How hard is this guy? He says he didn't tell Sydney that SD-6 were the bad guys, because telling her would reveal what he was doing. Later, he thanks Sydney for rescuing him in Cuba, and he tries to talk to her about fatherhood and what he should do as a parent.

Arvin Sloane: Sloane tells Jack he's glad to see him back, and was worried when he fell out of contact while in Cuba.

Michael Vaughn: Having discovered the codes in Jack's books, Vaughn is determined that he should be reported for suspicion of working for the KGB to kill CIA agents. He won't, however, do this alone – he wants Sydney with him to provide the evidence, and is determined to report Jack with her consent. When she stalls, he reminds her that agents died and their families' lives were destroyed by what Jack allegedly did. He says she's being selfish, neglecting the right thing to do because she will lose her newfound relationship with her father. Although he agrees to give her time, he's already taped her admission that Jack was probably involved. However, he can't bring himself to use the tape and instead admits he has a personal stake in the case – one of the agents Jack may have killed was his father, William C Vaughn.

Vaughn plays the hard man with Hassan, constantly threatening that Hassan is going to become some beefy prisoner's bitch in a maximum-security facility.

Will Tippin: Will has the baffling experience of Sydney visiting him without explanation, in tears, and lying with him on the sofa, almost wrapping him around her as she cries. While this is clearly a comfort she needs, it must be both incredibly confusing and frustrating for Will, considering his ongoing crush on her.

Marshall Flinkman: Marshall asks his SD-6 colleagues if they saw a TV documentary on monkeys the previous night.

Intelligence: A KGB agent killed Vaughn's father. That agent wasn't Jack, it was Laura Bristow. Hassan is captured by the CIA.

Lies: Sloane tells the SD-6 agents that Hassan has been murdered, and lets them believe Sakkoulas may be responsible.

Breaking the Code: The false code Hassan gives Sydney is 314159. The correct code is 766153. Location letters: E, S, R and G.

Plot Devices: In Greece, Sakkoulas's office has a retinal scanner on the lock. Marshall provides a retinal scanner in a pair of sunglasses, which Sydney can use to scan his eyes from up to thirty feet away, then transmit the scan to Dixon, who will be able to create contact lenses with the

retinal prints. The CIA provide her with a kit to record the specs for the CIA – a purse containing a camera (a compact), a voice recorder (lipstick) and a USB flash ram drive (lighter).
Action: Sydney and Jack fight side-by-side in Cuba. The exploding bunker in Crete is spectacular.
Undercover: In Greece Sydney wears a red summer dress and red wig, along with a matching choker. Dixon is also wearing holiday clothes, a black casual shirt with white patterns. On Crete, Sydney wears a very neatly fitted camouflage jumpsuit.
Reality Checks: Under the Patriot Act of 2001, the CIA are allowed to keep Hassan for as long as they like. The Uniting and Strengthening America by Providing Appropriate Tools Required to Intercept and Obstruct Terrorism (USA PATRIOT) Act was quickly passed after the terrorist attacks on 11 September (it became law on 26 October). This controversial piece of legislation gave the authorities a wide range of new powers, changed immigration laws, tightened controls on money laundering and expanded the legal use of surveillance. An immigrant such as Hassan could easily be held for a long period of time under an extraordinary interim regulation introduced by Attorney General John Ashcroft on 17 September 2001, which set aside the limitations on the detention of aliens.
Background Checks: James Handy has appeared in *NYPD Blue* and *The West Wing*, and in the movies *Anachrophobia* and *Unbreakable*.
Injuries: Jack takes a bullet in Cuba. Sakkoulas gets crispy-fried when the bunker explodes.
Music: 'Someone To Watch Over Me' by Sting and 'Rave Alarm' by DJ Teebee.
The Big Picture: Hassan's capture removes a major player from the *Alias* espionage world.
Debrief: 'For each of those lives lost, others were destroyed.' Episode **11**, 'The Confession' lives up to its name, blurting out a series of stunning plot twists and revelations. A major player (Hassan) departs; the truth is revealed about Vaughn's father, and Sydney's late mother is

exposed as a KGB assassin. This last revelation, while not entirely surprising (plot logic gives it a tragic inevitability), is a major twist that changes the entire shape of Sydney's world.

12
The Box (Part One)

Production #E641

1st US Transmission Date: 20 January 2002
1st UK Transmission Date: 10 April 2002

Writers: Jesse Alexander and John Eisendrath
Director: Jack Bender
Guest Cast: Quentin Tarantino (McKenas Cole), Joey Slotnick (Haladki), Agnes Bruckner (Kelly McNeil), Sarah Shahi (Jenny), Patricia Wettig (Dr Judy Barnett), Jennifer Tung (Toni), Ben Bray (Tchen), Christophe Konrad (Endo), Igor Jijikine (Chopper), Dave Lea (Ice), Jeff Wolfe (Gonov), Randy Hall (Security Agent #1), Lawence Lowe (Security Agent #2)

Briefing: A team, led by former agent McKenas Cole, breaks into the SD-6 office and holds the entire staff hostage. Sydney is considering quitting SD-6, but is advised against it by Jack and Vaughn, who think Sloane will have her killed. Sloane activates the failsafe security system before being captured.

Jack and Sydney are in the SD-6 elevator when the building locks down, and they are the only agents free as Cole's team swarm through SD-6. Cole wants something from the SD-6 vault. Jack knows that, with the failsafe activated, 5,000 pounds of C4 within the SD-6 building will be activated if Cole succeeds in entering the SD-6 vault. The building will collapse and all evidence of the Los Angeles cell of SD-6 will be destroyed. He wants to use a scrambler Marshall has been working on to scramble the vault codes and stop it from happening. Sydney goes through the airvents to get the scrambler.

Sloane is interrogated by Cole and gives him a code. Sydney gets the scrambler and activates it before Cole gets to the vault room, then disappears back into an airvent. Cole is frustrated to find the code doesn't work, blaming it on Sloane. Sydney makes too much noise as she crawls through the ceiling and Cole opens fire. Sydney tries to climb an airvent, but finds herself sliding.

Will wants to quit the SD-6 story because it's too dangerous, but McNeil's daughter persuades him to help her father, on condition she goes away where no one can threaten her.

OMG: It's Quentin Tarantino!

Mission: SD-6 is infiltrated by a team led by McKenas Cole, who get into the building posing as a maintenance crew. When Cole walks into the SD-6 office floor, an internal security system picks him up on the face-scanning database. When Sloane realises that he is in the building, he initiates a computer security failsafe, and tries to get the building locked down – but Cole has already taken out the security room. Knockout gas floods the office and Cole walks through it wearing a gasmask as all the agents collapse. Cole and his team tie up the SD-6 agents. Sydney and Jack escape and break into SD-6 through the maintenance corridors. Jack hacks into SD-6's security cameras via a switchbox and they observe the situation.

Cole was an SD-6 agent sent to blow up a pipeline in Chechnya in 1996. Sloane didn't send the chopper to the right location to pick them up, and the team was captured by the Russians after the job was done. Now he wants revenge on Sloane, as well as something his new employer, The Man, wants from the SD-6 vault. Cole takes Sloane to the 'conversation room', SD-6's torture chamber, and says that if he doesn't get the codes from him they can get in anyway, but if he gives them the codes he will not have to open 'the box'. Sloane refuses and Cole opens the small leather box, revealing the 'needles of fire'. Sydney breaks into Marshall's office through the airvents, trying to get a scrambler to disrupt the vault codes. The office is in full view of where the agents are being held, so Jack cuts the power to a camera pointing at Marshall, causing the light to blink on and off in morse code. Marshall sees it, and draws Dixon's attention, who fakes a seizure to distract the guard, following Jack's command, so that Sydney can drop into the office and grab the scrambler. Marshall provides another distraction, and gets smacked in the face with a gun butt for his trouble.

Cole talks about a Cajun restaurant where the hot sauce makes people cry, and how it's like vanilla ice cream compared to the needles of fire. He then tapes Sloane's hand open and gets ready to insert the first needle. Sloane tells Cole a code, but he sticks one of the pins into his hand anyway. He says that the powder takes a few minutes to kick in, and he can take it out – if Sloane gives them the right code. He takes the code to the vault, as Sydney rushes to use the scrambler on the vault keypad. Cole tries to use the keypad, and it fails – he blames Sloane.

Countermission: Sydney wants to quit. She wants out. Vaughn tries to persuade her that what she does is valuable and important, and that their mission to bring down SD-6 needs to be done. He offers her access to the Witness Protection Programme. Sydney refuses, saying she doesn't want to go into hiding. She doesn't think Sloane will kill her if she just quits, although Vaughn disagrees.

Destination: The entire episode takes place in LA, mainly within the Credit Dauphine building.

Transcripts: Sydney (to Jack): 'I can't believe, of all things, we're saving SD-6.'

Sloane (to Cole): 'I can't be the first person to have difficulty taking you seriously, can I?'

Marshall (distracting one of Cole's gang): 'Excuse me? As luck would have it, I'm feeling a kind of Stockholm Syndrome thing happening . . .'

Sydney Bristow: Sydney is left in shock and horror by Jack's revelation that the family life she thought had been taken away from her was a lie, and that her mother had been a killer and a spy who may never have cared for her family at all. Everything she has believed is reduced to nonsense by the revelation. The shock causes her to want to quit her countermission and leave both SD-6 and the CIA. She needs something real in her life, and wants to walk away from the world of espionage. She doesn't think Sloane will kill her if she resigns.

She tells Vaughn she's sorry for what her mother did, and hugs him. She invites him to go with her to a hockey match – an obvious date.

Jack Bristow: Jack believes that his entire relationship with Laura, and her desire to have a family, were just all part of her KGB mission. None of it was real.

He thinks that Sydney's plan to quit SD-6, without any exit strategy or plan, is suicide and that, while Sloane may be protective towards Sydney, his superiors would not be. If he let her go, they would both be killed by the Alliance. Once the Alliance consider Sydney a breach, they will eliminate all her friends and anyone she may have talked to, including Will and Francie.

It's Jack who realises the seriousness of the threat to the SD-6 office – when he and Sydney are trapped in the elevator, he tries the emergency phone and gets no answer. He knows that a power blackout wouldn't take down the security detail. His high-level clearance allows him to turn off some of the SD-6 security as he and Syd pass through the building. Sydney initially believes the team who invaded SD-6 are K-Directorate, but Jack corrects her – K-Directorate would expect retaliation for such an attack and no group that SD-6 know would risk such a gambit. He considers Cole's team unpredictable and dangerous, a rogue element.

For one hilarious scene, it seems like Jack is going to shimmy through the airvents, while Sydney stays and monitors the situation – it's a testament to our belief in Jack's abilities that, while this seems unconvincing, it doesn't actually seem impossible.

Laura Bristow: Sydney's mother was sent to America by the KGB to steal secrets from a CIA officer – Jack. She did this by pretending to fall in love with him.

Arvin Sloane: Sloane is trying to phone his wife's doctor when he notices Cole in the office. Sloane, tied to a chair and threatened with hideous torture, treats Cole's threats with contempt and indifference.

Michael Vaughn: Vaughn is a hockey fan and supports the Kings. He goes into a depressive gloom when Sydney wants to quit SD-6, knowing she's in danger. He's thrown by finding out who killed his father, a question which was always intellectual before. Vaughn has been ordered to report to Dr Judy Barnett, a CIA psychologist. He tells her that he thinks their appointment is a waste of time – there is no crisis; his father died over twenty years ago and he is used to the fact. Barnett asks him about his relationship with Sydney, about how often they meet and the circumstances. Vaughn says he's the only person Sydney can talk to and refutes any suggestion by Barnett that his relationship with her is inappropriate and breaks the rules about relations between agent and handler. Barnett has received reports about Vaughn's behaviour and, although she won't disclose who made the reports, he guesses it's Agent Haladki. He confronts Haladki and ends up fighting with him in the corridor before Weiss pulls him away.

Will Tippin: Will is baffled as to why everyone he talks to in his investigation seems desperate to get away from him. Jenny has found out that SD-6 is an ingredient in artificial sweeteners, but suspects it isn't the one Will is investigating. Will thinks his investigation may just be hurting the people he is trying to protect. Jenny disagrees – she thinks Will is the champion of the victims. Nevertheless, he wants out of the SD-6 story – he doesn't want to put McNeil's daughter Kelly in danger.

Will gets a call from his mystery source, directing him to an envelope on his office chair. He tells the voice to leave him alone if he's not brave enough to admit who he is, and throws the envelope away. Will then gets involved in a new story about a corrupt property developer, and finds he has been set up on a dinner meeting with Kelly McNeil (the property developer story is clearly a fake). Kelly wants to talk to him about her father, but he walks away. She visits him at work and tells him that the people involved in SD-6 killed her mother and framed her father. She's going to disappear, go away where she can never be found – McNeil will then be safe to talk. But she'll only do that if Will will fight for her father. Will agrees and picks the envelope out of his bin. Inside is a key.

Marshall Flinkman: Marshall sees some action in this episode, held hostage with the rest of SD-6 and knocked to the ground as he provides a distraction to help Sydney.

McKenas Cole: McKenas Cole is an ex-SD-6 agent, who has been away for five years. He tells Sloane that he looks older, but good, and that he wants to talk to him. Cole was left for dead in Grozny where he saw the rest of his SD-6 team tortured to death, and he blames Sloane for deserting them and for lying to him. When he was being interrogated by the Russians, he told them that he wasn't working for Islamic rebels but for the CIA. The Russians didn't want to torture an American citizen and contacted Langley. The CIA denied there was an agent called McKenas Cole – that was when Cole found out that SD-6 was a sham. The Russians retaliated by torturing Cole using 'the box', which contains a selection of needles. He now works for The Man, who wants something from the SD-6 vault.

Cole is, as you would expect from a Tarantino character, super-cool. When his team have got past SD-6 security, Cole pulls off his overalls to reveal a *Reservoir Dogs* dark suit. To complete the appearance of being there legitimately, his team pour him a cup of coffee from a thermal flask and he carries the cup as he walks into the office. Cole compliments Sloane on a witty retort when he says he can't take him seriously.

Intelligence: SD-6 is invaded by agents of The Man, who want something in the vault. Sydney wants to quit SD-6.

Office Politics: At the CIA, Dr Barnett deals with agents suffering from personal crises. Vaughn and Weiss despise Agent Steven Haladki, a tactless weasel of a man.

Plot Devices: Marshall's scrambler is disguised as a compact.

Action: Cole's team run through a corridor before the web of security lasers comes back on, the last member of the team sliding under a couple of beams as he gets to safety.

Undercover: Cole's team dress as an air-conditioning maintenance crew to get into the building.

Reference Points: The cover name for Cole's team is McTiernan Air Conditioning, named after John McTiernan, director of the ultimate office-under-siege movie, *Die Hard*.
Background Checks: Quentin Tarantino is the director of films such as *Reservoir Dogs* and *Pulp Fiction*, and has made acting appearances in both his own films and many others. Joey Slotnick appeared in the movies *Twister*, *Hollow Man* and *Idle Hands*. Patricia Wettig is married to frequent *Alias* director and sometime guest star, Ken Olin, and is best known for playing Nancy in *thirtysomething* and Joanne McFadden in *St Elsewhere*. Co-writer and *Alias* executive producer John Eisendrath has also worked on the shows *Malibu Shores* and *Beverly Hills 90210*.
Trivia: Originally a single episode, this was split into two during production when it seemed there was too much material to cram into one. This resulted in some hasty writing of new scenes to fill the space.
Injuries: Marshall gets knocked to the ground with a gun butt. Sloane has a needle of fire stuck in his hand by Cole.
Music: 'How Can I Keep From Singing' by Enya and 'Dragula (Si Non Oscillas, Noli Tintinnare Mix)' by Rob Zombie.
The Big Picture: A new player enters the scene, a mysterious character called The Man, who wants something from the SD-6 vault. The Man is audacious enough to successfully get a team into SD-6 and therefore is probably highly resourced and intelligent.
Debrief: 'There's something that happens when you discover the truth about someone. I know a little about this. The truth changes everything.' Without a pause for breath after the revelations regarding Laura Bristow, the first half of this two-parter is *Alias* as full-on action movie with thrills and jokes by the ton. Quentin Tarantino is excellent as McKenas Cole and has a wonderful tension with Ron Rifkin as Sloane. Anyone who can launch an attack on SD-6 on their home turf is a *serious* threat and it's great to see Jack and Sydney having to take on Cole's team without any outside help.

13
The Box (Part Two)

Production #E642

1st US Transmission Date: 10 February 2002
1st UK Transmission Date: 17 April 2002

Writers: Jesse Alexander and John Eisendrath
Director: Jack Bender
Guest Cast: Quentin Tarantino (McKenas Cole), Joey Slotnick (Haladki), Agnes Bruckner (Kelly McNeil), James Handy (Devlin), Jennifer Tung (Toni), Ben Bray (Tchen), Christophe Konrad (Endo), Igor Jijikine (Chopper), Dave Lea (Ice), Jeff Wolfe (Gonov), Geta Sesheta (CIA Secretary)

Briefing: Jack slides through the vents to where Sydney is hanging. He gives himself up to Cole's team, allowing Sydney to remain free. He has left her a map and instructions to find and disarm the three C4 packages in the building before the vault is opened. Meanwhile, a member of Cole's team, Toni, is trying to hack the scrambled vault code. Dixon uses a palm pilot to email Langley with a request for CIA help and the message is received by Vaughn. The CIA will not send in a team, so Vaughn goes to Credit Dauphine on his own and fights one of Cole's men. While Haladki blocks his request for back-up, Vaughn finds Sydney and helps her disarm the C4 packages, as well as taking out Cole's team. They find that Toni is working undercover for British SIS to try and identify The Man. Cole threatens to kill Jack, forcing Sydney to surrender before she can deactivate the last of the C4 packages (Vaughn doesn't have the map, so can't find it on his own). Vaughn calls Weiss and a CIA team is sent to prevent a new 'team' threat. Toni cracks the vault code and tells Cole, who then kills her in a violent rage because of Sloane's taunts. He goes to the vault to get the artefact he's been sent to retrieve. Sydney and the SD-6 agents escape their captors and Jack has to cut off Sloane's finger then rush it to his office to disarm the whole security system and the C4 as Cole opens the vault. Sydney goes to stop Cole, who has retrieved a small ampule bearing the Rambaldi symbol from the vault. She is beaten first time but, when Cole runs down to the car park, he's blocked from escaping by the CIA team. Sydney knocks him out and both he and the ampule are taken by the CIA, proving the value of Sydney's countermission.

OMG: Sydney and Cole kickbox.

Mission: Jack surrenders to Cole so that Sydney can stay free but, when Cole threatens Jack's life to smoke out the person killing his men, Sydney surrenders herself. Cole interrogates her and forces champagne down her throat. Sloane psyches out Cole as Toni comes to take him to the vault, but he loses his cool and shoots Toni, taunted by Sloane's accusation that he cracked under torture. He orders his team to shoot the SD-6 agents, then heads for the vault. On a signal from Marshall, Sydney drops an explosive earring. The agents fight back and beat their captors. Jack finds Sloane in the 'conversation room' and asks how to deactivate the failsafe. There's a biometric scanner in Sloane's office that requires his fingerprint. However, there's no time to free Sloane from the metal bracelets attaching him to the chair and Jack has to cut off his right index finger. In the vault, the codebreaker cracks the twelve-digit code. Dixon arrives to stop Cole but is easily taken down. Sydney comes in and she and Cole have a brutal kickboxing battle. Cole beats her but Jack gets to Sloane's office and uses the finger in time to stop the failsafe. Cole flees with the ampule from the vault.

Countermission: When he receives Dixon's email, Vaughn goes to Devlin to ask for an extraction team. However, with no independent confirmation of an attack on the Credit Dauphine building, Devlin insists they wait. Vaughn is currently suspended as Sydney's handler, with Haladki in charge of the SD-6 case. When Vaughn calls in asking for aid, Haladki doesn't pass the message to Weiss, who is angry when he finds out that Haladki intecepted a call from Vaughn for him. Haladki claims Vaughn was hysterical. Weiss goes in with a team, intercepting Cole as he tries to escape. The CIA get Cole and the Rambaldi box

– SD-6 will never know they were there. The silver box contains a small vial of liquid. Vaughn tells Sydney that they have it because of her.
Destination: As with **12**, 'The Box (Part One)', mostly within SD-6 itself.
Transcripts: Cole (to Sydney): '*You're* the badass that's been killing my men? I don't know, I just kinda thought you'd be an ugly guy.'
Sloane (to Cole): 'They broke you, didn't they? They made you beg? Is that what you did? You cried for mercy? You wept like a baby. A little baby.'
Vaughn: 'Think about it. What you do. Hockey can wait. I don't think what you're doing here can.'
Sydney Bristow: Sydney is exceptionally hard-nosed – at one point she threatens Tchen, who she has tied up, telling him to answer the call from his boss and say everything is OK. When he refuses, she brutally punches him out cold. However, when Jack is threatened, Sydney gives herself up – even though Vaughn can't deactivate the last of the C4 packages without her. She keeps her cool as Cole interrogates her. At the end of the episode, the victory she has scored on behalf of the CIA gives her reason not to resign.
Jack Bristow: At the end, Jack touches Sydney's shoulder, the most affectionate contact they've ever had. It seems their experience fighting together has brought them closer.
Arvin Sloane: Sloane taunts Cole into killing his own girlfriend, Toni. In the end, in spite of the box, and the threats, it is Cole who is broken, not Sloane. He lets Jack cut off his finger to save SD-6 and, even though he gets it back (Marshall has a surgeon ready in the last scene, and the digit on ice), this shows what he's made of. He tells Sydney that what happened is unacceptable and that whoever did it will pay.
Michael Vaughn: After his confrontation with Haladki in **12**, 'The Box (Part One)', Vaughn has been suspended as Sydney's handler. With the CIA unwilling to send in an extraction team to SD-6, he decides to go down on his own. He has to apply his – theoretical, untried – training in bomb disposal to disarm the C4 packages. He turns down Sydney's

invitation to a hockey game (made in the last episode), telling her that it can wait, while her mission at SD-6 can't.
Will Tippin: Will turns up at Sydney's house drunk and incoherent and rambles to Francie about how much his life sucks and the problems of the McNeil case. The key he received is labelled Pier 19, No. 305. With encouragement from Francie, he is back on the case and goes to Pier 19, where he finds the locker for the key. Inside is a pathology report revealing that Mrs McNeil did not commit suicide, which he passes to Kelly McNeil. He tells her to pass the file to her father and then go into hiding.
Marcus Dixon: Dixon wants to call Langley for help. He's left thinking the email never got through, not realising the CIA were ever there. Dixon, vulnerable since his surgery, gets whipped by Cole when they fight.
Francie Calfo: Francie laughs when Will says his investigation is dangerous and says that, if she were in his position and had a story that could help someone, she would do it.
McKenas Cole: Cole seems to be having a relationship with his lieutenant, Toni. He takes a bottle of champagne with him on every job, as a good luck charm. Five years before he was in the SD-6 coffee room and saw Sydney, who was wearing pigtails, and he asked her out. His technique cannot have been smooth because she said that, if he talked to her ever again, she'd break his kneecaps. He's thought about her ever since. He tells Sydney that, although she didn't want to kiss him, he backwashed in the champagne bottle he just forced down her throat.

Sloane tells Cole that it was his own fault those men died in Chechnya – the chopper waited but Cole was delayed because he tried to carry an injured man, sacrificing the rest of the team in the process.
Intelligence: Sydney decides to continue her mission at SD-6.
Office Politics: Haladki and Weiss clash when Haladki tries to stop Weiss from assisting Vaughn's unauthorised excursion into Credit Dauphine.
Lies: Jack tells Dixon that he can't call Langley because the CIA can't acknowledge the existence of SD-6, when of course the real reason is quite different.

Breaking the Code: The code for the vault is 927465398107.
Plot Devices: To disarm the C4, Vaughn and Sydney have to remove a crystal receiver without touching a web of lasers.
Action: Vaughn gets into a scrap with one of Cole's men, who is shot dead in the struggle. Cole and Sydney fight twice. First time he wins, but second time she beats him.
Reference Points: Vaughn mentions a CIA duty officer called Bendis – a reference to Brian Michael Bendis, writer and creator of the (unrelated) comic book *Alias*, which coincidentally began publication around the time of the TV show. The comic book has since returned the favour with similar in-jokes. Sloane's severed finger might be an allusion to the ear-removing scene in Tarantino's *Reservoir Dogs*.
Injuries: Marshall has a head injury from being assaulted in the previous episode. Jack gets another beating when Cole's team capture him. Sloane (at his own request) has his finger severed by Jack.
Music: 'Rockaway' by Jesse Harris and the Ferdinandos and 'Songbird' by Fleetwood Mac.
The Big Picture: There is a vial of liquid in a silver box bearing the Rambaldi symbol, an ampule so important The Man is willing to risk sending a team into SD-6 to get it. That ampule is now in the hands of the CIA.
Debrief: 'This has changed everything.' A thrilling conclusion to the two-parter, with Sydney brought closer to both Jack and Vaughn in the face of adversity (and isn't it cool to see Vaughn getting involved in the action?). Lots of funny lines, some real shocks and a severed finger. Very cool and, along with the first half, the centrepiece of the entire first season.

14
The Coup

Production #E643

1st US Transmission Date: 24 February 2002
1st UK Transmission Date: 24 April 2002

Writers: Alex Kurtzman and Roberto Orci
Director: Tom Wright
Guest Cast: Evan Dexter Parke (Charlie), David Anders (Mr Sark), Allison Dean (Stella), Keone Young (Professor Choy), Ray Laska (Floor Manager), Stephen Liska (Ilyich Ivankov), Jorgo Ognenowski (Lawro Kessar), Patrick Pankhurst (Brandon Dahlgren), Christopher Grey (Security Guard), Douglas Robert Jackson (Dealer), James Lew (Quan Li), Joe Toppe (Security Officer), Frank Patton (Roulette Dealer), Bobby Rodgers (Reverend), John Fletcher (1st Card Player), Hamilton Mitchell (2nd Card Player)

Briefing: The same day as Cole's attack on SD-6, a young blond man led a raid into FTL headquarters, stealing Rambaldi artefacts and killing FTL's leader. The FTL network is now in ruins. The young man was a representative of The Man and is set to arrange a meeting with K-Directorate to discuss Rambaldi knowledge. Sydney and Dixon go to Vegas to observe a K-Directorate go-between and find details of the meeting.

On that mission, Sydney takes a quick break to stop Francie from marrying her cheating boyfriend. She considers giving up her studies, but Jack persuades her she will make a great teacher.

The information from Vegas leads Sydney and Dixon to a meeting in Moscow, where the young man, Mr Sark, demands K-Directorate hands over all Rambaldi knowledge in exchange for a nominal fee. When Ivankov, the head of K-Directorate, refuses, Sark has him killed and repeats the offer to his deputy. Sydney, swinging outside the window on a line, dislodges some masonry, drawing attention and gunfire as she dangles helplessly . . .

OMG: FTL is wiped out overnight.

Mission: A young blond man shoots Quan Li, the head of FTL, dead outside Tyno Chem Engineering, the front company for FTL Headquarters in Hong Kong. The young man led a unit into FTL Headquarters, massacred Li's security detail, then gunned down Li himself. This took place at the same time as Cole assaulted SD-6. Both missions had the same objective – the acquisition of Rambaldi artefacts. FTL are now finished – their network crumbled within hours of the assault. SD-6 are shaken that an outside party could assault both SD-6 and FTL at the same time, without SD-6 knowing who they are. The Man now has the most significant collection of Rambaldi artefacts on earth. The Man's organisation has contacted K-Directorate to arrange a meeting to discuss the sharing of Rambaldi knowledge. Brandon Dahlgren is a K-Directorate go-between living in Vegas. Sydney and Dixon are sent to Vegas to find out the time and location of the meeting.

Sydney is on communications, heading behind the scenes at the casino to monitor the action in the gaming room. She is distracted when she sees Charlie and Francie there. Sydney avoids her friends and breaks into the security system, downloading Dixon's picture into the system so he can impersonate Buchanan, a Jamaican politician. Dixon is identified as a VIP by casino security and goes to a private gaming room where he is to plant a bug on Dahlgren. Sydney uses the security system to monitor the game and direct Dixon on how to cheat. The card game in the private room soon comes back to Dixon and Dahlgren, and Dixon hits a winning streak, thanks to Sydney.

Sydney spots Francie and Charlie about to get married and leaves Dixon while she goes to stop the wedding. She then runs back in time to help Dixon play his game.

Dixon gets Dahlgren to stake his fraternity ring, the ring they've had duplicated. Dixon loses, but manages to make the switch, leaving Dahlgren with the fake ring. Dixon is taken outside by security, who know the real Buchanan is still in Jamaica. Sydney and Dixon fight their way out.

The mission is a success and the transmitter in the ring intercepts a signal between K-Directorate and Dahlgren. Linguistics translates the phone call. They still don't know who The Man is, or his agency, but they do know that the meeting is to take place in an office building in Moscow, where Sydney and Dixon are to monitor the meeting and find out what they can. In Moscow, Sydney rappels between two buildings, while Dixon stays in the van to monitor her. As the representatives of K-Directorate enter the building, Sydney lowers herself towards the window of the correct floor, points a camera at the window and attaches a microphone for audio. The young man – Mr Sark, head of operations – arrives to meet Ivankov, head of K-Directorate. He refuses to reveal the identity of The Man. The proposal is for $100 million to K-Directorate's Cayman Islands 'shell' bank account in exchange for the Rambaldi manuscript acquired in Argentina and all associated translations and analysis. Ivankov considers it a good opening offer but, when Sark insists it is a final offer, Ivankov says that the manuscript is not for sale. Sark gives K-Directorate a sixty-second deadline. Ivankov and the guards are shot dead. Kessar, a surviving K-Directorate representative, inherits control with twenty seconds left to accept Sark's offer, which he does. Outside, Sydney's foot catches some masonry, dislodging it, which attracts the attention of men on the ground and in the room and she is fired upon by both.

Countermission: Haladki reported Vaughn for an alleged over-involvement in Sydney's case and for fighting with him (see **12**, 'The Box (Part One)'), but Devlin didn't discipline either party. Vaughn and Sydney meet on a train and later at the LA Observatory. He gives her a flash memory card for her Moscow mission to attach to the fibre-optic camera from SD-6; she is to drop the card, with a recording of the meeting on it, in seat pocket 15C on the flight home.

Destination: Hong Kong, Las Vegas, Los Angeles, Moscow.

Timescale: It's a week since **13**, 'The Box (Part Two)'.

Transcripts: Marshall Flinkman: 'Casino security is like an onion: it's layer after layer after layer, and the more you peel back, the more you want to cry.'

Casino Security Man: 'Apparently, you're stuck in Jamaica.' Dixon: 'I suppose there are worse places to be stuck.'

Sydney Bristow: Sydney is considering giving up school after finding out her mother wasn't the person she thought:

she went to graduate school because that was what her mother had done. Sydney goes to her professor asking for his signature to leave the course. She's stretched too thin, and doesn't feel like she can be a teacher any more. Her professor tells her that she's one of the best students he's ever had and asks her to think a bit more before making a final decision. Her latest paper got an A. After talking to her father, Sydney decides to stay in school.

Sydney puts up posters for Charlie's latest gig and meets Stella, the woman who went out with him while he's been dating Francie. Sydney kicks herself that, in spite of all her training to read people, she never realised Charlie was a cheat. When she spots Charlie and Francie about to get married in the casino, she pulls on a black suit over her showgirl outfit and runs over to talk to them. She tells Charlie she met Stella Campbell and insists Charlie tell Francie about his relationship with her. Back in LA, when Francie still doesn't know, Sydney tells her.

Jack Bristow: Jack makes a polite enquiry about Sydney's college work and mumbles through the sentence as if polite, normal small talk is a foreign language he barely knows. When she tells him that she's considering dropping college, he says he doesn't feel capable of advising her. Later, he arranges to meet her at a carousel the Bristows used to go to when Sydney was two. It was there Jack talked to his wife about work sometimes, but he hasn't been to the park for twenty years. He tells Sydney the decision to go back to school was hers, not her mother's, and that if she sticks with it she'll be a great teacher.

Arvin Sloane: Sloane waylays Sydney in the briefing room, so the SD-6 team can assemble to give her a round of applause for saving their lives during the Cole incursion. He sympathises with her over the revelation about her mother.

Michael Vaughn: Vaughn tells Sydney that he would have liked to have been able to go to that hockey game, to be in public with her, and makes it clear he would have really liked to be part of her life.

Will Tippin: Now that his daughter is safe, McNeil has another meeting with Will at the prison and he wants to talk. He sends Will to OT Technologies, where he claims he's there to interview the CEO, Larry Glassner, to get into the building – McNeil used to work there and left a trail in his encryption software. Whenever anyone used the software, their details would be sent to a dedicated server in the computer room at OT Technologies. At the office, Will goes to the computer room and, following McNeil's instructions, logs on and finds a file called 'Dolphin'. He downloads it – it is a roadmap to find SD-6.

Sydney finds a lovebite on Will's neck, which leaves him embarrassed. She jokes with him about how young Jenny is and how he's out of her league, but he thinks that, if there's a better league for him he doesn't know about it. There's a definite warmth between them as she applies make-up to cover his lovebite. He advises her to get Francie drunk before telling her about Charlie's infidelity.

Marshall Flinkman: Marshall doesn't understand why SD-6 aren't celebrating the downfall of FTL, an organisation that has been their enemy for a long, long time. It's then explained to him that, if The Man can take down FTL, he must be an even bigger threat.

Francie Calfo: Francie's and Charlie's parents have been introduced over brunch and got on so well that they're going on holiday together, where they'll plan the whole wedding without the actual participants. Francie wants to go to Vegas with Charlie and Sydney. Charlie asks Sydney to put posters up around campus for his next gig, which leads to her making her discovery about him. In Vegas, Francie spots a wedding chapel and suggests to Charlie that they get married there and then, avoiding their parents' plans for the wedding. They're about to do it when Sydney comes forward to tell Charlie that, if he doesn't admit to Francie he's been cheating on her, she will. Charlie calls off the wedding on the grounds that their families should be there, but doesn't tell Francie about Stella. Francie doesn't believe Sydney and says that Sydney never liked Charlie and has never been supportive of them. She thinks she should have stayed living with Charlie, instead of moving in with Sydney. Francie goes to three movies after seeing Charlie to delay going home to talk to Sydney but, when she does, she tells her that she was right – Charlie confessed and it's all over.

Mr Sark: Mr Sark is very young, in his early twenties, with boyish features and blond hair. He wears smart black clothing and has a cut-glass English accent. He's The Man's head of operations, a highly proficient killer who manages to eliminate the heads of both FTL and K-Directorate.

Intelligence: Mr Sark is introduced, destroying FTL and mauling K-Directorate. Francie and Charlie break up.

Lies: Charlie has been cheating on Francie.

Breaking the Code: The passcode for the computer room at OT Technologies is 4747. Sydney's dead-drop is at Seat 15C. Location letters: G, E, E and W.

Plot Devices: For Vegas, Marshall gives Sydney a laser prism that allows her to cut into the fibre-optic systems of the casino without interrupting the data stream and setting off the alarms.

Action: Sydney rappels between buildings in Moscow.

Undercover: Dixon's alias in Vegas is Darien Buchanan, a Jamaican politician planning to visit Vegas. As Buchanan, Dixon wears a smart suit, short dreadlocks and a beard. He also has a very arch Jamaican accent and walks with a notable swagger. Sydney is on communications for the mission, going behind the scenes at the casino disguised as a showgirl in a spangly dress.

Background Checks: David Anders was only 21 when cast as Sark but has previously worked as a stunt double in the film *Rancid Aluminium*, as well as an actor in *The Source*. Tom Wright, sometimes credited as Thomas J Wright, has directed episodes of *Angel*, *CSI* and *The X-Files*.

Injuries: Sydney is still bruised from the previous week. Sloane's finger is healing, tied up in a splint.

Music: As the story moves to Las Vegas, there's an awesome version of the theme tune in full, show tune Vegas style, with funky brass and cocktail piano. The songs are 'Shoot the Moon' by Norah Jones and 'Green Apples' by Chantal Kreviazuk.

The Big Picture: FTL are destroyed. The Man is amassing the greatest collection of Rambaldi artefacts in the world.
Debrief: 'I don't even know who you are any more. And I don't want to.' From the opening tracking shot of the harbour in Hong Kong, which seamlessly integrates into the action shot in LA, to the cliffhanger in Moscow, this is big epic fun all the way. The Vegas scenes in particular are a blast, with Sydney juggling her mission with her attempts to stop Francie marrying Charlie. Skirting the edge of farce with its comic deceptions and silly secret identities (what is it with Dixon's Carribbean accent?), this is hugely, hugely entertaining. All the while, the mystery over The Man deepens as Mr Sark casually massacres his way through the series' previously invincible organisations (FTL, K-Directorate). Way cool and the perfect episode with which to introduce a friend to the series.

15
Page 47

Production #E644

1st US Transmission Date: 3 March 2002
1st UK Transmission Date: 1 May 2002

Writers: JJ Abrams and Jeff Pinkner
Director: Ken Olin
Guest Cast: Sarah Shahi (Jenny), Amy Irving (Emily Sloane), Michelle Arthur (Abigail), Jorgo Ognenovski (Kessar), Bryan Rasmussen (Cohen), Don Took (Agent Grey), Thomas Mills (Delivery Man)

Briefing: In Moscow, Sydney cuts the line she's hanging from, swinging across to crash through a window in the building opposite. Dodging her pursuers, she then runs to Dixon and safety.

K-Directorate are set to hand over the Rambaldi book Anna stole in Argentina to The Man. Sydney and Dixon go to Tunisia and steal the book, with her photographing the pages for the CIA's benefit. The CIA find that page 47 is blank in the photos – the number 47 is significant, so the CIA want the page to examine. Jack, disguised under a balaclava, leads a team to kidnap and threaten Will to put him off the SD-6 story. If he does not drop the story, Sloane will have him killed. Sydney uses a dinner party thrown by Sloane and his cancer-stricken wife Emily as a chance to plant a bug in his office and replace page 47 of the Rambaldi journal with a counterfeit. Will tells McNeil he's no longer on the case. Sloane's assassin stands down.

Vaughn shows Sydney the uncovered page 47, the ink on which is revealed when the liquid from the Rambaldi ampule retrieved from SD-6 (in **13**, 'The Box (Part 2)') was sprinkled on it. The page is written in code, but includes an image of a woman who appears to be Sydney . . .

OMG: Sydney finds that Rambaldi drew a picture of her in his journal.

Mission: Sloane says it will take time for the implications of Ivankov's murder to become clear. Ivankov's body was delivered in a freight container to K-Directorate's headquarters in St Petersburg, while Kessar is believed to be a hostage of Sark, held to force K-Directorate to deliver the Rambaldi manuscript. Sloane has pinpointed the handover as taking place in Tunisia – Sydney is to retrieve the Rambaldi book and bring it back. In Tunisia, Sydney speedboats over to K-Directorate's boat, saying she has run out of petrol and needs to borrow some. She knocks out the guards with a spray and punches out the man with the briefcase before opening it to get the Rambaldi manuscript. She takes photographs of the pages, steals the K-Directorate boat and escapes just as Sark arrives at the jetty. When it transpires that the crew of the boat are civilians who don't know anything, Sloane orders them killed. SD-6 have so far been unable to break the code most of the documents are written in. Intelligence agencies and corporations worldwide are investing millions in cracking the Rambaldi mystery.

Sloane has found out about McNeil's contact with Will. He tells Jack that McNeil created an encryption program SD-6 wanted, but he wouldn't sell. Sloane wants Will eliminated but Jack argues that they should find out more first. Will has a bug planted on him by an SD-6 agent and he is then picked up by SD-6, beaten up a bit and interrogated by a balaclavaed Jack, who speaks through a voicebox. It is made clear that he, along with his friends and family, will be dead if he keeps investigating SD-6. Sloane had Security Section monitor Jack and is not convinced that the threats will put Will off the case. When Will goes to visit McNeil at the prison again, Sloane has an SD-6 man follow him there. If he does not tell McNeil he is dropping the story, he will be killed.

Countermission: The CIA retrieved the camera Sydney dropped for them in Argentina and got some good shots of the Rambaldi book, which seems to be an instruction manual in Italian. It refers to one hundred segments, continuing on a page the CIA don't have. In Tunisia, Sydney is to photograph the pages for the CIA and deliver the originals to SD-6. The photographs Sydney gets on this mission are useful as well, but page 47 is blank – in previous Rambaldi documents, the forty-seventh page is always significant. Jack is working on a strategy to replace the real page with a counterfeit, so the CIA can get it.

The CIA want Sydney to use her friendship with Emily Sloane to get an invite to the Sloane house, so that she can plant a bug. She argues that it's not right to use Emily, while Vaughn insists that it's her chance, albeit unknowingly, to do something good. Emily responds, inviting Sydney over. Vaughn gives Sydney a paperclip-shaped bug to plant in Sloane's office. When Jack finds out that Sloane is keeping the Rambaldi book at home to show Sydney that night, before its couriered to Germany the next morning for analysis, he plans for her to replace page 47. Vaughn will call Sydney on her mobile and she will leave the table to take the call, before switching the pages and planting the bug. Jack will be at dinner too and able to help her. Sloane comes into his study just after she has made the move. She dead-drops the page to the CIA.

Cohen from Sci-Tech presents Vaughn with the revealed page 47, which he then takes to Sydney. The vial of liquid from the SD-6 vault reveals the ink on the page to show a picture of Sydney. They can't crack the code and don't know what it means.

Destination: Tunisia, Los Angeles.

Transcripts: Sloane (on Will): 'What concerns me is that this doesn't seem to concern you.' Jack: 'There is a difference between concern and assassination.'

Sloane (on Rambaldi): 'Who was this man, Sydney? What did he see? What did Rambaldi see?'

Sydney Bristow: In a big step towards closure, Sydney finally stops wearing her engagement ring, partially to help Francie stop wearing hers. She is initially disgusted by the idea that she should use her friendship with Emily Sloane, a woman dying of cancer, to get invited to the Sloane house. When she is invited to bring a friend, she gets Will to come along. She tells Sloane that she doesn't know yet whether she believes in Rambaldi.

Jack Bristow: Jack kidnaps Will, threatens him and has him beaten up in an attempt to get him to drop his investigation. Jack knows that Sloane will have Will killed if he doesn't back off and he doesn't want Sydney to lose another friend. As usual, he is using violent means to protect his daughter. After that encounter, Jack is understandably shocked when told that Will is going to be at Sloane's house.

Arvin Sloane: Sloane wants Will eliminated – McNeil is a threat to SD-6, and Sloane tells Jack that Sydney must never be exposed to certain truths. His persona at home is incredibly civilised and urbane: black polo neck and thick-rimmed reading glasses, along with a beautiful house full of books and antiques, a far contrast from the brutal technological world of his working life. His fixation with Rambaldi is clear as he leafs through the documents Sydney brings back from Tunisia and he admits that Rambaldi is becoming an obsession for him. Sloane listens to Will and Emily explaining the story of Louis Marona (see **Will Tippin**), and considers it interesting, echoing as it does his own role as a monster who controls his employees through fear. He then asks Will what he's working on now.

Michael Vaughn: Vaughn's loopy Aunt Trish believes in crop circles, spirits and the like, and the Rambaldi story reminds him of her. When Sydney is dressed up ready for Sloane's dinner party, Vaughn compliments her.
Will Tippin: Will interviews McNeil again. He has found 42 companies that use the McNeil encryption software, six of which have a common board member, Alain Christophe. Christophe is a retired CIA man who ran counter-intelligence at Langley from 1982 to 1989. McNeil is pleased – SD-6 should be afraid of him. Will is on his way back from the jail when his car is stopped and he is kidnapped by masked men and told that the deaths he is investigating were unfortunate but that, if he doesn't stop investigating SD-6, his friends and family will die, including his sister Amy, his parents Robert and Patsy, and Sydney. He is knocked out cold and wakes up later on the floor of an abandoned warehouse. He then has to keep his head together while talking to Sydney on his mobile. He tells McNeil he can't continue with the story, because he was kidnapped and threatened. McNeil can't believe he is giving it up and tells him the only way to survive is to publish the story, but Will refuses. McNeil is angry that his daughter has gone away because of Will's promises, but he says that he's in the same position that McNeil was before his wife was killed and if he could go back and do something differently, he would.

Will is winning a Caplin Award for writing an inspirational article about a fruit picker from Laventa. Jenny wants to celebrate with him on Friday, but he blows her off, saying he's got something on that night. He tells Sydney about the award and invites her to see a screening of *North By Northwest* on Friday, then have dinner afterwards to celebrate. Litvack gives him a cake for the Most Inspirational Article award, but is jealous that she's never won anything. Sydney cancels the film but invites Will to come with her to the Sloane house for dinner. He gets Jenny to pick him up from the warehouse and refuses to talk about what happened, but he decides this is a good time to break up with Jenny – she responds by leaving him in the middle of nowhere and resigning as his assistant. At dinner, Emily Sloane tells Will she loved his award-winning article and voted for it to win the prize.

Will's award-winning story is about a Mexican immigrant worker, Louis Marona, whose boss was, as far as Will is concerned, the devil, having people who spoke out against him killed. Marona led a revolt against his boss and won. He is now going to college and the monster he worked for is in jail.

Francie Calfo: Francie is busy returning engagement gifts with enclosed thank-you cards, but she's devastated by breaking up with Charlie and is still wearing her engagement ring. She apologises when Sydney shows she's still wearing the ring she got from Danny. Francie thinks they should get a new number to avoid all the calls for Joey's Pizza.

Marshall Flinkman: Marshall has always wondered whether there's a conspiracy or coincidence behind Rex Harrison starring in two films featuring characters called Dolittle.

Mr Sark: According to Marshall's analysis, Sark's speech patterns indicate that he is extremely clever and that he spends a considerable time in Ireland, probably Galway.

Intelligence: Rambaldi's writings seem to involve Sydney. Will drops his investigation into SD-6 after being threatened.

Lies: The cover for Jack working with Sydney and Sloane at Credit Dauphine, as told to Will and Emily, is that Sloane recruited him to work on investment strategies. Sloane tells Sydney that the Rambaldi book is being taken to England for analysis – in fact it's going to Germany. Sydney says she didn't open the Rambaldi book in Tunisia. Will tells Sloane that he got his bruised face from a basketball.

Breaking the Code: House numbers: 3723, 63034, 4250. Location letters: T and E.

Plot Devices: Two cool CIA devices for Sydney's suppertime spying – a paperclip bug to leave in Sloane's office and a lipstick-shaped device to open Sloane's safe.

Undercover: In Tunisia, Sydney wears blonde hair, a red bikini top and denim shorts, while Dixon disguises himself as a fisherman on the beach, complete with basket and big straw hat.
Reference Points: *North By Northwest*, the film Will wants to see with Sydney, is about an innocent man trapped within a baffling conspiracy – not unlike Will himself.
Background Checks: Amy Irving was the singing voice of Jessica Rabbit in *Who Framed Roger Rabbit?*, and her film career takes in *Yentl*, *Carrie* and *Traffic*. Michelle Arthur, who appears for the first time as Will's colleague Abby – a non-romantic replacement for Jenny – appeared in *Goldeneye*.
Injuries: Sloane is still knocking back pills, and his finger is heavily bandaged. Will takes a beating when he's kidnapped and is knocked unconscious.
Music: In Tunisia, the music hits an arabic theme. Tracks heard are 'No Such Thing' by John Mayer, 'Landslide' by The Smashing Pumpkins, 'Home' by Abra Moore and 'Feelin' The Same Way' by Norah Jones.
Debrief: 'Men would die for this book. Men have died.' Life at the family Sloane adds layers to his character, making him almost sympathetic, while Jack yet again does some very bad things in this morally grey episode. Most of all, though, this is an episode built around its ending, which places Sydney at the heart of the Rambaldi mystery.

16
The Prophecy

Production #E645

1st US Transmission Date: 10 March 2002
1st UK Transmission Date: 8 May 2002

Writer: John Eisendrath
Director: Davis Guggenheim
Guest Cast: Roger Moore (Edward Poole),
Lindsay Crouse (Dr Carson Evans), James Handy (Devlin),

Derrick O'Connor (Alexander Khasinau),
Joey Slotnick (Haladki), Castulo Guerra (Jean Briault),
Wolf Muser (Ramon Vesolo), Amy Irving (Emily Sloane),
Joe D'Angerio (Dr Watterson), Robert Arce (Hobbes),
Allen Williams (Senator Mark Townsend),
Lilyan Chauvin (Signora Ventutti), Anya Matanovic (Opera Student),
Joseph Vassallo (Vatican Station Chief)

Briefing: In Washington, a Senate sub-committee is formed to discuss Sydney Bristow and the Rambaldi prophecy. Dr Carson Evans of the Department of Special Research (DSR) presents evidence from semi-decoded Rambaldi pages that Sydney is of vital importance. He is authorised to investigate. Vaughn tells Sydney that the investigation is under way and she will be brought in for questioning soon. She is questioned, but refuses physical tests until she knows what the page says. She visits Emily Sloane, who is dying of cancer, and their conversation encourages her to face her fear and take the tests. She knows that if the DSR take her into custody, her mission at SD-6 will be over and her cover blown so Sydney and Vaughn steal Rambaldi's original code key from the Vatican, allowing a true reading of the page. She is out clubbing with her friends when she realises there are agents watching her. They bundle her into a van. Vaughn is sitting opposite as Evans cuffs her. She is taken into custody under Directive 81(a), pursuant to national security. The code key was the same as the one the CIA already had. The page was already correctly deciphered and the DSR is calling it The Prophecy. The medical tests were checking for three physical anomalies: DNA sequencing; platelet levels; and the size of her heart, and she matches all three. The Prophecy states that the woman bearing these marks, pictured on page 47, will devastate the greatest power . . .

OMG: Sydney runs off a cliff, opening her chute to paraglide past the famous statue of Christ in Rio.

Mission: Sydney completes a mission in Rio de Janeiro as the episode begins, getting surveillance photos of someone SD-6 thinks may be The Man. They use them to identify Alexander Khasinau as recipient of Sark's message reporting the loss of the Rambaldi book. Having been spotted and knowing he's a target, Khasinau has moved his headquarters. There's no immediate mission, as Sloane wants to make sure their next step is exactly the right one.

Sloane tells Jack that he wants Khasinau dead, but the Alliance is split on the issue – five will vote against war, four for decisive action. Three, yet undecided, control the vote, and one is Edward Poole of SD-9, who Sloane wants to persuade. Once he has Poole's support, that leaves two: Aska Dunst and Jean Briault. Sloane says that they should do whatever is necessary to get the declaration of war ratified. Poole promises intelligence to Sloane and comes to Los Angeles.

Poole tells Sloane that Briault is a traitor to the Alliance and shows him a photograph of Briault meeting Khasinau, along with evidence that Khasinau has paid millions to Briault. Khasinau has infiltrated the Alliance and Briault is his creature. Sloane tells him he can't believe Briault is a traitor. Poole suggests they see what happens, but Sloane sees the need for action. As a friend, he is the only man who can get close enough to Briault to eliminate him.

Sloane finds out from Kleinhoff in Berlin that the page 47 they have is fake. He knows the significance of the number 47 to Rambaldi and wants to see Sydney immediately to find out why they don't have that page. Jack tells him she's at the university. Sloane leaves for London to present his case for war, telling Jack to work with Kleinhoff and to have Sydney ready to talk to him when he returns.

Sloane meets Briault in Montreal and kills him. At the Alliance meeting in London, the death of Briault is taken as another tragedy. The vote is taken on whether to attack Khasinau or seek a diplomatic settlement with The Man. In the case of aggression, Alliance members will split the cost of the assault equally between them. The vote goes in favour of diplomacy – Poole has betrayed Sloane. Outside the meeting, Sloane accuses him of being the one in Khasinau's pocket. He has used Sloane and he promises to repay the favour.

Countermission: Sydney dead-drops copies of the photos from Rio to Vaughn.

Dr Evans is from the Department of Special Research at the National Security Agency with permission to investigate Sydney and the team have taken all Vaughn's files on her. Devlin confidentially fills in Vaughn on the situation, who then meets Sydney. He tells her that the DSR believe the woman in the picture is still alive, based on future dates listed in the text. They refer to the text as 'The Prophecy'.

Sydney is brought in for an interview, which Evans insists isn't an interrogation or suggestive of any wrongdoing on her part. The DSR refuse to discuss the content of page 47 with Sydney, much to her annoyance. The interrogator, Dr Watterson, asks her a series of logic and perception questions, while a monitor tracks her brain patterns via her eyes. Agent Haladki is involved in the investigation, to Vaughn's disgust. Evidence is presented to the interrogators and Sydney is asked to submit to a physical examination, but she demands that she's first told what page 47 says. Evans tells her she doesn't have clearance and she leaves, but later returns and submits to the tests.

The CIA and DSR have a face-to-face meeting where Devlin says he hopes their co-operation will be efficient. Evans complains that her requests for files have not been processed and insists that the CIA don't work with the DSR, but for them – it is for the CIA to do as they are told, not assess the instructions. Devlin fights his corner and the importance of Sydney. Haladki rebels against Devlin, railing against Sydney and saying that she met a Rambaldi expert at the exact time his death was prophesied, see **8,** 'Time Will Tell'. Haladki says they need to be vigilant and that's why they're testing for the physical anomalies mentioned by Rambaldi.

Jack tells Sydney that DSR are using a code key to decipher the Rambaldi text that was reverse engineered, and that they have been working on a key for the code for years. The deciphered text could therefore be incorrect. Sydney wants the original Rambaldi code key, but the CIA won't get the original code key because it's in the Vatican, and for political reasons they can't steal it. Devlin refuses to approve a mission to get the key.

Sydney approaches Vaughn to be her partner to break into the Vatican and he agrees. They have an inventory number to go on and nothing more – as it's a Rambaldi artefact, the key could be in any form. In Rome, Sydney and Vaughn go into a nearby building dressed as engineers, where they break into the secret archive with explosive. Once in, Sydney has twenty seconds to disable the alarm system – but she likes working under pressure. The code key is hidden around the frame of a painting of Pope Alexander VI, Rambaldi's employer, and they photograph it. Guards find them and they fight their way out. Vaughn passes the code key to DSR and tells Sydney the insanity is almost over. However, the code simply confirms the DSR's translation and Sydney is taken into custody.

Destination: Rio de Janeiro, Los Angeles, Rome, Los Angeles, Montreal, London, Los Angeles.

Transcripts: Rambaldi's prophecy: 'This woman here depicted will possess unseen marks, signs that she will be the one to bring forth my works . . . at vulgar cost this woman will render the greatest power unto utter desolation.'

Sydney Bristow: Sydney believes the whole Rambaldi picture issue is ridiculous, that it could be anyone, including her mother. Vaughn points out that her mother is dead and the woman is supposed to be alive. Sydney is unco-operative with the DSR, but when Emily Sloane tells her about her fear when she found out about her cancer, she realises that it's fear of what The Prophecy might mean that is holding her back and decides to submit to the tests.

Sydney tells Emily that she and Will are just friends and that she feels guilty even thinking about dating again.

Jack Bristow: Jack doesn't know anything about The Prophecy or what the DSR may know. He can't get the code key from the Vatican himself because, while Sloane is in London, he has been left in charge of SD-6 operations. He knows Devlin well enough to call him by his first name, a sign of his seniority within the CIA.

Arvin Sloane: Sloane wants Khasinau dead for the assault on SD-6 and considers the five members of the Alliance who reject an assault to be cowards for failing to respond to the threat. When Edward Poole tells Sloane that Jean Briault is a traitor, Sloane refuses to believe it as he is a friend, the man who recruited him. However, he kills Briault, even after Briault has affectionately shown him a picture of his new grandson.

Sloane tells Sydney that he's never seen Emily's spirits as high as the night she came to visit and asks if she could give her a call. When Jack says Sydney is at the university, Sloane says that her school work is a liability and she needs to re-examine her priorities.

Emily Sloane: In her conversation with Sydney, Emily alludes to knowing more about what Sloane and Sydney do, but then covers up, saying she meant working for Sloane (at the bank), who has had a difficult time. Emily knows she won't be alive by the next Christmas. Even though she looks fine, she has not much time left because of the cancer. It's too far advanced to be cured.

Michael Vaughn: Vaughn reluctantly agrees to partner Sydney in breaking into the Vatican. Once there, he tells her about his favourite restaurant, Trattoria de Nadi, which is in the city, and suggests going that night, but their rapid escape precludes it. He insists that, next time they're in Rome, they should go out to eat, which Sydney says she would like. When she is seized by the DSR, he promises they will work it out.

Will Tippin: Will invites Francie to a Lakers game – he knows what it's like to want someone you can't have and wants to help her forget about Charlie for a couple of hours.

Francie Calfo: When Will invites her to the ballgame, she asks if he's asking the right flatmate. She is obsessed with sitting close to one of her favourite players, Coby Bryant, who she considers the perfect man for her.

The Man/Alexander Khasinau: SD-6 believe they have identified The Man as Alexander Khasinau, a former high-ranking KGB operative who went private, working as a liaison between the Russian mafia, rogue states and the global arms market. The Russian mafia is the source of finance but Khasinau and his organisation operate at a higher order.

Edward Poole: Poole is head of SD-9, and one of the Alliance members Sloane needs to persuade to vote in favour of war with Khasinau. He is a distinguished older Englishman and a ruthless operator within the Alliance. When Sloane finds out Poole has betrayed him and promises to repay him in kind, Poole coolly denies everything and asks him to pass on his regards to Emily. He then gets into the back of a car where his associate Khasinau is already sitting.

The genius of Poole's character is that he's sufficiently malevolent and manipulative to make Sloane look like the wronged party – quite an achievement, considering Sloane has just murdered one of his close friends in cold blood.

Steven Haladki: Haladki tells the DSR that he has been worried about Sydney Bristow, that there are discrepancies and questions. He claims to be terrified of her potential.

Intelligence: Rambaldi's prophecy is revealed. The Man is identified by SD-6 as Alexander Khasinau.

Office Politics: The Department of Special Research, a sub-division of the National Security Agency, was formed during World War II to investigate Nazi involvement with the occult. Since then the DSR have been assigned to investigate paranormal issues. Ben Devlin, a CIA director, has to defer to the DSR, so they clearly have a lot of clout.

Five out of twelve members of the Alliance are ex-Eastern bloc and believe in the Cold War policies of détente; as such they don't want to go to war with Khasinau.

Home Front: Sydney, Will and Francie discuss prophecies, ostensibly based on a dream of Sydney's: Will and Francie both think that having a prophecy about you sounds bad. Sydney gets back from Rome to find a note on the fridge directing her to a club that Will and Francie have gone to after the ballgame.

Lies: When Sydney goes to Rome, she tells her friends that she'll be in Boston. When she is about to be picked up by the DSR agents in the club, she says she has to make a phone call to Hong Kong and she may be some time.

Breaking the Code: The inventory number for the code key is 14547. Location letters: O, O, G, R, L and E.

Action: There's an amazing action sequence where Sydney is chased by men with guns and fierce dogs and that ends with her running off the edge of a cliff, then paragliding to safety – the most spectacular sequence the series has managed yet.

Reality Checks: In his conversations with the DSR, Devlin alludes to the vigilance required for National Security at the time, a reference to the heightened alert against terrorism following the attacks of 11 September 2001. The DSR are fictional.

Reference Points: Sydney's big jump in the pre-credits sequence is a visual reference to a similar stunt performed by guest-star Roger Moore's James Bond in *The Spy Who Loved Me*.

Background Checks: Roger Moore is the longest-serving and (inflation-adjusted) the most financially successful James Bond and originally came to fame in long-running TV series *The Saint*. Lindsay Crouse is a respected character actress and her most notable credits are in work by her husband, writer/director David Mamet, such as 1987's *House of Games*. Derrick O'Connor had roles in Terry Gilliam's *Time Bandits* and *Brazil*, as well as *Lethal Weapon 2* and Jennifer Garner starrer *Daredevil*. Davis Guggenheim has also directed episodes of *24*, *ER* and *NYPD Blue*.

Injuries: The DSR take a sample of Sydney's spinal fluid, a painful-looking operation.

Music: 'Hate To Say I Told You So' by Swedish band The Hives, 'World Gone Mad' by Bill Bonk, 'Feels Like Home' by Hathaway and 'From Rusholme With Love' by Mint Royale.

The Big Picture: Rambaldi predicted that the woman pictured on page 47 would destroy the greatest power. But what is the 'greatest power'? The DSR clearly consider it to be America, the last superpower, but could it be something more abstract?

Debrief: 'This drawing is five hundred years old. Millions of women have looked like that. My mom looked like that. Maybe it's a picture of my mother.' As Will and Francie say, a prophecy is unlikely to be a good thing for the subject. The Rambaldi prophecy and the Vatican's vault of treasures take the series further into *Indiana Jones* territory, balanced out by the technocratic aspect of the DSR. Genre-bending fun, with another huge cliffhanger.

17
Q and A

Production #E646

1st US Transmission Date: 17 March 2002
1st UK Transmission Date: 15 May 2002

Writer: JJ Abrams
Director: Ken Olin
Guest Cast: Terry O'Quinn (Kendall), Joey Slotnick (Haladki), Jon Simmons (FBI Officer), Andrew A Rolfes (Guard), Lisa Dinkins (Baker), Frank Hoyt Taylor (Dunn)

Briefing: Later. A disguised Sydney sits in a car, police cars massing behind her. She stops to think, then drives straight off the edge . . .

Earlier. Sydney is handcuffed to a chair. An FBI tribunal, led by Special Officer Kendall, is convened to interview her and decide her fate. If she asks for legal counsel, the tribunal will disperse and decide her case based on current evidence – which is enough to convict her as a possible threat. She says she has nothing to hide and explains her time with SD-6, how she was recruited and trained as an agent. She tells Kendall what happened to Danny. He implies that she knew what SD-6 was well before she went to the CIA. She tells him about SD-6's history and the Alliance and how she swore to destroy them, becoming a double agent. She discusses her discoveries about her parents, Rambaldi's life story, along with the scavenger hunt for his artefacts in the intelligence world. Kendall asks if she thinks Rambaldi was a prophet but, when she returns the question and he doesn't answer, she realises they're not going to let her go.

Sydney is abducted as she is about to be transferred to a more secure location, taken by masked men – Vaughn, Weiss and Jack. She needs to get to Mount Sebastio in Italy to prove to the FBI she is not the woman in The Prophecy (see **Countermission**). Sydney is angry that she is now a fugitive, but Jack argues it's the only way to protect her as a CIA asset. She gets a car and a disguise and is chased by the police, before driving off the pier.

Under water, she survives by breathing air from the tyres, before emerging under the pier after the police have left. Before going to Mount Sebastio, Sydney meets Jack to tell him what she has realised – that her mother could have survived her car crash the way she did, using it as a method to avoid her pursuers. She believes Laura Bristow is still alive and that she is the woman in The Prophecy.

OMG: Laura Bristow lives!

Mission: The official SD-6 mission statement, as passed to its agents, is to retrieve military and industrial information necessary for the survival of the United States. The 'SD' in SD-6 stands for 'Section Disparu', literally 'the section that doesn't exist', a term invented by Alliance founder Alain Christophe. The Alliance is a board of directors, mostly former Intelligence agents but with some from the private sector. They trade in secrets, mostly technological but taking in blackmail-worthy or politically sensitive information. SD-6 was responsible for the Bangalore chemical leak of 1992, the Kyoto subway derailment of 1996 and a plane crash outside Munich in 2001.

Sloane wants to meet with Sydney on Tuesday morning.

Countermission: Vaughn tries to get Haladki to tell him what is happening with Sydney and the DSR. When Haladki says he knows nothing, Vaughn goes to Jack, who can't get access to the information either – Sydney's case has been classified as highly sensitive: Omega 17. A friend of Weiss's used to see Haladki dining at the Webster

Rotunda in the John Adams building – a place where only ranking FBI officers can sit. Vaughn confronts Haladki about being FBI before joining the CIA, demands to know where the FBI would hold Sydney and what they would do to her. Haladki says that the CIA have decoded 47 distinct Rambaldi predictions, all of which proved to be correct – Sydney could be a threat. Vaughn obsessively reads the detail of The Prophecy and finds that the woman in the picture is said to never see the sky behind Mount Sebastio, the region in which Rambaldi was born. If Sydney can get there, she will have proven she is not the woman in The Prophecy. Vaughn presents this plan to Jack, who agrees it's the only way. Devlin can't get co-operation from the FBI, though, so Jack decides they need to extract Sydney and send her to Italy themselves. Vaughn tips off Jack about Haladki's FBI ties. Jack finds Haladki, slams him against a car bonnet and puts a gun to his chin. Haladki tells him when Sydney will be moved to a safehouse. Jack and Vaughn extract Sydney, but Haladki reports them to the FBI. Haladki traces the vehicles they have taken out, allowing the cops to follow her.
Destination: Entirely within Los Angeles, mainly within the FBI building where Sydney is interrogated.
Transcripts: Jack (to Haladki): 'Just so we're clear, you report this conversation and you'll never wear a hat again.'

Sydney (facing her father, who has just kidnapped her): 'Dad?' Jack (in balaclava): 'Hey, honey!'
Sydney Bristow: At college, Sydney took some time to decide whether to accept the offer to take tests for the US government, accepting the offer so that she could see if she could actually pass the tests and get the job. She had no social life, a dead mother and an estranged father. She believed she was being recruited by the CIA. She did six months in an office job at Credit Dauphine (the 'evaluation' phase) before being trained as an agent (the 'transitional' phase). SD-6 had all the right answers to her questions. After the transitional phase, she was taken to SD-6 headquarters in sub-level 6 of the Credit Dauphine building – SD-6 had been beneath her feet all along. She

was initially assigned desk work but within a year was being sent on reconnaisance missions. She remained in school throughout the entire period, refusing to give up her teaching ambitions. She had been with Danny for two years when he was killed. She doesn't know why she was specifically recruited by Sloane and is certain Jack wasn't behind her recruitment. Sydney gets angry for the first time when Kendall makes accusations about Jack.

Sydney hates lying to her friends and also despises the constant jet lag in service of a man she hates.

Jack Bristow: Jack is concerned that Sydney gets to her meeting with Sloane at SD-6. If she doesn't make it because of being held by the FBI, her cover is in danger. He argues that, if Rambaldi was right and Sydney is the woman in the picture, everything is predetermined and there's nothing to be lost by trying to do things differently.

After Laura's death, Jack hired a nanny to look after Sydney.

Arvin Sloane: When Sydney is introduced to Sloane on her first day at SD-6, he's clean shaven.

Michael Vaughn: Vaughn is increasingly baffled and convinced by the Rambaldi prophecy, even though he thinks it's insane. He never thought that Rambaldi could be right about Sydney – he has faith in her.

Home Front: As Sydney is being chased by the police, Will and Francie watch the chase on the TV live newsfeed, not realising who is at the wheel.

Breaking the Code: The number of predictions the CIA have verified as coming true is, of course, 47.

Action: There's some brilliantly edited sequences of all the best action from previous episodes, both fights and stunts.

Undercover: Sydney, on the run from the LAPD, wears an unflattering wig and tracksuit.

Reality Checks: The disasters Sydney claims were caused by SD-6 are not real-life events, although the Bangalore chemical incident does bear a similarity to an incident in Bhopal in 1984.

Background Checks: Terry O'Quinn starred in horror film *The Stepfather*, the TV series *Millennium* and also appeared in comedy hit *Old School.*

Trivia: Some of the clips of Sydney's past activities were newly shot for the episode, rather than sourced from previous instalments.

Music: A return airing for 'Diggin' Your Scene' by Smashmouth, see **9,** 'Mea Culpa'.

Debrief: 'We're just trying to determine how a girl as brilliant as yourself could believe that an agency that could order the assassination of an innocent civilian could actually be affiliated with the US government.' So it's come to this, an *Alias* clipshow. Recapping the plotlines of the series for the inattentive and latecomers, episode **17,** 'Q and A' also features a huge chase sequence and some further background on Sydney's recruitment. It even manages to get a big plot revelation in there – not bad for an episode mostly made up of old clips.

18
Masquerade

Production #E647

1st US Transmission Date: 7 April 2002
1st UK Transmission Date: 22 May 2002

Writers: Roberto Orci and Alex Kurtzman
Director: Craig Zisk
Guest Cast: Peter Berg (Noah Hicks), Angus Scrimm (McCullough), Patricia Wettig (Dr Judy Barnett)

Briefing: Sydney climbs Mount Sebastio, proving she is not the woman in the Rambaldi prophecy. She then calls the FBI for extraction. Back in LA, Jack tells her that the FBI are now searching for her mother. Jack has broken into Langley's archives and found that an Internal Commission, including Sloane, had investigated Laura Bristow's death. The Commission had kept from Jack the fact that Laura didn't die for the sake of his mental health.

Sydney asks Sloane to help her find her mother. He asks her about the year her mother died. She thought that her father was away on business, but he tells her Jack spent six months in a Federal prison, suspected of being in collusion with Laura. Although he was eventually vindicated, he began to unravel, drinking and taking unnecessary risks. It took a long time for him to recover and Sloane was under orders not to tell him that Laura had survived. Unfortunately, this also meant not telling Sydney the truth. Sydney wants to go off active duty and find out what happened to her mother, but Sloane can't let her go on a rogue operation that could compromise SD-6.

When Sydney is assigned a mission to pick up information on Khasinau, she protests to Sloane, who tells her that the operation against Khasinau has everything to do with Laura Bristow – Khasinau was her KGB superior. It is the only clue he can give her. On a mission in Vienna, Sydney encounters Noah Hicks, an old lover who has spent the last few years in deep cover, and he has to be extracted after his cover is blown.

Sydney and Hicks go to Archangelsk to retrieve a computer datacore of Khasinau's. After completing their mission they retreat to an SD-6 safehouse to wait for a pickup. Sydney says she was looking for information about her mother in Khasinau's computer, but she doesn't want to tell him about it all just yet. She says she was hurt by him leaving. They make love.

OMG: Sydney has sex.

Mission: Jack's analysis indicates that thanks to Khasinau's old connections his organisation has the legitimacy of a fledgling government. For five years, SD-6 has had two deep-cover agents in the Russian Embassy in Vienna. One, Kyle Wexler, reports that Khasinau has converted $250 million worth of assets into cash and Sloane wants to know what he is spending it on. Wexler has encoded details of Khasinau's transaction on to a microchip. A brush pass has been scheduled for Saturday night at the Embassy, under the cover of a party. Sydney is sent to pick up the intelligence.

In Vienna, Sydney and Dixon attend a masked ball. A young masked man dances with Sydney and tells her that Wexler is dead. He claims to be the other agent within the

Embassy and gives her several facts about SD-6 to persuade her of who he is. They go to retrieve the microchip, while Dixon gets their escape route ready. Sydney and the agent unmask and they recognise each other. The agent, Noah Hicks, says that Khasinau has the Embassy in his pocket. Wexler's body is in the basement and Hicks cuts it open to get the chip, which he'd swallowed. They escape, using a shower of balloons from the ceiling as a distraction. Meanwhile, a guard intercepts Dixon in the car. Dixon has obtained a horse and carriage as a vehicle instead.

Sloane is angry that Sydney and Dixon pulled Hicks from his position at the Embassy, destroying a five-year operation. Hicks argues that, if he had stayed, he would also be dead. Sloane orders him to be checked by Security Section. He gets through the debriefing and works on the files from the microchip with Sydney.

Khasinau has bought two Westbury 23 supercomputers, ideal for simulating engineering designs. Sloane thinks he's using them to analyse how the Rambaldi artefacts fit together and work out what pieces are missing. SD-6 need the datacore on which both computers store their data. The datacore needs to be kept in a cryogenic storage facility maintained at a temperature halfway to absolute zero – cold enough to freeze human flesh solid. The core is kept a mile beneath a heavily guarded facility in Archangelsk, Russia. Sloane thinks it's being used as Khasinau's personal archive. Hicks says he knows the area well, so he rather than Dixon goes with Sydney.

They wander into the Archangelsk facility posing as lost American tourists, allowing themselves to be captured, and they're taken into the compound. They slip on their sunglasses as one of the guards fiddles with Sydney's camera – when the film casing is opened, a magnesium flash stuns everyone in the room except the two SD-6 agents. Sydney triggers a secret door and they go down into the base, putting on protective containment suits. She disengages the core from the computer, using the access to do a computer search for Laura Bristow. Hicks keeps a scientist at gunpoint while Sydney goes in to get the core.

The scientist attacks Hicks, but is thrown across the computer control panel when Hicks knocks him out. Sydney is knocked over by the robot arm as the scientist falls against the controls and her faceplate cracks in the low temperature. Hicks blasts the window to the frozen room with a machine gun and rescues Sydney as the cold air escapes. He has to give her the kiss of life to revive her after her exposure. They take the core and escape to a safehouse with six hours to wait for their extraction.

Sloane thinks Jack is affected more than he admits by the discovery that Laura Bristow may be alive and he wants him to take a few days off from active duty to recover.

Countermission: All files relating to Laura Bristow have been classified Omega 17 by the FBI, including her connection to the Rambaldi prophecy. Vaughn can't help Sydney with her search.

On her debrief from Vienna, Sydney tells Vaughn that she met Hicks in training and dated him for a while, albeit in secret. Both SD-6 and the CIA discourage fraternisation. Vaughn asks Sydney where her father is – the CIA have lost track of him.

Destination: Los Angeles, Vienna, Los Angeles, Archangelsk.

Timescale: Sydney has been away from home for a week.

Transcripts: Jack: 'I thought by now you'd know not to ask Sloane for a favour. You'll spend more time than you care to paying it back.'

Hicks: 'You were the last person that I ever wanted to see again, ever, and you were the only person that I ever wanted to see again.'

Sydney Bristow: Sydney wants to find her mother, but doesn't know what she expects, or even whether she is still alive. She remembers breaking her leg when she was camping with her parents and her father picking her up. She thought he was strong back then, but now believes he is damaged, scared of her trying to find her mother. She uses the revelation about her mother's possible survival as an excuse for her recent absence from SD-6. She's so desperate for help to locate her that she even asks Sloane.

Sydney dated fellow agent Noah Hicks. When he was reassigned, she thought he had left her without saying goodbye. In fact, he had sent her a message encoded in a junk email – but her computer was set to delete junk, so she never saw it. As such, their relationship ended on false pretences – leaving the door open for it to resume. It does so, as they have sex, the first time anything like this has happened to her since Danny died.

Jack Bristow: Jack's mental state after Laura's 'death' was not good and he seems to regress now that he's found that she's alive, losing his cool when Sydney says she wants to find her mother. He tells her that there's nothing that Laura could say that will change what she did and that Sydney had better decide what she expects before she does find her.

Jack is angry about Sydney talking to Sloane, telling her she'll have to repay that debt many times over. He first talks to Sydney, then Sloane. He doesn't understand why Sloane would lead her into disappointment. When Sloane asks Jack to take a few days off active duty to clear his head, he says he doesn't feel comfortable leaving Sydney alone at present – if she were Sloane's daughter, he would understand.

Nonetheless, Jack ends up at a loose end and Sydney finds him in a bar close to his home, drinking, at 2 p.m. She wants him to talk to someone about his problems and he says their current lack of communication is temporary. She advises him to go to a CIA counsellor and he says she is only responsible for herself. She feels it isn't irrational for her to be worried about him. As she didn't think he would listen, she made it official and she passes him an order from Devlin to attend trauma evaluation.

Jack visits Dr Barnett and tells her that he takes Sydney's interest in Laura as a criticism of himself. He says that a normal family would be one where the members aren't ordered to lie to one another. He is pleasant and humble in counselling and Barnett notes that he's just fed her a pack of lies telling her what she wanted to hear. She congratulates him on being a master of deception, keeping all his subconscious signals in order. Barnett recommends that he come to her once a week. He says she doesn't have the slightest idea what it takes to lead his life.

Arvin Sloane: Sloane was part of the Internal Commission formed to investigate Laura Bristow, a fact with which both Jack and Sydney confront him. He says that he has always acted in her best interests, acting as a father to her when Jack was not there.

Will Tippin: Francie is helping Will find a tuxedo for his awards ceremony, but he doesn't want Syd or Francie there. Will spits out his coffee when Francie suggests Sydney may be sleeping with her boss – after all, he has *met* Sloane.

Marcus Dixon: Dixon advises Sydney not to get too close to Hicks until he's gone through debriefing.

Francie Calfo: Francie borrows one of Sydney's coats – and finds a ticket from Italy in the pocket, dated for the week she claimed she was in Seattle. Francie speculates to Will that her trip may have been with a man she hasn't told them about and that she may not have told them because he's beating her. Will says Sydney would never tolerate that.

Marshall Flinkman: Marshall has hives, due to problems with a dermal pigmentation capsule he's working on.

Alexander Khasinau: Khasinau was Laura Bristow's superior at the KGB.

Noah Hicks: Hicks was recruited from Berkeley University. He had a relationship with Sydney, which ended when he was assigned to Vienna. When he was given the deep-cover assignment, he sent her a message to meet him, then believed she had rejected him when she never turned up.

Hicks has a lot of nerve – he argues openly with Sloane, cheekily calling him by his surname. During interrogation by the frankly terrifying McCullough, Hicks bluffs out a claim that he was recruited by K-Directorate and refuses to answer questions on his motivation. When questioned further, he says that he took the deep-cover assignment because he was in love and was scared that it was incompatible with the life he led. He has had five years to regret that mistake. He refuses to give McCullough the name of the woman in question, says he's a valued commodity and therefore won't cave in to McCullough's threats and, as a gentleman, he won't kiss and tell. Hicks probably has a fair idea that Sydney is watching . . .

He tells Sydney that he doesn't know how long he will be around. He remembers her as a trainee, the fun she seemed to have, and he worried that one day she would not feel that way. She admits that he was right – she isn't having fun any more.

Intelligence: Sydney has sex with Hicks, an old flame. The CIA always knew Laura Bristow survived her 'accident'.

Lies: Francie sees a large bruise on Sydney's arm – she claims someone accidentally hit her on the arm with his bag.

Breaking the Code: Location letters: N, A, O and G.

Plot Devices: In Vienna, Sydney wears earrings which emit an infrared (IR) beam. Sydney's contact will be wearing IR-sensitive lenses and will see the signal to perform the brush pass.

Action: Sydney climbs Mount Sebastio as the episode opens.

Undercover: Sydney and Dixon attend a ball in Vienna, wearing evening dress and masks. Dixon's half-mask has a sunburst of stripes, while Sydney's is full face and mostly white.

Background Checks: Multi-talented actor Peter Berg wrote and directed the movie *Very Bad Things*, but is probably best known for playing Linda Fiorentino's easy mark in *The Last Seduction*. Craig Zisk has directed episodes of *Smallville* and the short-lived *Birds of Prey*.

Music: 'Plus Bele Que Flor . . .' by Anonymous 4, 'Lay Your Weary Body Down' by Gigolo Aunts, 'Break Me Gently' by The Doves and 'Dream On' by Depeche Mode.

The Big Picture: Alexander Khasinau was KGB trainer to Sydney's mother.

Debrief: 'Searching for that woman will accomplish nothing. No good can come from her.' Sydney abandons her role as grief-stricken fiancée, falling into the arms of old love Hicks in this fun, peppy episode. There's a screwball, almost farcical aspect to the romance between the two spies, an impression helped by Peter Berg's excellent, urbane performance. While things look up for Sydney – especially in the last scene – it's Jack turn to be the tormented one, as he loses his grip now he knows his deceitful wife is still alive.

19
Snowman

Production #E648

1st US Transmission Date: 14 April 2002
1st UK Transmission Date: 29 May 2002

Writers: Jesse Alexander and Jeff Pinkner
Director: Barnet Kellman
Guest Cast: Peter Berg (Noah Hicks), Natasha Pavlovich (Young Irina Derevko), Stephen Spinella (Kishell), Boris Lee Krutonog (Young Alexander Khasinau), Angus Scrimm (McCullough), Paul Lieber (Young Bentley Calder), Patricia Wettig (Dr Judy Barnett), Richard F Whiten (Officer Pollard), Don Took (Agent Grey), Scott Vance (Agent Douglas)

Briefing: Sydney is woken by Hicks – Khasinau's men have found the safehouse and raid it, blasting away, but Hicks and Sydney have already escaped through a trap door. The couple find a motorbike and Sydney calls in for an early pick-up. They escape on the bike and are chased by a jeep. They are extracted on the move, Hicks driving the bike as Sydney lets a balloon on a cable loose, which shoots up and is grabbed by the SD-6 plane. They hold on to one another as they are dragged into the air before the bike crashes into the jeep, causing an explosion.

Back in LA, Hicks asks Sydney to come away with him – he has some money, and they can disappear forever, but she is more interested in finding her mother. The datacore contains footage of Laura Bristow (real name Irina Derevko) being debriefed from her mission by two KGB men

– Alexander Khasinau and another man Sydney recognises as Calder, the supposed FBI man who was alleged to have died in the crash while pursuing Irina. His real name is Igor Sergei Valenko and his death was faked at the same time. Sydney wants to find him and proposes an SD-6 mission to a bank in Cape Town where he was seen recently. Hicks is under suspicion of treachery – there are questionable sums of money in his accounts – but he is released so that he can go with Sydney to Cape Town, where they steal information from the bank's computer. When they return to SD-6, the information is corrupted, but Marshall manages to reconstruct it enough to locate Calder in Mackay, Australia, and Sydney and Dixon are sent to abduct him.

Meanwhile, Vaughn searches for legendary hitman the Snowman, who has been hired by K-Directorate to eliminate Khasinau and his associates. Too late, he finds out the Snowman has gone to Mackay to kill Calder – and he has no way to warn Sydney.

Sydney finds Calder dead and confronts the Snowman. In a fight, the Snowman falls on a knife and is killed – she removes his balaclava, and finds that Hicks was the famed killer all along.

Mission: Sydney and Hicks bring back the datacore to SD-6. Jack says that the information from the datacore is useless – highly theoretical information, none of which gives any clue regarding the Rambaldi artefacts, or Khasinau's whereabouts.

Sloane gets a requested report on Hicks and calls in McCullough, demanding that Hicks should not leave the building. Hicks is taken away and interrogated about his accounts by McCullough. He says he opened the accounts under an alias as an SVR (Russian foreign intelligence agency) agent and was operating undercover. He denies knowing who was the recipient of $45 million missing from one account. SD-6 consider the bank activity ties Hicks to K-Directorate.

Sydney proposes an operation. The FBI's spy hunter, Calder, was in fact Igor Sergei Valenko, an associate of

Khasinau, and his initials were on the memo liquidating $200 million of Khasinau's assets, while a man matching his description was caught on an SD-4 camera entering a bank in Cape Town, a money-laundering operation. Sydney wants to hit the bank in Cape Town to get their records and she wants Hicks on board as he knows the city. Jack takes the operation to Sloane and recommends that he use Sydney and release Hicks to go with her.

In Cape Town, Hicks and Sydney have to break into a server room armed with motion and sound detectors. They can't touch the floor or make any noise above .05 decibels. Marshall provides them with a device that creates an out of phase audio signal, blocking any noise in a 200ft radius. Sydney hangs over the server on a wire, holding a wireless modem three inches away from the server (it's alarmed too), while Hicks downloads the intelligence to a laptop. The rope holding Sydney begins to slip and, without sound, Hicks can't hear her cry out. At the last moment he grabs the rope and pulls it back, wrapping it painfully around his forearm, while she pulls herself back.

When they get back to LA, the laptop has no data on it – Marshall presumes that the server room had active countermeasures, perhaps an EMF generator which erased everything. Hicks wears a bandage on his arm where he grabbed the rope and had 26 stitches. Sloane has a new deep-cover assignment for Hicks, for which he volunteered, and he will leave for Baku that day to work at Kazar University.

Marshall interrogates the laptop and reconstructs the data. He finds Calder/Valenko in a private house in Mackay, Australia, where Sydney is to go that night, capture Calder and return him to SD-6 for questioning. In Mackay, she finds a bloodbath. The guards are dead, cut, and a masked man, the Snowman, has killed Calder with an icepick. They fight in the kitchen, the Snowman hesitating, using non-fatal implements on her. He falls on a knife, fatally wounding himself. She notices the bandage on his arm and pulls off the balaclava. Hicks, the Snowman, dies and his last words are that he tried to keep her away from this. Dixon runs in.

Countermission: The CIA have found that K-Directorate have hired a freelance assassin, the Snowman, to find Khasinau and kill him. Vaughn wants to find him by following the Snowman and wants to make sure Sydney can get to him first. He goes to Bogotá to talk to Kishell, a man who used to work with the Snowman and who survived an attack by the assassin, although he was severely disfigured by the attack, and rasps through a punctured lung. He never met the Snowman, who contacted him by telephone, and used him to arrange travel across tricky borders. In one operation the Snowman was ambushed and thought Kishell set him up and attacked him while he slept. Vaughn asks him if he has any leads since he was last interviewed by the CIA. He says that for years he was afraid to seek revenge, but now he is not scared and has leads. He promises to contact Vaughn with any leads he can establish and asks him to promise that the Snowman will suffer.

Sydney asks for a countermission regarding Cape Town, but Vaughn is angry that he wasn't told first that Calder was KGB. Sydney didn't want the information passed to the FBI, who would classify it and stop them from doing anything with the information.

Devlin wants a full report on Sydney's Australian mission. Vaughn is still waiting for a reply from Kishell on the Snowman. Sydney is already in Australia when Vaughn receives a call – the Snowman is in Mackay and is going after Calder himself. There's no way to get a warning to Sydney.

Destination: Los Angeles, Bogota, Cape Town, Mackay.

Transcripts: Hicks: 'Syd, I want you to come with me. I can't tell you where, but I can tell you we won't need locks on the door and you will learn how to surf.'

Jack (on Hicks): 'Sydney, you have no perspective on who that man is. You're as lost now as I was years ago.'

Irina Derevko: 'Jack Bristow was a fool.'

Sydney Bristow: Sydney seems almost guilty when Vaughn asks her about the Archangelsk mission. When Hicks asks Sydney to join him in his departure from SD-6, she has a million reasons why she can't. When he asks to know the reasons so he can refute every one, she mentions her mother. The files recovered from Archangelsk may help her find Laura Bristow but, until then, she can't go anywhere. When Hicks offers to wait and asks if she'll ever come with him, she smiles. When Jack tells her that Hicks is being held by Security Section, under suspicion of connections to K-Directorate, she defends him, saying that he is a patriot who believes SD-6 is genuinely part of the CIA and that he could never be a traitor.

Sydney is understandably reluctant to do anything for the FBI after their recent treatment of her. She promises Vaughn that Khasinau will not walk free, but she is unwilling to let the FBI get in her way.

When Will and Francie confront her about the ticket to Italy, she tells them that it relates to a new job at the bank, dealing with international clients who don't want a global paper trail and she flies to them on the bank's behalf. She claims to have had to sign non-disclosure agreements and is therefore unable to talk about it. She insists that this job is legal, but secret. Lying to her friends again drains her and she drifts towards accepting Hick's offer. She's shocked when Hicks is given another deep-cover assignment but, when he says that he requested it, Sydney realises he isn't really going. He tells her he's going to an island in the South Pacific and again asks her to go with him; she's tempted but she has her own reasons to stay. Hicks gives her a ticket for the following night and asks her to come with him for one week so he can prove it will work. They can find her mother together, without the CIA.

Sydney doesn't go with Hicks, instead opting for a mission to retrieve Calder and find a link to her mother. She lies to him, saying there are no leads. He stops her from making a final speech, saying it isn't goodbye.

Jack Bristow: When Sydney asks Jack if he saw the person he was supposed to – a counsellor – he replies bluntly that he has taken care of it. He insists he has no interest in her pursuit of her mother or any information pertaining to that search. He is frosty – the search for Laura Bristow has driven a wedge between them, as has Sydney referring him for counselling. He is frustrated by her faith in Hicks, as it reminds him of his belief in his wife. However, he tells Sloane that killing Hicks could be squandering a potentially valuable asset, one who could be useful in getting to Khasinau. When Hicks is released by Sloane and Sydney is close to him again, Jack looks on with what seems to be a kind of sadness – perhaps because he suspects it can only lead to heartache for Sydney?

The tape of Irina reveals Jack's full name – Jonathan Donahue Bristow. Needless to say, he eventually watches the footage and has to see his wife saying how easy to fool he was. Afterwards he goes to see Dr Barnett, who agrees to make some time to see him.

Laura Bristow/Irina Derevko: The datacore included files regarding Sydney's mother. Jack says these are purely archival, but they do include video footage. The footage of her being debriefed confirms that she was alive after her supposed death. The footage confirms Laura's Russian name (as glimpsed on a computer screen in **18,** 'Masquerade'), and shows her talking to Khasinau, who recruited her to the KGB in 1970. Phase One of her operation was to pose as an American student of literature. Phase Two was to make contact with a certain CIA officer and insinuate herself into his life. Phase Three was to acquire information on the project he was working on – Project Christmas. Irina went through his briefcase every night, listened in on all his private conversations, planted bugs on him – she says he knew nothing.

Arvin Sloane: Sloane talks to his wife on the phone, saying that if she's in pain she should have stronger medication. This caring side is contrasted with his ruthless dealing with possible treachery within SD-6. He thinks Hicks is hiding something, and he's also suspicious of Jack constantly lobbying for mercy towards the men in Sydney's life. Sloane knows that Sydney and Hicks are in a physical relationship – presumably due to surveillance of the safehouse.

When Sloane gives Sydney the mission to bring in Calder, he tells her that, as promised, he has brought her closer to her mother and he's always there for her.

Michael Vaughn: Vaughn is hesitant as he asks Sydney about her mission with Hicks and he is left alone at the meeting place as she leaves. He has a dog called Donovan, and leaves his keys with Weiss so that his friend can feed it while he is in Bogota. He is visibly unnerved when Kishell asks him to make sure the Snowman suffers. Vaughn tells Sydney that she can talk to him off the record, but her issues with Hicks have driven them apart.
Will Tippin: Will wants to work out a strategy for how he and Francie should ask Sydney about her mystery trip to Italy, as he is worried about accusing her of lying to her friends. They are relieved when she says the secret simply relates to a new job at the bank.
Marcus Dixon: Dixon doesn't trust Hicks and thinks that, in a situation where they have to rely on each other to survive, Hicks will be the only one of them who is truly safe.
Francie Calfo: Francie thinks Sydney may have left the ticket in her pocket because she wanted it to be found – she thinks it's some kind of cry for help. Francie accuses Will of cheating when he beats her at a football video game.
Noah Hicks: Hicks tells Sydney that Russia has a huge bootleg software industry and while he was over there he worked out how to take money from the Russian mob. He claims to have a lot of cash stashed away in offshore accounts because of this and asks Sydney to go away with him. He wants to walk away from the espionage life forever and he wants her with him. He repeatedly says that the life they're in isn't worth all the lies. After he's released by Security Section, he is seen laughing with Marshall.
The Snowman: The Snowman has been on the CIA's wanted list for twelve years and has been presumed dead since 1997. Who else has been missing since 1997? His name comes from a preference for the icepick as a weapon, although he also uses knives. The Snowman, alias Noah Hicks, is killed in a fight with Sydney after falling on a knife. Notably, he uses only blunt, non-lethal objects to fight back.

Home Front: Sydney gets back from the exertions of her Cape Town mission to find Will and Francie playing video games on her sofa.
Lies: Hicks tells Sydney he wants her to come with him to his tropical paradise – but considering the revelations about him, can we be sure that was his true intention?
Breaking the Code: Sydney's SD-6 callsign in Archangelsk is White Rabbit, the extraction plane callsign is Skyhook. Location letters: G, G, C and C.
Plot Devices: Marshall's active noise control-device cancels out sound and comes in the form of a strap around the upper arm. He demonstrates it by creating complete silence in a room containing a loud stereo. Hicks and Sydney are suitably amazed, miming their shock.
Action: Hicks and Sydney are winched off a moving bike by the SD-6 plane. Their second mission involves some impressive acrobatics, as Sydney hangs on a cable to get to the server in Cape Town. Sydney and Hicks fight each other in Calder's kitchen, using various kitchen implements.
Background Checks: Barnet Kellman has directed episodes of *ER*, *Felicity* and *Ally McBeal.*
Injuries: Hicks's arm is injured when he wraps a rope around it in the server room in Cape Town. It's the bandage around the dying Snowman's arm that tips Sydney off to who he really is.
Music: 'From The Summer' by Matt Beckler, 'Lover, You Should Have Come Over' by Jeff Buckley, 'Ready Steady Go' by Paul Oakenfold, 'There's Something Better' by Hathaway and 'My Favourite Regret' by Gigolo Aunts.
Debrief: 'Killing is his job. He likes his job.' Episode **19,** 'Snowman' is that dumbest of stories, the mystery with only one suspect, and as such it's a testament to Peter Berg and the *Alias* team that the episode is still highly entertaining, even with such an obvious twist.

20
The Solution

Production #E649

1st US Transmission Date: 21 April 2002
1st UK Transmission Date: 5 June 2002

Writer: John Eisendrath
Director: Daniel Attias
Guest Cast: James Handy (Devlin), David Anders (Mr Sark), Tony Amendola (Barcelo), Kirk BR Woller (Exterminator), Amy Irving (Emily Sloane), Michelle Arthur (Abigail), Alec Maray (Sial), Al Faris (Salim Wahid), Zuhair Haddad (Sayyad), Nameer El-Kadi (Algosaibi)

Briefing: Distraught after Hicks's death, Sydney hits the punchbag and punishes herself. She's losing faith in her mission. A comment by Francie about catching rats leads her to think up a CIA mission to draw out Khasinau, baiting him with the vial of solution the CIA got from the SD-6 vault. After robbing a vault as a cover for the emergence of a supposed second vial, Sydney meets with Sark to make the exchange. The meeting is interrupted by Dixon, sent by SD-6 to get the vial.

Will discovers that Jack kidnapped him and confronts him. They strike a deal – Jack will give Will the answers he wants, but first he needs to lead him to his source.

Emily knows about SD-6 and when the Alliance find out they want Emily dead.

Mission: Sydney Bristow takes leave from SD-6 for a few days to spend some quiet time in the desert.

SD-6 surveillance captures footage of Emily referring to SD-6 in conversation with Sydney. The Alliance want Emily killed, as knowledge of SD-6 is treated like a virus. Sloane has a meeting with the head of Alliance Security at which a decision on Emily will be made. Sloane says that his wife is dying and there is nothing to gain by killing her now. He is told that the time and date has been set and replies that he will not sit back and see this done. The Head of Alliance Security tells Sloane he was a friend of Jean

Briault – who was murdered in mysterious circumstances. When Briault died, Sloane didn't talk of decency. The Alliance know that Sloane has been pursuing Khasinau, against their instructions, and want evidence of his loyalty.

Sloane orders Marshall to bring up the last bioscan of Alliance member Edward Poole. Marshall finds that the scan revealed Poole was carrying two phones – Sloane asks him to locate them. He wants to know what the other phone is for – he believes it is Poole's link to Khasinau. Marshall's tap on Poole's secure telephone unit finds Khasinau's number and they put a tap on that. They intercept a call between Khasinau and Sark arranging for Sark to buy a second ampule similar to the one taken from the SD-6 vault by Cole. Sloane wants this second ampule and sends Dixon to the meeting between Sark and the Raslad Jihad, with orders to use all necessary force to get the ampule. In Denpasar, Dixon shoots his way into the exchange and holds the participants at gunpoint, demanding the ampule.

Countermission: Vaughn shows Sydney the map of SD-6 again, see **2,** 'So It Begins', and overlays a plan showing the parts which have been taken down thanks to her. These achievements don't even include the number of Rambaldi artefacts she has obtained for the CIA. He tells her that these are major accomplishments.

The previous year, SD-6 unsuccessfully tried to steal some priceless artwork, including an alleged Rambaldi artefact, from the Kherfu Art Museum in Algiers after which Sloane had the captured agents killed before they could be questioned.

Vaughn goes to Devlin suggesting Sydney's plan to set up a black-market sale of priceless objects including another ampule of liquid akin to the one Khasinau tried to get from SD-6. Sydney wants to stage a robbery of the Kherfu museum, then start rumours of a second ampule. The artwork would be returned to the museum through back channels after they have made contact with Khasinau. Devlin is alarmed that Vaughn wants the CIA to steal priceless artworks, but approves the mission.

In Algeria, Sydney and Vaughn pose as insurance agents and are given a tour of the security. Vaughn handles the shutdown of the security system (ostensibly to analyse the security) while Sydney knocks out her guide and climbs through the ventilation system to get to the vault room. She uses an electronic device to crack the lock to the vault, which gives her two minutes to get out before the alarms start. Meanwhile, the curator of the museum turns up and insists on the security system being turned on and that Vaughn and Sydney be thrown out. The reactivated ventilation system pulls Sydney's cable back and she's dragged through the system, dropping her explosive. There's an explosion in the vault as she pulls herself out through a vent. They meet up in the lobby and walk out as the alarms go off.

Vaughn finds a broker in Lisbon and claims to be from a splinter group of the Raslad Jihad responsible for the robbery. They set up a meeting with interested parties for the merchandise. Jack has sabotaged the SD-6 satcom intercept so that SD-6 can't intercept satphone calls during the agreed window for bids. The price for the Rambaldi ampule is $10 million. Khasinau offers double the asking price – in diamonds. Each side is allowed to bring two people to an exchange in Denpasar and Khasinau is sending Sark. Each side has the means to test the other's merchandise. Sark will authenticate the real Rambaldi ampule, then Sydney will swap it for a duplicate containing liquid with a radioactive isotope that can be tracked by the CIA.

In Denpasar, Sark challenges Sydney (who is disguised by a veil) to an ancient form of combat in which the Raslad Jihad are supposed to be proficient. Vaughn doesn't want her to, but watches from a distance, a sniper at his side in case of emergency. Sydney uses the traditional weapons, sticks with crescent-shaped blades at each end. She fights him to a standstill, until he is satisfied she is who she says. They test the merchandise. Vaughn sees Dixon shoot the guards outside the meeting place, heading for where Sydney and Sark are meeting. Dixon walks in, gun raised, as Sark pockets the ampule. Dixon demands the vial, as he holds Sydney and Sark at gunpoint.

When he realises that Will's source must be getting information from within the CIA, Jack goes to Devlin. He tells him that their entire operation is in danger. The source clearly has access to Omega 17 files. Haladki is Jack's first suspect. Devlin retorts by saying that Haladki reported Jack for threatening him at gunpoint. Devlin wants Jack to stop – he's going too far – and says he will deal with the possible leak in his own way, in his own time.

The CIA still have a bug in Sloane's home office.

Destination: Algeria, Denpasar.

Transcripts: Devlin: 'You're a good agent, Jack, but lately I find your methods . . . reprehensible.'

Sloane: 'Are you suggesting that I allow you to kill my wife to enhance my standing within the Alliance?'

Sydney Bristow: Sydney is finding that not trusting anyone, expecting betrayal, is becoming a part of her. She killed Hicks and, although he was a bad guy and she was justified in her actions, it's affecting her that she killed someone she cared about. She feels she's losing control; that she's out for revenge rather than justice. The one thing she wants is to find her mother, but by helping SD-6 find Khasinau she fears she really will help them.

Sydney tells Francie that she recently had sex with Hicks on a business trip and that they picked up where they left off, but that it didn't end well.

Sydney finds herself sympathising with Sloane when the Alliance want to kill Emily for her knowledge of SD-6.

Jack Bristow: Jack denies everything when Will approaches him about his kidnapping. He is angered that Will's source within the CIA is threatening Sydney's safety. After failing to persuade Devlin to investigate Haladki, he goes back to Will and works out a plan to expose his source.

Arvin Sloane: The threat to his wife leaves Sloane a quieter man, thoughtful, slow and slightly broken. He breaks down when he sees his wife in hospital.

Emily Sloane: Emily is worse, and she is hospitalised. She tells Sydney that, when you look back over your life, work doesn't matter as much as family and friends. She says that even working for SD-6 isn't that important – revealing that she knows something of her husband's work. Sloane has never told her, but she picked up on clues and overheard conversations and she realised that he never truly left the intelligence world. She's proud of him.

Emily has a biopsy scheduled for the following week.

Michael Vaughn: Vaughn is clearly in awe of Sydney's achievements in fighting SD-6 and desperately wants to rekindle her faith. He tells her that they'll find Khasinau and her mother. He is concerned about her meeting Sark – he's worried that Sark may recognise her from Moscow and fears what he may be capable of after his recent assassinations.

Will Tippin: Will is helping Francie find an alleged rat in the house when he gets a call from his mystery source. He tells his source about his kidnapping and that he's off the story. The source calls back and tells him that it was Jack who kidnapped him. While waiting for an exterminator at Sydney and Francie's house, Will finds a photo of Jack, lays clingfilm over the top and uses a permanent marker to draw a balaclava over his face. He realises what the voice told him was true. He talks to his colleague Abby, telling her that, if anything happens to him, she's to publish his file on the story. He gets her to promise she won't open it otherwise. Then he finds Jack and follows him to a bar, where he sits by him and asks if Sydney knows that he had him kidnapped. He tells him about the story and that it will get published if he dies. He says that his source is driving him insane and he doesn't even know who it is, so Jack can't beat it out of him. He asks Jack to tell him what he knows, to confirm that he's on Sydney's side. He wants Jack to help him stop what has been going on and in return he can help Jack find his source. Jack initially denies it all.

Later, Will receives a note to meet Jack. In a deserted industrial area, Jack tells Will that he works in intelligence, and that is all he needs to know. Jack will arrange their meetings and Will will never call him. Jack wants to go after the source first – answers to Will's questions will come later. He says that Sydney has nothing to do with any of this. Will agrees to Jack's terms. He tells him about the brooch and Jack admits that he planted it on Eloise Kurtz, but denies killing her, although they both have some responsibility for her death.

Jack tells him to use the brooch to talk to his source and to say that he's terrified of Jack and is back on the story. Will talks to the brooch and waits for the call.

Francie Calfo: Francie expounds her theory on rats – that they're clever, and you need to be clever to catch them: the only way to do it is to put out stuff they really want. When Sydney tells her that she slept with Hicks, she says that he was never good enough for her, especially after the way he dumped her. Francie isn't surprised it didn't end well. She promises to try and be nice to Hicks, should he call, not realising how unlikely that is.

Marshall Flinkman: Marshall is playing with a pop-up book on company time.

Intelligence: Will finds out that Jack was his kidnapper and later that he works in intelligence. They team up to find out who his source is.

Home Front: Sydney's house has rats, or possibly mice.

Lies: Jack denies Sydney is involved in Will's story.

Breaking the Code: Location letters: G and P.

Action: Sydney and Sark fight with ancient weapons, twirling and weaving.

Undercover: In Algeria, Sydney and Vaughn adopt French accents. In Denpasar, posing as a member of the Raslad Jihad, Sydney goes fully robed with a veil.

Trivia: Michael Vartan's effective French accent is not surprising – he was born and raised in France before moving to America when he was eighteen.

Music: 'Coming Down' by Trickside and 'I'm Gone' by Alison Krauss and Union Station.

Debrief: 'I am becoming what I despise.' A placeholder episode, **20,** 'The Solution' is all set-up and very little delivery, a slow build towards the season finale. Nonetheless, the individual missions are a lot of fun, as is the fight between Sydney and Sark.

21
Rendezvous

Production #E650

1st US Transmission Date: 5 May 2002
1st UK Transmission Date: 12 June 2002

Writers: Erica Messer and Debra Fisher
Director: Ken Olin
Guest Cast: David Anders (Mr Sark), Derrick O'Connor (Alexander Khasinau), Joseph Ruskin (Alain Christophe), Wolf Muser (Ramon Vesolo), Kamala Lopez Dawson (Dr Shah), Amy Irving (Emily Sloane), Philippe Bergeron (Lucques Trepainer), Christopher Dukes (Alpha Team Leader), Yvans Jourdain (Second Door Guard), Angela Nogaro (Make-up Artist), Tom Waite (Interrogator)

Briefing: Vaughn's CIA sniper prepares to give covering fire, as Vaughn runs down and throws a gas grenade into the meeting area. Everyone starts shooting. Vaughn chases Sark while Sydney heads to the extraction point. Dixon chases Sydney through the streets. Vaughn slams Sark against a gate, knocking him out. Sydney fights Dixon while Vaughn retrieves the ampule. Vaughn handcuffs Sark, while Sydney's arm is cut by Dixon's knife, who stands over her, gun raised, but Vaughn comes up behind him and knocks him out. Vaughn gets back to the gate to find that Sark has escaped.

Sloane wants the Alliance to allow Emily to die in peace.

SD-6 have Sark and Sloane makes a deal with Sark to betray Khasinau. Sydney, Dixon and Sark go to a dinner club in Paris owned by Khasinau. Meanwhile, Will goes to meet his source in the same city and is taken to the club by Khasinau's men. While Dixon steals a Rambaldi page from Khasinau's office, Sydney spots and rescues Will. Sark escapes SD-6's grip. Will is baffled by the Bristows' lives.

The Alliance accept that Emily should be allowed to die. Sloane then finds out that Emily's cancer is in remission.

In LA, Will is kept at a CIA safehouse. Sark takes out the CIA agents guarding Will and then shoots him in the chest.
OMG: Sydney sings!
Mission: The Alliance meet in London with Sloane in attendance. He asks them to let Emily die of cancer in an SD-6 hospital, where information can be contained. He says that if the Alliance kill his wife he will be forced to resign. In the previous twelve years, SD-6 has raised hundreds of millions for the Alliance in arms sales and transactions with Hassan, as well as amassing a greater collection of Rambaldi artefacts than any other SD cell. The Alliance knows Sloane killed Jean Briault. Poole isn't in attendance because the Alliance have realised his connection to Khasinau, which he admitted under duress. Poole has admitted to manipulating Sloane. The Alliance are willing to wage war on Khasinau. Sloane wants to assassinate him, but the Alliance have a different plan – they want to know how Khasinau works and what he knows. They want information on Khasinau's organisation from Sloane – then they will decide on Emily's fate.

SD-6 gained one thing from the Denpasar operation – they captured Sark. Sloane tells Sark he isn't in the mood for torturing him, but he wants him to help find Khasinau. Sark says that Khasinau doesn't tell him everything. Sloane gets a bottle of wine at Sark's request and drinks some before allowing Sark to take a sip. Sark agrees to lead him to Khasinau.

The information Sark has provided so far has been confirmed by other sources. He has told Sloane that he is set to meet with Khasinau at a dinner club he owns in Paris, this Thursday. Khasinau needs the ampule to decode a Rambaldi page written in invisible ink and Sark is to meet him with a counterfeit ampule, while Sydney steals the Rambaldi page and replaces it with a fake. Sydney can't believe they're not going to abduct him. She is to replace an employee of the club, who has called in sick.

Sydney and Dixon go to the club in Paris, Sydney as a performer, Dixon as her manager. She uses a ring given by Marshall to detect Khasinau's heartbeat and pass the signature to Dixon's cellphone, which will unlock the biometric scanner to get into his office. Sark goes into the club and meets with Khasinau, who wants to go straight to his office, but Sark, having ordered some wine, asks that they spend a while in the club. Sydney comes on stage to sing a number, walks down to their table and places the ring against Khasinau's chest. Meanwhile, Dixon heads for Khasinau's vault and gets in with the phone. Once in, he replaces the page and tells Sydney that he'll meet her outside in two minutes. Shortly after, Dixon gets a message from her saying that she can't meet him, and he agrees to meet her at the extraction point in thirty minutes. In the debrief, Sydney tells Sloane that Sark must have tipped off Khasinau – that's why his men came after her. Sark has been lost, but Sloane isn't despondent – the wine he drank at SD-6 was laced with a non-lethal dose of a radioactive isotope, so SD-6 can track him by satellite. He is on a transatlantic flight, probably with Khasinau, and when they land (in Geneva) SD-6 will send in a team. They find medical equipment revealing that Sark has had a full blood transfusion, getting the isotope out of his system.

Sloane gets a call from Alain Christophe of the Alliance, congratulating him on his operation in Paris. Emily will be spared and allowed to die in an SD-6 hospital.

Countermission: Sydney's countermission for Paris is not, as she hopes, to abduct Khasinau, but to switch the Rambaldi page for a counterfeit. After completing her song and getting Khasinau's heartbeat for Dixon, Sydney spots Will being brought into the club. She apologises in French to the audience and hastily exits the stage. She rescues Will, high-kicking his interrogators unconscious, then stalls Dixon while she gets him out of there. Sydney has to fight her way out of the club as Khasinau's men shoot at her. She and Will jump in a car with Jack, who shoots one of Khasinau's men over their heads. Jack arranges for a CIA team to give Will a makeover and passage back to the USA. When Jack and Sydney discuss the situation, Jack realises that Khasinau is using Will to bring down SD-6 by publicising their activities.

The CIA have lost the Rambaldi document to SD-6. Back in LA, Vaughn says that the Office of Securities is working on a plan to keep Will safe – witness protection, possibly recruitment. Sydney wants Will kept out of this life, but Vaughn says he is already involved. She visits him at a CIA safehouse in LA.

At the safehouse, the guards are down. Sark walks into the room and shoots Will in the chest.

Destination: Denpasar, Los Angeles, London, Paris.

Transcripts: Jack (to Will): 'I wouldn't let you do this if I thought the odds were in favour of your murder.'

Sydney (on Will): 'You should have seen his face in Paris. It was like he was looking at a stranger.' Vaughn: 'But he wasn't. He was looking at you, maybe for the first time. He was looking at you.'

Sydney Bristow: Sydney hugs Will before he's packed on the plane to LA, telling him he can't tell anyone about what he has seen. She's in tears, promising to see him at home. Another part of her life has been left tainted. Later, she tells Vaughn that, while he gets to say he works for the CIA, she looks for some tiny moment in her home life when she can be honest with anybody. Now that Will knows, she doesn't think he will ever trust her again – the shock on his face is etched in her mind.

When she visits him at the safehouse, she says that she told him not to follow the story. Danny was killed because he knew about what she did, and they were going to kill her too. She can't answer any of his questions and she's terrified that he knows anything about her. When he tells her he loves her because of who she is, not what she does, she thanks him.

Sydney finds herself having some sympathy with Sloane when he shows regret for Danny's murder.

Jack Bristow: Jack tells Sydney that the Denpasar operation was sloppy and that her search for her mother is clouding her judgement. He can't protect her, as he hasn't been reinstated to active duty by Sloane yet. When Sydney gives him hell for dragging Will into this situation, he says there were circumstances she didn't understand. He says that Will was already being used and Khasinau is using him to try and expose the Bristows.

Arvin Sloane: Sloane strikes a deal with the Alliance to allow Emily to live. He tells Sydney that he knows about her visit to Emily and that Emily mentioned SD-6. He says she will not be killed because of her forthcoming demise, and thanks Sydney for not reporting Emily and for being her friend. He tells her that she showed more mercy than he did for Sydney in similar circumstances.

Emily Sloane: Sloane thinks Emily's forthcoming bone marrow biopsy results will be a formality, revealing that she has not got long to live. She wants to be at home when she dies and gets him to promise she won't die in hospital. She jokes about not making plans for next week and when he doesn't laugh she tells him he needs to keep his sense of humour.

Emily's biopsy reveals the pain is due to rapid regrowth of her bone marrow. The cancer is in remission and she's heading for a recovery.

Michael Vaughn: Vaughn leaves Sark unattended to save Sydney, in spite of Weiss telling him over the satellite feed not to do so. Weiss takes a reprimand from Devlin for the loss of Sark, telling him that he misread the feed and told Vaughn to go help Sydney. Weiss wants to retire fully vested and doesn't want Vaughn to endanger his career any longer by requiring him to cover his back all the time. Vaughn tells him he doesn't know how to be Sydney's handler without it being personal. But he takes Weiss's guidance, briefing Sydney in a very formal manner for Paris. She notices something is wrong with him, although he denies any change.

Will Tippin: Under Jack's instruction, Will tells his source he wants a meeting, at the source's discretion. Jack tells him that the source only gave him his name so that he would know that Jack would never hurt Sydney, as claimed during his kidnapping. Jack presumes the source never thought Will would have the nerve to contact him. When Will's source refuses a meeting, he tells him he knows something about the circumference. Jack refuses to explain what 'the circumference' is. Will's source tells him he'll be contacted with instructions for their meeting.

Will is given lessons by Jack in avoiding being followed, which he uses before meeting him. Jack tells him that he will be picked up by armed men, blindfolded and taken to a secure location, but he will not be hurt. The source's men need Will alive. Jack gives him a jacket with a built-in transmitter, and his instructions are to go to a street corner in Paris. Jack goes with him and gives him a time-released metamphetamine to counteract the effects of the truth drug sodium pentathol. Jack will get a recording of Will's interrogator's voice and will be listening in case he gets into trouble. Will is picked up at gunpoint and taken to the club and, as expected, he is injected with pentathol and asked about the circumference. Sydney rescues him and when he sees the face of the person who has just kicked the guards over he screams. Outside, Jack hears Sydney's voice and starts driving. Will is completely spaced as he is extracted, disturbed by what is going on.

Later, when she explains why Danny was killed, he realises that this was why she had to borrow his sister's identity. Will tells her that he only investigated the story because she didn't seem to have any explanation for Danny's death – he couldn't stand it and wanted to help. He tells her he isn't going to ask her anything, or say anything else to anybody about it. He loves her, regardless of what she does, but he can't believe what her life is and what she keeps from everyone. He thanks her for saving his life.

Marcus Dixon: Dixon is wary of Sydney after Denpasar, having seemed to recognise her there. Nonetheless, he tells her he missed not having her on the mission. He notices when she bumps her wounded arm – from where he cut her. Later, he remembers her using the codename 'freelancer' after he was shot. He asks her about her wounded arm and she claims she was hiking in Palm Springs and fell down a rockslide. He tells her she should have told him, as they need to know about each other's injuries.

Marshall Flinkman: When talking about the friendship ring device, Marshall implies that it's impossible for men and women to be platonic friends – then takes it back when he realises he's talking to Sydney.

Mr Sark: Sark knows SD-6 is not part of the CIA. When captured, he expects Sloane to have him cut open in retaliation for Cole's incursion into SD-6. He prefers conversation over a Chateau Petrus '82, but is surprised when Sloane actually has a bottle delivered to the interrogation cell.

Intelligence: Khasinau is behind Will's source, feeding him information on SD-6 and endangering the Bristows' cover there. Dixon becomes suspicious of Sydney.

Home Front: Syd, Francie and Will watch a ludicrous soap opera.

Lies: Sydney tells Dixon that she has spent the week in Palm Springs and that she found time to read a book.

Breaking the Code: Location letters: A, O, D and A.

Plot Devices: For Paris, Marshall gives Sydney a friendship ring which records a cardiac pattern. Khasinau's heartbeat is very distinct, as he suffers from atrial fibrillation. The ring will detect that pattern and transmit it to a cellphone held by Dixon, which will then replicate the biopattern to allow him access to Khasinau's office, locked with a biometric scanner.

Action: Sydney's rescue of Will is spectacular, as she fights her way through an entire club full of goons. As they run out of the club, Jack pulls up in a car and shouts for them to duck as he shoots their pursuers.

Undercover: As a nightclub singer, Sydney has maroon hair, black trousers and a tight black bodice top. For his trip back to the USA, Will is given fresh clothes, a black floppy wig and the name Patrice Lafont.

Background Checks: Joseph (sometimes Joe) Ruskin has appeared in all incarnations of *Star Trek* (including the original series) to date, as well as *The Scorpion King* and *Prizzi's Honor*.

Injuries: Dixon has a plaster on the back of his neck from being knocked out by Vaughn, while Sydney has a painful arm from where Dixon cut her.

Music: The song Sydney sings in the club is 'Since I Fell

For You'. The tracks in the episode are 'Autumn Leaves' by Jacintha and 'Just Like You' by Maren Ord.

Debrief: 'Who the hell are you people?' The various plots begin to come together as *Alias* limbers up to the end of its first season. Everything set in Paris is a joy, from Sydney's song to Will's amazing reaction to seeing his friend in action for the first time. Seeing the barriers between these two friends taken away and Sydney able to tell Will the truth about herself, makes the cliffhanger ending even more shocking.

22
Almost Thirty Years

Production #E651

1st US Transmission Date: 12 May 2002
1st UK Transmission Date: 19 June 2002

Writer: JJ Abrams
Director: JJ Abrams
Guest Cast: David Anders (Mr Sark),
Derrick O'Connor (Alexander Khasinau), James Handy (Devlin),
Joey Slotnick (Haladki), Elaine Kagan (June Litvack),
Wolf Muser (Ramon Vesolo), Ric Young (Suit and Glasses),
Amy Irving (Emily Sloane), Michelle Arthur (Abigail),
Emily Wachtel (Worker)

Briefing: Will is tortured for information by Suit and Glasses, while Sark makes an offer to Sydney – he wants the Rambaldi page they stole from Khasinau's office, along with the ampule of liquid to reveal the page. The exchange will be in Taipei. Jack makes a plan – he will get the ampule from the CIA and Sydney will get the page from an SD-6 facility. Dixon is increasingly suspicious of Sydney, remembering her mentioning the callsign 'freelancer' – he confirms with Marshall that SD-6 have never used that name. Sloane tells Emily the truth about SD-6. Jack and Sydney steal the items. Dixon confronts Sydney, accusing her of being a traitor, but doesn't stop her.

The Alliance make Sloane an offer – kill Emily, and become a full member. Will is injected with a truth serum that causes paralysis in one in five cases. Sydney spreads the solution over the Rambaldi page, revealing the writing – the page shows the Mueller device from **1**, 'Truth Be Told', and she remembers the burst of water when she took it from Taipei. Jack says that 'the circumference' is a method of applying the Rambaldi technology Khasinau has acquired and that the instructions on the page must be the circumference. The page will tell Khasinau how to use a Mueller device. Jack tortures Haladki to find the location of Khasinau's base in Taipei, then kills him. Vaughn meets with Sydney and agrees to partner her to rescue Will.

Sydney, Jack and Vaughn fly out to Taipei. To prevent Khasinau from using the circumference, Sydney and Vaughn must destroy the device and the lab before Jack hands over the page in exchange for Will. Jack gives Sydney a red mercury explosive to destroy the lab. She says destroying the Mueller device won't be a problem, as it's only the size of a shoe. Suit and Glasses finds Will catatonic, and gets the soldiers to unchain him – at which point Will jumps up and stabs Suit and Glasses in the throat with a syringe of the potentially paralysing truth serum, elbowing a soldier in the face when he tries to stop him. He is dragged away laughing as Suit and Glasses begins to keel over under the influence.

At the beach house, Sloane breaks tablets into a wineglass, then takes it through to Emily and they sit down for dinner. Emily says she can't judge him for what he did and forgives him for his life with SD-6, then raises the glass in a toast.

In Taipei, Jack makes the exchange, while Sydney and Vaughn find the lab. Sydney locates the Mueller device, which is over a storey high. When she blows it up, a tidal wave of water fills the lab. She runs out as the lab door closes, but Vaughn is left behind, completely submerged as water fills the corridor. Sydney is knocked out by guards.

She wakes up tied to a chair. Khasinau comes over to her with a tray holding a bowl and a spoon and says she

should eat, but she says she's not hungry. As he walks away, she says she has questions and Khasinau says she can ask his boss. She thought The Man was the boss. Khasinau says The Man is – but he is not The Man. He walks out and a female figure walks in – Sydney's mother.
OMG: The season's closing moments – when the enemy walks in.
Mission: Sloane talks to Alliance member Ramon about Emily. Ramon says she was only allowed to live because she was already dying. Sloane argues that Emily should be brought in – she has valuable experience the Alliance could use. Ramon says it won't work – the Alliance's principles are well set, but Sloane says the Alliance is crumbling under bureaucracy and infighting and if Emily dies he won't help save them. He says the Alliance need new leadership. With Briault and Poole gone, there are two empty spaces in the Alliance and Sloane wants one. Ramon says that the Alliance have already voted – Sloane will be admitted as full partner, contingent upon his dealing with the Emily issue. He appears to deal with Emily, crushing tablets into her wine then proposing a toast.
Countermission: Vaughn tells Sydney the people who kidnapped Sark only used tranquillisers so she shouldn't presume the worst. He says they should wait to be contacted with demands, but thinks that Sydney may be planning to get Will back through illegitimate channels. Weiss tells Vaughn he should inform Devlin of his suspicions.

Weiss reports Vaughn's suspicions about Sydney to Devlin and Vaughn is called in before Devlin and Haladki. Vaughn says he simply thought Sydney seemed troubled. Devlin asks Vaughn directly if he thought she was hiding something from the CIA and he says he did. Devlin calls to get Jack held at the CIA vault, but he has already left. Jack calls Devlin himself and says the CIA will get the vial back, along with a copy of the Rambaldi page. Devlin says he has had enough of Jack's methods and has given Haladki authority in the mole hunt. Jack says he'll only come back to the office when the job has been done.

Destination: Los Angeles, Taipei.
Timescale: The exchange is to take place on Tuesday night.
Transcripts: Will (stabbing Suit and Glasses with the syringe): 'One in five, you little bitch! One in five!' (See **Will Tippin**.)

The Man: 'I have waited almost thirty years for this.'
Sydney: 'Mom?'

Sydney Bristow: When Jack says they can't just give things to the enemy to free Will, she asks him if he has any close friends, whether there is anyone he loves. She talks to Sloane about her mother and how Emily gave her a similar connection. Sydney likes to go to the train station when she wants to be alone, because there are normal people there going to their normal jobs.

When Vaughn tells her about his father and offers to help her rescue Will, she is reduced to tears – she's not as alone as she thought.

Jack Bristow: Jack knows Khasinau has a man inside the CIA. He grabs Haladki in his car and knocks him out, then ties him up on a bench in a warehouse, his hand in a vice. Jack demands to know how long he has worked for Khasinau. He turns the vice and crushes his hand. Haladki admits to working for Khasinau for two years and gives Jack the information he wants. He accuses him of telling Khasinau about the safehouse, about Sydney acting as a double agent for SD-6 and generally putting her life in danger. Haladki asks Jack to come with him, saying Khasinau can save him, but Jack shoots Haladki dead, his desire to protect Sydney yet again causing him to commit a horrendous act of violence.

While Sydney wants nothing other than to rescue Will, Jack is looking at the bigger picture more strategically and advises her to do the same. He says that Khasinau wants the ampule to read the page – he was so desperate to read the page that he sent Cole into SD-6 to get the ampule, a risk he wouldn't have taken if it wasn't important. Jack wants to get the ampule and page, so they can read it themselves. From that position, they can decide what to do with the page. After his conversation with Sydney about having friends, Jack asks Devlin if they're friends. Devlin says he thought they were, but isn't sure any more.

When Vaughn takes a risk by joining Sydney in her mission to help Will, he earns Jack's respect at last. When Sark asks Jack if he's comfortable exchanging priceless artefacts for a low-grade reporter, he replies that Will's writing isn't that bad. Sark complains that Jack has exposed the page, but he would have done the same. Will staggers over to Jack and hugs him, thanking him as he begins to cry. Jack uncomfortably raises a comforting hand, unable to cope with such an emotional situation.

Arvin Sloane: With Emily in recovery, Sloane has to tell her the truth about what he does. He also seems to tell her more about their predicament – but the audience is not privy to exactly what he says.

Sloane is given the chance to become a full member of the Alliance and lead the charge against Khasinau. After being cast in a sympathetic light, as a man threatened with a terrible personal loss, he proves himself to be even worse than we suspected, grinding pills into his wife's drink.

Emily Sloane: Emily looks shattered and distressed after her husband explains the true nature of SD-6 to her, but she loves and forgives him. Her initial cancer diagnosis was that she would only live six months – and that was three years ago. When her husband passes a glass of wine to her, Emily toasts their future.

Michael Vaughn: Echoing Sydney in the previous episode, Vaughn realises something is wrong with her because she's unresponsive during their briefing. He knows her well enough to become suspicious when she doesn't seem to be proactively addressing Will's kidnapping.

Vaughn's father used to keep a diary. He punished himself whenever he made mistakes. He questioned operations, but only in his diary, writing out things he could never say in real life. He was a loyal company man, but being a company man killed him. He was blindly devoted to the job and Vaughn isn't going to go that way – that's why he offers to help Sydney rescue Will.

The last time we see Vaughn he's trapped under water,

a door between him and Sydney. As such he can be considered missing, presumed drowned.

Will Tippin: In Taipei, Will is dentally tortured by Suit and Glasses, who finds a cavity. Will is asked about the circumference and when he doesn't know anything, he loses a tooth. Suit and Glasses injects him with a truth serum which results in paralysis and other symptoms for one in five men it is used on. Will shakes as the drug is injected and begins to cry. Suit and Glasses asks again about the circumference. Will demonstrates he may have the right stuff to be a spy after all, faking paralysis so that, when the Taiwanese guards untie him, he has an opportunity to grab one of the syringes of serum and jab it into Suit and Glasses' neck. Will is jubilant as he is dragged away by the guards, screaming his victory. However, by the time he is handed over to Jack, he is more subdued – he hugs Jack, thanking him.

In his absence, Abby goes to Litvack and gets her to publish the story.

Marcus Dixon: Dixon confronts Sydney about the callsign 'freelancer', which he knows isn't an SD-6 callsign. He wants to know who she has been working for and says he can't believe anything now that he knows she has been lying to him. She asks him to trust her, saying that she can't tell him what any of this is about. She asks him to remember that he knows her, knows she wouldn't betray what they both believe. She says what she is doing is classified and that she would never betray her country. He says he needs a reason not to report her to Security Section and walks away.

Francie Calfo: Francie has decided to open a restaurant, and has found a location in Silver Lake. She's just about to graduate from business school.

Steven Haladki: Haladki is revealed, as Jack suspected, as having worked for Khasinau for two years. He cracks under Jack's torture, telling him that Khasinau is the future and can save him. There's a fanatical gleam in his eyes as he says this, just before Jack shoots him dead.

Mr Sark: Sark congratulates Jack on his daughter's singing voice, saying he enjoyed the stage show in Paris.

Alexander Khasinau: . . . is not The Man.

Intelligence: Judging purely from what we see on screen: Dixon suspects Sydney of working against SD-6; Jack kills Haladki; Will's story goes to press; Sloane murders Emily; Vaughn drowns; The Man is revealed.
Lies: Jack tells Sydney and Vaughn he found out about the lab in Taipei from a source.
Breaking the Code: SD-6 passwords: Rule, Dear, Choose. Sydney's SD-6 password in Okenagwa was 'bluebird', not 'freelancer'. Location letters: A and T.
Plot Devices: To get the Rambaldi page from an offshore facility, Sydney requires Sloane's voice ID and fingerprints. Jack gives her a shirt made of heat-sensitive material which she needs to get Sloane to touch so Jack can pick up his fingerprints and make a copy. She does this by acting emotionally, so Sloane squeezes her shoulder comfortingly. Jack gives her a transmitter with a modem, allowing him to get the passwords to the SD-6 facility by hacking into Sloane's computer while Sydney talks to him. At the same time a microphone allows him to pick the correct syllables for each password from Sloane's speech. When Sloane is about to leave, Jack tells Sydney he still needs a 'ch' consonant, so she asks him about children.

In Taipei, Vaughn has a surge inducer which knocks out the security cameras.
Action: The Mueller device explodes, flooding the lab in Taipei. Sydney and Vaughn run from the water, but Vaughn is lost, apparently drowned.
Undercover: In Taipei, Sydney and Vaughn wear clubbing gear – she wears tight black PVC trousers with a transparent top over a black bra, along with a dog collar hung with chain-links and blue-dyed hair. Vaughn wears a long leather coat.
Injuries: Will gets the full Suit and Glasses treatment, but gets his own back by stabbing his torturer with a syringe of truth serum, which seems to have a paralysing effect judging by the way he collapses afterwards.

Jack crushes Haladki's hand in a vice, then blows his head off. Vaughn seems likely to have drowned.
Music: 'My Skin' by Natalie Merchant, 'Music Response' by The Chemical Brothers and 'Supermoves' by Overseer,

as well as 'Canzone Del Salce' from Verdi's *Othello*, performed by Miriam Gauci.

The Big Picture: The circumference consists of instructions for an energy battery that Khasinau has built – the Mueller device. It's in an underground lab below the Pang Pharmaceuticals warehouse in the Hui Sing district of Taipei, Room 47. The Mueller device is bigger than the one Sydney saw in her last visit to Taipei – it's two storeys high, complete with a giant red floating ball.

The Man is revealed to be Sydney's mother.

Debrief: 'Trust is a tricky thing.' The first season comes full circle with this perfect season finale, ending as it began, with Sydney tied to a chair in Taipei. Echoes of episode **1**, 'Truth Be Told' appear throughout the episode: Will suffers the same torture as Sydney at the hands of Suit and Glasses; there's the Mueller device, writ large; Sydney's look is a mirror of that in the first episode, blue hair replacing red hair; and then there's the big parental revelation, the flipside to Jack's stellar entrance in that pilot instalment. The pieces of plot throughout the season click together, showing that it wasn't all random, or made up by the production team as they went along – there's a shape to the season, a great story behind all the revelations and twists. There's also an emotional drive to the episode – Sydney, Jack, Vaughn, Will and Sloane all get key character moments, developing them in interesting directions. The Bristows and Vaughn in particular seem to be breaking away from the authorities more than ever, putting loved ones above an abstract cause.

Never ones to skimp on the big plot moments, the *Alias* team start piling on the cliffhangers from around halfway through the episode. Aside from the big shock at the end and the fate of Vaughn, there's the question to ponder of whether Sloane has killed Emily, along with worries about what Dixon will do next and what the fallout will be from the publication of Will's SD-6 story. By the end credits virtually every aspect of the series' format has been thrown up in the air, with hardly any clues as to how they will land at the start of the next season.

Season Two

Regular Cast:

Jennifer Garner (Sydney Bristow)
Ron Rifkin (Arvin Sloane
Michael Vartan (Michael Vaughn)
Bradley Cooper (Will Tippin)
Merrin Dungey (Francine Calfo)
Carl Lumbly (Marcus Dixon)
Kevin Weisman (Marshall Flinkman)
David Anders (Mr Sark)
Victor Garber (Jack Bristow)
Lena Olin (Irina Derevko/Laura Bristow)

Created by JJ Abrams

23
The Enemy Walks In

Production #E652

1st US Transmission Date: 29 September 2002
1st UK Transmission Date: 4 March 2003

Writer: JJ Abrams
Director: Ken Olin
Guest Cast: Derrick O'Connor (Khasinau), Greg Grunberg (Weiss), Patricia Wettig (Dr Judy Barnett), Stuart Yee (The Tester), Jamie McShane (CIA Agent), Dayna Adams (Receptionist), Chris Harrison (Reporter #2), Todd Karli (Newscaster), Roger Lim (Gasping Body), Tricia Nickell (Reporter #3), Danny Romero (Reporter #1), Lancaster Dean Grimes (Stunt Junkie), Ron Yuan (HazMat Guy), Clayton Landey (Wilcox)

Briefing: Irina shoots Sydney in the shoulder when she refuses to say who sent her. As she tells her therapist, Dr Barnett, she escaped and looked for Vaughn, but he was nowhere to be found. Will's story has been published and Jack saves him from SD-6 by getting him to 'confess' that he's a heroin addict who made it all up. Sydney is arrested by SD-6 after Dixon tells Sloane he's suspicious of her.

Jack covers for her and she is released. She's sent on a mission to France, where she discovers Vaughn. She then goes on a mission to Barcelona for the CIA to recover valuable documents from Khasinau. Irina is also there and she kills Khasinau and takes the documents. Sydney returns to LA for Emily Sloane's funeral. Afterwards, Jack tells her that Irina has handed herself in to the CIA.
OMG: Irina shoots Sydney!
Mission: Once Sydney returns from her mission in Taipei (which successfully shuts down Khasinau and Irina's operation there; see **22**, 'Almost Thirty Years'), she is sent to France to bug the telephone of Jean Luc Rave, a member of the French National Assembly and one of Khasinau's financiers.
Countermission: Sydney's countermission is to place a CIA device on the tapped phone that allows them to listen in, but also control SD-6's access to the phone calls. She successfully completes the mission. She then goes on the CIA mission to Port of Barcelona, where she intends to intercept 'the Bible' before Khasinau can get his hands back on it. Irina foils this and takes 'the Bible' for herself.
Destinations: Taipei (Taiwan), Los Angeles (USA), Cap Ferrat (France), Port of Barcelona (Spain).
Timescale: Dixon says he caught Sydney in Santa Barbara last Thursday (see **22**, 'Almost Thirty Years'). On the day of Emily's funeral, Will says it's a few days since he found out about Sydney's secret life. Sydney says at the funeral that she was six when she lost her mother. She tells Dr Barnett that it's twenty years since she saw her mother.
Transcripts: Irina (to Sydney): 'I could have prevented this . . . you were so small when you were born.'
Sydney Bristow: Sydney comes face to face with her mother, but says at Emily's funeral that she was the mother she never had. As for Irina, Sydney concludes, 'All anyone needs to know about that woman is that she's a bad guy' – black and white thinking in a world that's never less than a murky grey. Sydney sees a therapist, Dr Barnett, which conveniently allows her to explain the story so far. During her first two sessions – both in this episode

– Barnett thinks she's made progress. Like her father, Sydney is very suspicious of therapy.
Jack Bristow: Jack seems surprised to learn that Irina is The Man, but displays no emotion at the news she's alive – although he is concerned that Sydney's been shot. He seems genuinely concerned to help Will out, despite his anger that he left the SD-6 story with his editor.
Arvin Sloane: Jack manages to get two plans past Sloane: first, he tricks him to save Sydney from Dixon's revelation that she's a double agent; second, he gets Sloane to agree that killing Will would only draw attention to SD-6. Sloane says he wished he'd killed Will earlier, then tells Sydney that he saved him because he didn't want to hurt her. Sloane asks Sydney to speak at Emily's funeral. There are no Alliance people at the funeral, presumably as they don't want to be seen in public.
Marcus Dixon: With deep regret, Dixon tells Sloane that he thinks Sydney is a double agent. When Jack convinces them otherwise, Dixon swiftly apologises for doubting her.
Will Tippin: Will hears Vaughn's name for the first time, and discovers that Sydney's mother is alive and that she shot her daughter. As they leave Taipei, an LA TV channel is breaking Will's SD-6 story but he says he's only heard the name and he doesn't know much else. The Bristows fill him in ('he thought it sounded preposterous . . . which is appropriate,' as Sydney tells Dr Barnett). Jack comes up with a number of plans to salvage the situation, only one of which doesn't involve killing Will – he discredits him by injecting him with heroin and setting him up with the police. Will publicly announces that the whole SD-6 story was a drug-fuelled fantasy. He's sacked from his paper.
Michael Vaughn: Vaughn didn't drown; he swam to a ventilation shaft and by an amazing coincidence he had a screwdriver with him. He unscrewed the vent and made his escape. He goes on the field mission to Barcelona. He and Sydney, pumped full of adrenaline, almost kiss when they've escaped from the facility at Cap Ferrat. Sydney protests too much to Dr Barnett, saying her relationship with him is professional.

Irina Derevko: Irina was apparently very young when she married Jack and had Sydney – Lena Olin was born in 1956, so was 46 when this episode was made. Sydney is (by most accounts, anyway) 26. (While there's no indication how old their characters are, Victor Garber is seven years older than Lena Olin.) Irina has many of the same mannerisms as Sydney. For example, she tucks her hair behind her ear when she's worried. Sydney says Irina has killed twelve CIA agents. It's unclear what Irina's doing in Barcelona – she's there as a sniper, presumably to kill the operative who's handing over 'the Bible' if he causes trouble (or even if he doesn't). Khasinau seems to know she's there, but isn't expecting Irina to kill him. Was that always Irina's plan once 'the Bible' was secured? Is it a coincidence after Vaughn's praise of the humble screwdriver that Irina lodges one into her sniper rifle to cover her escape? Like Sydney in the first episode, Irina walks into CIA reception at Langley and hands herself in.
Marshall Flinkman: Marshall inadvertently reveals he's nervous around his Aunt Ruthie.
Intelligence: Irina asks Sydney who sent her – she knows Sydney works for SD-6 so it's actually a big clue that she knows Sydney *also* works for the CIA. Or perhaps she thinks Jack has sent her. Jack still doesn't explain how he knew about the facility at Taipei.

Khasinau has a Hazardous Materials (HazMat) team investigate the water from the Mueller device. Vaughn swims through it without any obvious ill effect and it seems to be ordinary water. Is this evidence that Khasinau doesn't fully understand the device? Or that he was expecting something more? He is also conducting experiments on living people at Cap Ferrat: he's planning to cut open the head of one Taiwanese man; he's done something to the eye of another; and Sydney narrowly prevents him cutting open Vaughn's chest. It may be pure sadism, a further investigation into exposure to the Mueller device or it may be an entirely different scheme.
Office Politics: A fairly straightforward episode – SD-6 send Sydney on a mission, the CIA organise a countermission, before sending Sydney on another mission.

Home Front: Francie is now the only regular cast member that doesn't know Sydney is a spy. During this episode, she meets an estate agent and buys a restaurant. She sees Will in hospital and tends to him afterwards.
Lies: Will and Sydney have a heart-to-heart where they agree that it's hard to keep her secret. Sydney is visibly pained at lying to Dixon. On the other hand, she's perfectly at ease telling Dr Barnett everything she knows and feels. Sydney gives a heartfelt eulogy at Emily's funeral – but lies about her mother during it. Jack deceives Sloane, telling him that the 'freelancer' code was one he arranged for Sydney (rather than her CIA codename) because he didn't trust Sloane. Irina double-crosses Khasinau, killing him.
Plot Devices: Sydney has no idea what the Mueller device is, just that it's unusual. Marshall supplies her with a revolutionary phone tap that taps the line, rather than the phone, so it can be fitted to any phone, anywhere in the world. She tells Will that the front room of her apartment has a bug killer in the lamp so they can't be overheard. Presumably there are similar devices in her other rooms and they are CIA issue (she's free to speak to Will about being a double agent). So, even if her room isn't bugged, her phone line may be tapped, see **24,** 'Trust Me'.
Action: Sydney escapes her Taipei captivity by breaking her chair, using a fire extinguisher as a missile to smash down the door and then using the broken-off chair arms as weapons. In France, she parachutes in, then has a fight with Khasinau and he lasts a lot longer than most people who fight her. He wins the first fight by knocking her to the floor and making his escape to raise the alarm. In Barcelona she gets a rematch and, although it's a long and even fight, she prevails.
Undercover: Sydney starts the episode in the blue wig and fishnet gear she was wearing in **22,** 'Almost Thirty Years'. On her mission to France, she parachutes in wearing a black jumpsuit, which she quickly unzips to reveal a low-cut black full-length dress with white embroidery and a wide slit almost up to her waist. She wears a platinum blonde wig. For the Barcelona mission, she wears sensible

SWAT gear, like the CIA men – although, unlike theirs, hers shows a flash of midriff when she's fighting.

Background Checks: Swedish actress Lena Olin came to international attention with *The Unbearable Lightness of Being* and has demonstrated her versatility in films such as *Mr Jones*, *Romeo Lies Bleeding* and *Chocolat*. She isn't related to Ken Olin, an executive producer on the show and the director of this episode.

Trivia: There's a new opening voiceover, an unidentified man filling in the story so far. The end of episode **22,** 'Almost Thirty Years' was reshot for this episode to include Lena Olin.

Music: 'I Wanna Stay' by Gemma Hayes, 'Farewell' by Rosie Thomas and 'Spy' by Daniel Lenz.

Injuries: Sydney is shot in the left shoulder by Irina, but this doesn't slow her down too much. After fighting her way out of Taipei, she's soon parachuting into France with only a token wince when she lands. The black dress she's wearing there has a relatively thick strap by Sydney's standards, but there's no evidence of a dressing on the 'wounded' shoulder (ironically, there is in episode **24,** 'Trust Me'). In Barcelona, during their fight, Khasinau grabs Sydney's shoulder seemingly knowing it will cause her excessive pain (and it does); he also gives her a visible bruise on her left cheek (which she has to cover up with make-up for Emily's funeral). Sydney explains her ability to run and fight to Dr Barnett by saying she's learned there's no drug like adrenaline. This is, of course, ironic considering she plunges a (very large!) syringe full of adrenaline into Vaughn's chest to revive him in France. Vaughn hadn't suffered too much under water, but was quickly captured and knocked out by a guard. His chest is nearly cut open by Khasinau, who knows he's still alive. Will is still recovering from his torture – he has a black eye, scars on his forehead and apparently a broken nose. These heal in time for Emily's funeral. In the meantime, though, Jack has injected him with enough heroin to render him semi-conscious and he's hospitalised after he's arrested. Weiss gets a flesh wound to the neck.

The Big Picture: Khasinau is killed by Irina. The destruction of the Taipei facility has seriously damaged their operation. At this stage, SD-6 know nothing about Irina, and talk about her cartel as 'Khasinau's operation'. It's unclear what Irina has done with 'the Bible'.

Debrief: 'Mom?' For most television shows, three big action sequences and a mother shooting a daughter after telling her she wished she'd killed her at birth would represent half-a-dozen episodes' worth of material. For *Alias*, it seems almost a low-key reintroduction to the characters and their world. Vaughn's resurrection is a cop-out and everyone but Francie now knows Sydney's a spy. But *Alias* hits its second season with the confidence to play against expectations and start with a reminder of the state of play, rather than an hour of mindless action.

24
Trust Me

Production #E653

1st US Transmission Date: 6 October 2002
1st UK Transmission Date: 11 March 2003

Writer: John Eisendrath
Director: Craig Zisk
Guest Cast: Terry O'Quinn (Kendall), Tony Amendola (Barcelo), Wolf Muser (Veloso), Joseph Ruskin (Christophe), JD Hall (Judge Freid), Wendle Josepher (Vicki Crane), Soren Hellerup (Petr Fordson), James Kohli (Concierge), PJ Marino (Felon), Scott A Smith (Schmidt), Benson Choy (Soldier), Joel Guggenheim (Agent On Call), Alex Morris ('Homeless' Man), Sam Aylia Saka (Security Guard), Krikor Salamian (Naj), Kevin Sutherland (Monitoring Agent), Michael Yavnieli (Driver)

Briefing: Irina is brought in chains to her cell. Jack arrives at Sydney's house to say her mother hasn't told her captors anything and finds her in denial about Irina. Assistant Director Kendall puts pressure on Vaughn to get Sydney to talk to Irina. Sloane is initiated as a full member of the Alliance. On his return, Sloane sends Sydney and Dixon to

Rabat to recover Irina's blackmail disc. Sydney succeeds, but ignores intelligence given to Vaughn by Irina. Sydney sees Irina, who says SD-6 will use the disc to get a T-wave camera from its Finnish inventor. Sydney and Vaughn go to Helsinki to retrieve the T-wave camera before SD-6 can get it. Sloane is there, but Sydney snatches the camera in time. She sees Irina again – she'll talk to her mother, but only on strictly professional terms.

Will is sentenced to, and starts, community service.

Destinations:: London (UK), Rabat (Morocco), Los Angeles (USA), Helsinki (Finland) and back to Los Angeles (USA).

Timescale: It's 21 years since Laura Bristow died, according to Sydney.

Transcripts: Jack (to Francie): 'I'm not really into interior decorating.'

Sydney Bristow: Sydney hates her mother. She doesn't support the death penalty, but wants to see Irina executed for what she has done. Sydney agrees to talk to her mother, but she must be addressed as 'Agent Bristow' and she won't allow personal questions or comments. Irina agrees, but gives an evil smile as soon as Sydney isn't looking.

Irina Derevko: There is no indication why Irina has handed herself in. She hasn't brought 'the Bible' with her and she isn't answering any questions. Irina thinks big – she has a 'blackmail disk' full of compromising photos and data that allowed her control of members of NATO, the UN, the World Bank – all multinational organisations. Irina warns her captors to tell Sydney to trip the fire alarm before she opens the safe in Rabat. Jack tells them not to pass on the advice, but they do, although (against Vaughn's advice) Sydney doesn't take it. The alarm goes off as the safe is opened. Irina correctly guesses that Sydney didn't trust the information – she wouldn't have done either in her place.

Jack Bristow: Jack warns Sydney about Irina, from bitter experience: 'The minute you depend on her, she'll gut you.' He tells Vaughn not to pass on the advice about the fire alarm to Sydney.

Arvin Sloane: Sloane flies to London and is made a full

member of the Alliance following an initiation procedure. The Alliance are very impressed that he killed Emily.

Michael Vaughn: Kendall (somehow) knows Vaughn helped bust Sydney out from his custody (see **17,** 'Q and A') and threatens him with charges unless he convinces Sydney to talk to Irina. Vaughn comes face to face with Irina and tries to maintain a professional air with the woman who killed his father (he could only be identified by his dental records after what she did to him). He doesn't tell her about their history. As he leaves, Irina tells Vaughn he looks just like his father.

Irina spots that Vaughn calls her daughter 'Sydney' and not 'Agent Bristow', so immediately guesses a close connection. Vaughn, for his part, seems overawed by a woman who is, after all, a sort of über-Sydney.

For the first time, Vaughn is in the same room as Sloane. He's clearly not worried if Sloane sees him.

Marcus Dixon: Dixon helps Sydney in Rabat, accessing the hotel computer and jamming the lifts so Sydney can make her escape.

Will Tippin: Will is put on probation, sentenced to one hundred hours' community service (he picks up litter with fellow junkies, including copies of his old paper) and a course of drug rehab. He gets sunburn picking litter.

Francie Calfo: There's a lovely scene when Jack comes round to Sydney's house and Francie engages him in small talk. She doesn't want to wait six months for a liquor licence, so she's talking to the Mafia. Will is horrified and offers to help her with the paperwork.

Intelligence: SD-6 know that Irina and Khasinau's operation is vulnerable and move to seize some of its assets. Top of the list is Irina's blackmail disk. Once Sloane has it, he sends it straight to Alliance HQ in London. Irina knows, or correctly guesses, that SD-6's first target on the disk will be Petr Fordson and his T-wave camera. The disk has compromising photos of Fordson's daughter. It's not clear what Irina knows about T-wave technology. Sydney uses the 'freelancer' code in Helsinki. Surely that callsign is compromised now, see **23,** 'The Enemy Walks In'.

Office Politics: Irina isn't held by the CIA but by the US Joint Task Force on Intelligence in a huge underground facility (callsign: 'Boot Camp') that Sydney reaches by passing an elaborate series of checkpoints. Irina herself is behind a sheet of bulletproof glass, at least four sets of barred doors accessed by a handprint reader and is under armed guard. A camera in Irina's cell constantly monitors her. Sydney has an ID card which means she can see Irina without seeking further authorisation.

Irina is being held by Assistant Director Kendall (last seen in episode **17,** 'Q and A'), who approaches Sydney directly, rather than going through the proper CIA channels.

Mission: SD-6 send Sydney on a simple mission – retrieve the 'blackmail disk' from Mohammed Naj's safe in Rabat.

Countermission: Sydney is to swap the disk for an almost identical one containing false information. Dixon gets to her before her CIA contact, so she succeeds in the mission, but not the countermission. She's then sent on a mission to retrieve the T-wave camera before SD-6 can get it. She succeeds. As she hands the camera to Kendall, it might not, actually, be the CIA sending her on the mission.

Lies: Did Irina tell Sydney the truth about the fire alarm? It is, as Jack says, still entirely possible that it was a trap.

Breaking the Code: The combination to Naj's safe is 0925. Location letters: D, B, E, H and O.

Plot Devices: Sloane is injected in the neck with some sort of device (a metal capsule) as part of his initiation into the Alliance. He says he understands the reasons why, but these aren't clear. Is it a surveillance device, or something more sinister? For the Rabat mission, Marshall has an 'old school' metal detector for Sydney and a device for cracking the safe that clamps over the dial and is activated when Sydney taps 739793 into her phone (793 is SYD on a telephone keypad). The CIA give Sydney a subvocal mike that means she can talk to them during the Rabat mission. In Helsinki, the CIA give Sydney abseiling gear and a pen laser for cutting the glass of the hotel room window.

The T-wave camera (the T is short for terahertz) is a device small enough to be portable, capable of seeing into

anywhere, even NORAD (the North American Aerospace Defense Command – in charge of protecting US air space).
Action: Fairly restrained – a fight for Sydney escaping from Rabat and then an abseil in Helsinki.
Undercover: In Rabat, Sydney poses as Beatricia Cunelli, a rich Italian wife. She keeps the concierge talking long enough for Dixon to change the hotel register to include her alias on it and so gain access to Naj's room. She's dressed in a short zebra dress, designer glasses and carries a silver-tipped cane. Her hair is pushed up and has either a blonde or grey streak in it. In Helsinki, it's more practical – a black fur-trimmed coat comes off to reveal black trousers and black leather halter top with a black bob wig.
Reality Checks: There aren't any skyscrapers in Helsinki. There are, however, many Joint Task Forces in the US between the FBI (domestic) and CIA (international) that are concerned with such things as organised crime, the drugs and arms trades and terrorism. There's no one 'US Joint Task Force on Intelligence', as seems to be implied by this episode. Terahertz cameras exist in prototype form. They detect ultra-high-frequency energy, just below infrared on the electromagnetic spectrum.
Music: 'Shelter From The Storm' by Bob Dylan, 'Touch Me' by Supreme Beings of Leisure and 'Fusco's Song' by Catie Curtis.
Injuries: Sydney has two bandages on her shoulder from where she was shot, which she tells Jack is healing. Irina seems concerned about Sydney, asking about her shoulder wound. This might seem maternal, except that it was, of course, Irina that shot her. Agent Weiss is in hospital following his wounding in Barcelona see **23,** 'The Enemy Walks In' – he's getting better, but Vaughn's looking after his fish for him. Sloane has Fordson shot in the leg when he can't produce the T-wave camera.
The Big Picture: Sydney states that SD-6 know that Khasinau is dead and they think Irina is on the run – but how do they even know Irina's alive, let alone that she's The Man? Sloane later tells Sydney he knows she saw her mother in Taipei – if Sydney hasn't told someone that at a debriefing, has Jack?

Mystery surrounds Irina – why has she handed herself in only to keep silent? Where is 'the Bible' which she made such an effort to retrieve? Did Irina want the T-wave camera for a particular purpose? How does she know Sydney so well, when she hasn't seen her since she was six?
Debrief: 'The true loyalty of Agent Bristow's mother is unknown'. Did they really go a whole season without Irina? Lena Olin's an excellent addition to one of the strongest casts on TV and this is her episode, from her baiting Vaughn to two dynamite scenes with Sydney. This is a really strong episode, one that's subtly shifting the emphasis of the show while brilliantly exemplifying it.

25
Cipher

Production #E654

1st US Transmission Date: 13 October 2002
1st UK Transmission Date: 18 March 2003

Writers: Alex Kurtzman-Counter and Roberto Orci
Director: Dan Attias
Guest Cast: Terry O'Quinn (Kendall), Janet MacLachlan (Jane Banks), Patricia Wettig (Barnett), Mark Colson (Ops Director), Endre Hules (Vashko) Strahil Goodman (Techie #2), Tom Kiesche (Agent Cooper), Keith Lewis (Agent Novak), Ilya Morelle (Techie #1), Weston J Blakesley (Barfly), Joel Guggenheim (Agent On Call), Paul Mendoza (Bartender), Alex Morris ('Homeless' man), Kavita Patil (Desk Attendant)

Briefing: Sydney tells Kendall that Sark is back and he's got a T-wave camera. She sees Irina, who tells her Sark is looking for the secrets of zero point energy. Sloane confides in Sydney about Emily saying her garden has died without her – but returns home to discover it in full bloom.

Sydney goes to Sri Lanka and plants a bug on Sark's satellite, narrowly escaping the blast from the rocket in a luge. Vaughn wants Will brought to CIA for hypnotic regression to find some clue to Sark's motives. Will reveals a code Sark had on his laptop. SD-6 know that Sark is after a Rambaldi artefact, a music box, in Siberia. With the help of Will's hypnosis and Irina's decoding of the information, Sydney heads to Siberia, where she finds the music box and records the music – but Sark ambushes her and she ends up falling into icy water.

OMG: During the luge ride a million pounds of thrust is coming straight for Sydney – but it's almost a damp squib compared to Jack and Irina's first onscreen meeting.

Mission: SD-6 send Sydney and Dixon to Sri Lanka to attach a tap to Sark's satellite feed from the T-wave camera. They succeed. They then go to Siberia to retrieve the Rambaldi music box.

Countermission: The CIA give Sydney their own version of the tap, identical to the SD-6 one, but which also allows them to see what Sark is seeing. The countermission is a success. The CIA want a recording of the music box, but want Sydney to destroy it before SD-6 can hear it.

Destinations: Sri Lanka, Los Angeles (USA), Siberia (Russia).

Timescale: Sydney spoke to Irina 'last week'. At the start of the episode, it's 72 hours before the launch of the satellite – she's sent out the day before and it's a fifteen-hour flight there, another fifteen back.

Transcripts: Jack to Irina: 'She spent most of her life thinking you were dead. She'll get used to it again.'

Sydney Bristow: Sydney's mother 'died' around Thanksgiving. Irina asks what part Sydney had in the Thanksgiving play. Sydney can't remember, but Jack says she was the one turkey who was spared. Sydney realises that a lot of her memories around the time her mother died are little more than blurred impressions. Once again, she retains her composure while talking to Irina, but breaks down as soon as she's got away. When Sydney was six, Miss Adams taught her the piano.

Jack Bristow: Jack starts the episode by trying to enlist Dr Barnett to come up with a strategy to prevent Sydney from seeing Irina. He calls her 'Irina' at first, but Dr Barnett notices that when he's agitated his ex-wife becomes 'Laura'

– he still thinks of her that way. Barnett refuses to help. Jack then tells Sydney that he trusts her judgement and she's doing fine – apparently a huge shift and a sentiment that pleases Sydney, but clearly part of Jack's strategy. When he watches Sydney and Irina discussing the Thanksgiving play later, he's uneasy. He then confronts Irina and warns her that, if Sydney is hurt, he'll kill her.

Irina Derevko: Vaughn says that Irina is a Rambaldi expert. She knows about the music box, what the music it plays means and that it relates to zero point energy. Irina keeps herself fit in her cell with press-ups and by the way she gets up from them, it's clear she's at a peak of physical fitness. She knows a circadian meditation technique that gives all the benefits of sleep in a fraction of the time. Displaying none of the charm or vulnerability she does with Sydney (or even with Vaughn), perhaps we see the true Irina when she talks to Jack. She's cruel and knows exactly where to hurt him – first by telling him there were times (especially when Sydney was born) when she loved him – but no longer. Jack gives as good as he gets and there's the intriguing possibility that this is *his* true face, too.

Marcus Dixon: In Sri Lanka, Dixon cues Sydney that Sark has arrived, then does his familar trick of hacking into the computers and surveillance systems of the ASA complex. In Siberia, he's part of a three-man perimeter team that's guarding Sydney as she goes for the music box. The other two members are killed as Dixon realises their attackers are coming from under the ice.

Michael Vaughn: Vaughn trusts Sydney's judgement over whether she should talk to Irina again. He reminds Kendall that the two of them were effectively countering SD-6 before Irina was on the scene. Vaughn is hoping Will will remember facts about Sark under hypnosis. He meets him and is happy to delay the session by a day so that Will can help Francie out. He's clearly jealous of Will when Sydney rushes to his side after the hypnotherapy.

Will Tippin: Will meets Vaughn for the first time. He'd assumed he was older and is also clearly jealous of Vaughn's knowledge of Sydney and her life. He discovers that Vaughn gave Sydney the picture frame (see **10, 'Spirit'**). The CIA bring in Will and hypnotically regress him to his flight to Taipei. He remembers seeing Sark working at a laptop and confesses to being worried that he would die – as would Sydney.

Arvin Sloane: Sloane gives Sydney a seed box that belonged to Emily and her mother before her. It dates from 1910. He tells her that he's not touched his house: Emily's clothes are still in the closet and anyone going into the house wouldn't know she was dead – until they saw the garden, which has died without Emily's expert touch. Sydney reassures him that Emily's death wasn't his fault. Later, Sloane discovers that the rose garden is mysteriously in full bloom once again. Sloane says he is not a spiritual man but he thinks Emily is still with him. Jack suggests he has been traumatised by Emily's death and is hallucinating. Sloane asks him to monitor his behaviour and take him aside if he's letting his emotions show. Sloane tells Jack that, just before she died, Emily booked them into a B&B in Sonoma – she was still thinking about the future. Later, Sloane gets a crackly call which he traces back to the same B&B.

Francie Calfo: Francie tells Sydney off for drinking beer in front of Will while he's in rehab.

Mr Sark: Sark is now the top operative of what's left of Irina's organisation.

Intelligence: The CIA's covert ways of contacting people are SOPs: Special Operating Procedures.

Home Front: Will is helping Francie with the opening of the restaurant.

Lies: Jack did something to Sydney's memories after her mother died – presumably some sort of CIA brainwashing (and surely it's not a coincidence that this episode shows the CIA using the same methods on Will). What has he told her? All the evidence is that he's planted an idealised version of her mother in her memory. Why? Did Irina really want to know about Sydney's school play, or was she just testing her memory?

Breaking the Code: Sark's code is 'Dostoevsky, Nabokov, Tolstoy, Chekov'. Irina can decode this cipher text (only by using a pencil and paper), but it is not clear how. Irina reveals that it means that the code to start the music box is 311254. Location letters: A, O and B.

Plot Devices: The Asiatic Space Agency is based in Sri Lanka and consists mainly of ex-Soviet rocket scientists. They have rockets that can put satellites into space and appear to be a commercial organisation. It's not clear if they know Sark is anything other than legitimate.

The T-wave – Terahertz Imaging Camera – is designed to be mounted on a satellite and can see through up to a hundred metres of solid matter. Sydney retrieved the prototype in Helsinki, but Sark has the final version.

The Rambaldi music box is quite a large padlocked metal box which works like a primitive record player. The music is, according to Irina, a code that when deciphered reveals the secrets of zero point energy, and Sark has stolen the camera to locate it. The box has somehow ended up in Siberian ice caverns that form a twenty-mile-square version of the Rambaldi symbol <○>.

For Sri Lanka, Marshall kits out Sydney with a wristwatch that can deliver a puff of knockout gas or dust, and with a luge disguised as a suitcase which can propel her along at 150mph (although, oddly, the speedo seems to stick at 125mph in the field). For the Siberian mission, the SD-6 agents get palmtop motion sensors. The CIA give Sydney a spray that damages the music box once they've got a recording of the music. Sark has at his disposal a four-man submersible capable of travelling under the ice.

Action: Sydney luges down the exhaust vents as the ASA rocket launches, narrowly outrunning the blast. For the first time in ages, she doesn't need to dodge or fight any guards. In Siberia, Sark's men attack the SD-6 team, with Sark confronting Sydney. She falls through the ice trying to escape him.

Undercover: Sydney goes to Sri Lanka as Joanna Kelly, a VIP representative of Euro Teledyne. She has a very passable English accent, a ginger wig and a tweed suit with (naturally) a short skirt. To get to the rocket, she disguises herself in a red all-over fireproof suit and goggles. In Siberia she wears a white ski suit with a dark fur trim, completing the ensemble with matching white headband and gloves.

Reality Checks: It's not normally possible to access a satellite inside a rocket on the launch pad by unscrewing one flimsy panel on the side of the rocket. Sydney manages to screw the panel back and climb down the ladder from the top of a rocket that's got to be over a hundred feet tall, going by the countdown, in seventeen seconds. If Sydney really fell into freezing water, as she does at the end of the episode, then her body would probably go into a coma within seconds. Zero point energy is theoretically possible, according to quantum physics. At absolute zero, classical physics says that a particle is at a complete standstill – it has no energy. But the uncertainty principle states that we can't measure both the position and momentum of a particle. If a particle was at a standstill, we *would* be able to. In the 30s Paul Dirac suggested that particles in a vacuum possess what he called 'residual negative energy': they can, indeed they have to, spontaneously create tiny amounts of energy for tiny amounts of time. Essentially there is a vast amount of energy in a vacuum, but it cancels itself out very quickly. If one could harness this energy, it literally would be 'energy from nothing'. No one, obviously, *has* managed to harness it and, up until now, it's tended to be the preserve of the same fringe scientists who in previous generations would have claimed to have discovered perpetual motion or cold fusion.

The one thing prototype terahertz cameras can't see through is wet material, so they'd be useless at looking through ice, as they do in this episode.

Music: 'Spanish Moss' by Saint Low. The music box plays the *Alias* theme music.

Injuries: Sydney throws an icepick into Sark's left leg.

The Big Picture: Zero point energy – is this 'the greatest power' mentioned in the prophecy? Who's making Sloane's garden bloom and phoning him from the B&B? Is it somehow connected to the thing injected into his neck?

Debrief: The show manages to go up *another* gear. An episode that mixes 60s spy caper staples – sabotaging space rockets and adventures in ski suits – with character moments ranging from the subtle to the explosive. Even a predictable development – Emily's death wasn't the whole story – generates suspense and (a really clever trick) makes Sloane perhaps the most sympathetic character in the show. All this and the return of the Rambaldi plotline. An expertly balanced hour of television drama and quite a good one to give a newcomer to *Alias* to show what it's all about.

26
Dead Drop

Production #E655

1st US Transmission Date: 20 October 2002
1st UK Transmission Date: 24 March 2003

Writer: Jesse Alexander
Director: Guy Bee
Guest Cast: Terry O'Quinn (Kendall), Marisol Nichols ('Rebecca Martinez'), Daniel Feraldo (Manolo), Patricia Wettig (Dr Judy Barnett), Jim Hanna (Claus Richter), Carol Androsky (NA Moderator), Kevin Sutherland (CIA Operative), Dato Bakhtadze (Russian Security Guard), Scott Donovan (American Tourist), Ira Heiden (Techie), Commodore James (American Tourist)

Briefing: Dixon rescues Sydney from the ice. Sloane tells Jack about the call from the B&B. Dixon checks and returns with news that Emily was signed on the register.

Jack sends Sydney on a mission to Moscow, but she guesses he's keeping her away from Irina. Sydney recovers a map that reveals the location of 'the Bible'. It is in Madagascar and Sydney is sent to retrieve it. Jack hires an operative to booby-trap the building it's in. Irina says it's safe, but it explodes. Sydney has been betrayed and Irina is led away in chains for full interrogation. Sydney hugs Jack and tells him she was a fool not to trust his judgement.

In rehab, Will meets a girl who believes SD-6 set him up as an addict – he denies it, and it turns out she's an SD-6 agent checking his level of discretion.

OMG: Jack frames Irina!

Mission: Sydney is sent to Moscow to recover Richter's map from FAPSI (see **Reality Checks**) headquarters.

Countermission: Jack gives Sydney her countermission before SD-6 have given her the mission! She's to give SD-6 a fake map. The countermission is a success and SD-6 get the false map. However, Sark also gets a copy. The CIA then send Sydney to Madagascar to retrieve 'the Bible'. The building is rigged with explosives and is destroyed.

Destinations: Los Angeles (US), The Falkland Islands, Moscow (Russia), Sambavar (Madagascar).

Timescale: Will was hypnotised 'last week' and has four weeks left of community service. Barcelona (see **23,** 'The Enemy Walks In') was 'three weeks ago'. Jack's operative has twelve hours to get to Madagascar before Sydney and has to parachute in to beat her to it.

Transcripts: Jack (on Irina): 'She has destroyed countless lives.' Dr Barnett: 'Even yours.'

Jack Bristow: Jack lobbies to have Irina 'sent away'. He warns Sydney and Vaughn that nothing she says can be taken at face value and thinks Sydney is showing too much emotion in dealing with her. She objects – but Jack eavesdropped on her talking to Irina about the Thanksgiving play (see **25,** 'Cipher'). Sydney is shocked when she discovers this. He tells her she's wanted a mother all her life, so she's highly vulnerable to Irina's manipulation.

Jack tells Barnett that Sydney and the CIA are playing with fire. He's not sure whether Irina is trying to recruit Sydney or whether she's after something at the CIA. He's clearly losing his temper as he discusses her. He admits he's afraid of losing his daughter. Interestingly, he doesn't seem to think Irina wants to *kill* Sydney. Jack also loses his temper with Vaughn when he seems to take Irina's side.

Jack puts a plan into operation. He meets with a mysterious operative (named as Manolo DeSouza in **27,** 'The Indicator') who owes Jack in someway. This operative parachutes to the map co-ordinates in Madagascar and rigs the building where 'the Bible' is to explode with thirty pounds of Semtex. Jack allows himself a smile as Irina is led away and Sydney admits she was wrong.

Sydney Bristow: Sydney reminds Jack she's taking down SD-6 to get out of life as an agent as soon as possible. She realises Jack's given her the Moscow mission direct so that she avoids contact with Irina. Sydney still sees Irina before going to Moscow. Irina smiles and tells her to be careful. Sydney finds herself mirroring the smile. She feels utterly betrayed by Irina after Madagascar, confiding in her father that he was right and she was stupid to trust her mother. She hugs him and apologises for doubting him.

Irina Derevko: Irina has been allowed a book in prison. She asks that a pair of earrings she was wearing are returned to her. These are scanned, the sharp edges are blunted and she is given them. She tells Sydney they have great sentimental value: they were given to her by her mother (Sydney's grandmother) when she was 21 and graduated from 'the Academy' (presumably the KGB's). The earrings are conspicuous by their absence when Irina is removed from her cell at the end of the episode. In return for the earrings, Irina gives Sydney a better route through the FAPSI building, one with an escape route that emerges in Lenin's tomb. The CIA can't decipher Richter's map, but Irina can. Richter describes Irina as 'a great woman'. In the aftermath of Madagascar, Irina is taken to Camp Harris for 'unrestricted interrogation'. She seems confused and doesn't resist as she is removed.

Will Tippin: Sydney assures Will that what he revealed under hypnosis allowed a big victory against SD-6. At his AA meeting, Will says that one good thing has come from all this: he can now speak to a friend of his in a way he never could before. He is approached by Rebecca Martinez, a junkie with a conspiracy website, who flirts with him, trying to get him to admit that SD-6 is real and that they set him up as an addict. Will twice denies it, which is lucky for him – 'Rebecca' is an SD-6 agent checking to see if he's keeping silent. She records his replies and Security

Section pass Will as not a security risk. He does let slip a big secret to Rebecca, though, that he was investigating the death of Sydney's fiancé because he hoped it might mean he got closer to her.

Arvin Sloane: Sloane hugs Sydney, pleased she survived Siberia. He believes her story about the music box, but sends a team (which doesn't include her) to recover the corroded music box from Sark. He admits to Jack that the phone call from Sonoma (see **25,** 'Cipher') has left him unsettled and asks him to discreetly send someone to see who made the call; he doesn't want news to get back to the Alliance (so the device in his neck isn't a microphone allowing the Alliance to constantly listen in). Jack sends Dixon, who reports back with the news that Emily signed herself into the B&B that night – after her death.

Michael Vaughn: Vaughn tells Sydney that he's her ally and there's no need for her to question that. Irina saves Sydney in Moscow, but Vaughn refuses to thank the woman who killed his father. Once again, although he's not a field agent, Vaughn goes on a mission. This time it's to Madagascar.

Marcus Dixon: Dixon rescues Sydney from the ice. He's the agent picked by Jack to look into the phone call from Sonoma.

Mr Sark: Sark is in Moscow when Sydney gets there, also in disguise. He tells Sydney he'll pay her more than Sloane is, as part of a 'comprehensive offer' and acts like she will accept. She thinks he's cute, but turns down his offer. Sark follows her to 'the Bible' in Madagascar and wonders if her success is because she has another source of information besides SD-6, but he is caught out by the explosion. He makes his escape in the confusion.

Intelligence: Sloane can't understand why Rambaldi went to the unimaginable lengths of building ice caverns in Siberia only to put a music box there that would corrode. He has the ruined box retrieved and SD-6 now hold it. The music Sydney recorded is at Langley for analysis. SD-6 refer to Irina's old operation as her 'syndicate'. Sark had a hideout in the Falklands, which is stormed by SD-6. He gets away, but they discover Klaus Richter was being tortured there and SD-6 bring him back to Los Angeles. He's got some condition that means he's in pain and bleeding from his fingernails. He's screened for all known diseases, but nothing shows up and the doctors conclude it's an allergic reaction to something. Jack dips into his morphine stock again to relieve Richter's pain. Unless Richter co-operates, Jack will withdraw the supply. Richter was in Barcelona when Sydney was there (see **23,** 'The Enemy Walks In'), and knows where 'the Bible' is, having hidden it. It's too difficult to describe the location, so Richter created a coded map and hid it in a copy of *War and Peace* in the FAPSI building in Moscow. Irina seems to be about to pass 'the Bible' to the CIA, before Jack sabotages her plan. It's her only leverage: once it's handed over, what's stopping the CIA from throwing away Irina's key or having her executed? Clearly, according to Jack, Irina has a plan.

Home Front: Francie's restaurant is due to be graded by the Health Department.

Lies: The big one – Jack frames Irina by blowing up the building in Madagascar. He claims that Irina was just using Sydney for her own ends and that she wanted to kill Sydney and destroy 'the Bible' in one move.

Breaking the Code: 'Rebecca' says she has a website, www.conspiracychick.com (this site exists as part of the *Alias* webgame). Is it a coincidence that a book by Tolstoy features, when he was part of Sark's code, see **25,** 'Cipher'? Irina decodes Richter's map – 'the Bible' is hidden at Latitude 14° 26′, Longitude 49° 57′ 20″. Location letters: S and A.

Plot Devices: For Moscow, Marshall supplies Sydney with fake medals that are actually keys to get her into various places in the FAPSI building. Her belt buckle is a disguised cellphone to call the CIA.

Action: Once again, one of Irina's group beats Sydney in a straight fist fight. This time it's Sark, in Moscow. It's just the start of a long chase scene, with Sydney barely getting out alive.

Undercover: For Moscow, Sydney disguises herself as a much-decorated Russian army major, wearing a short black wig with a red tint. She can speak Russian well enough to hold a conversation with two Moscow security guards without arousing suspicion. In Madagascar, she wears combat gear, complete with nightsight.
Reality Checks: The FAPSI is the Russian Federation's communications intercept organisation (it stands for Federal'naya Agenstvo Pravitel'stvennoy Svayazi i Informatsii). Even assuming Sydney didn't enter an immediate coma from the shock of being in ice water, there's little chance her gun would still work. Once again, in Madagascar, Sydney uses the 'freelancer' code when on a mission for the CIA.
Music: 'Oh Do Not Fly Away' by The Innocence Mission and 'Stay' by Michelle Featherstone.
Injuries: Sark doesn't seem troubled by the fact Sydney threw an icepick at his leg in **25,** 'Cipher'.
The Big Picture: Irina retrieved 'the Bible' in Barcelona. Richter subsequently hid it in Madagascar. So she must have given it to Richter before handing herself in to the CIA. Sark takes Richter to the Falklands to torture him – the implication being that Sark is trying to extract the location of 'the Bible' from him. This suggests Sark and Irina aren't in league, or at least that Irina isn't sharing everything with Sark. Was Irina really willing to hand over 'the Bible'? If so, what leverage would she still have? What else does she have to offer the US government? And was 'the Bible' destroyed in Madagascar, or does Jack now have it? Is it significant that Sark explicitly calls Sydney's SD-6 boss 'Arvin Sloane', rather than just 'Sloane'? Is there another Sloane out there? And what's happening with Emily? What condition is Richter suffering from? Are Irina's earrings really just of 'sentimental value'? And where are they?
Debrief: 'Good guys or bad guys?' 'Neither. It's my father.' Jack makes his move to discredit Irina and in doing so we see him with the gloves off – it's not a pretty sight. An episode where Sydney is almost an incidental

character, despite getting a great Moscow action scene. Exquisite pacing and storytelling has Irina dragged off just at the point when she and Sydney have made a connection and there's the first possibility that Irina may not be as malevolent as we first thought. But Jack – wow.

27
The Indicator

Production #E656

1st US Transmission Date: 3 November 2002
1st UK Transmission Date: 31 March 2003

Writer: Jeff Pinckner
Director: Ken Olin
Guest Cast: Amy Aquino (Agent Virginia Kerr), James Lesure (Agent Craig Blair), Stephen Markle (Sen. Douglas), Kevin West (SD-6 Agent Kelsey), Daniel Faraldo (Manolo), Newell Alexander (Congressman), Dan Istrate (Public Employee), Vladimir Skomarovsky (Kholokov), Kevin Sutherland (CIA Agent), Loren Hayes (CIA Strike Team Leader), Sarah Peterson (Six-year-old Sydney)

Briefing: In Vienna, a man is killed in his car by a hit team. This is an SD-6 informer who worked for the Triad. The Triad has next-generation weapons in Budapest and Sydney discovers that these are brainwashed children. The man running the project in Budapest is Kholokov, based in Buenos Aires. Sydney goes there and abducts him, but discovers a familiar logic puzzle. After hypnotic regression, she realises that her father was running a similar project in the 70s, and that she was a test subject. She confronts her father, telling him she never wants to speak to him again.

Vaughn is suspicious of Jack and discovers he hired Manolo to sabotage their operation in Madagascar.

OMG: The weapons are children. Jack appears in Sydney's flashback.

Mission: Sydney and Dixon are sent to Budapest by SD-6 to download the specs and photograph the next-generation weapons. Sydney succeeds – and discovers that they are children.

Countermission: Sydney's CIA countermission is to feed Dixon false specifications, and to get the real specifications to the CIA. (No mention is made of photographs in the countermission.) The CIA send Sydney with a team to Buenos Aires to abduct Kholokov. This mission is a success.

Destinations: Vienna (Austria), Los Angeles (US), Budapest (Hungary), Buenos Aires (Argentina).

Timescale: It's five weeks since Irina handed herself in. Sydney's mission to Madagascar was last week. It's summer, as the kids in Budapest are at summer school. It's weeks since Emily died. Sydney's flashback takes her back to when she was six, just after her mother had died, and shortly before Christmas.

Transcripts: Jack (to Vaughn): 'Your consistent shortcoming is a sense of morality.'

Michael Vaughn: Vaughn is suspicious of Jack. Jack only noticed the explosives when the satellite was switched to detect infra-red emissions. But before the mission, he retasked the only satellite in the area with an IR detector – it was as if he knew he'd need it. Vaughn thinks that he set up Irina like he set up Russek (see **10,** 'Spirit').

Vaughn meets Manolo DeSouza, the man who Jack used to plant explosives in Madagascar, tells him it's not a good time to be a terrorist and that he has no civil rights. Manolo says he was working for the CIA – for Jack Bristow – and that he won't take the fall for him. Jack confronts Vaughn the next day and warns him not to tell Sydney.

Sydney Bristow: Sydney wants to stand in Irina's cell just once. Her father joins her there. She apologises for doubting him and thanks him for saving her life. They leave arm in arm. Sydney is angry at Vaughn for doubting her father. One of Will's friends has a theory that what you are like in sixth grade is what you're really like. Sydney confesses that she had big teeth, little eyes and was a foot taller than everyone else. She confides to Will that her mother is facing the death penalty and that she's unsure how she feels.

Sydney sees a logic puzzle in Kholokov's house and completes it straight away, somehow remembering the solution. She asks Agent Kerr to hypnotically regress her. She is worried that Irina programmed her to be a spy when she was a child. Sydney says she can usually compartmentalise, a necessary part of her job, but she can't concentrate until this issue is resolved. She is hypnotised and sees herself as a six-year-old. Going downstairs, she hears her father say he's 'taking care of Christmas'. The logic puzzle is there and she completes it. Next she field strips a pistol – and Jack congratulates her. Sydney wakes with a start. She confronts her father – she'd always thought what she'd overheard was about the Christmas holiday, but it was a reference to the Project. She accuses him of trying to shield her from Irina so that her mother couldn't tell her that he'd brainwashed her. She tells him she'll never forgive him. Sydney speaks and reads Hungarian and Kerr says she has stellar spatial intelligence.

Arvin Sloane: Sloane seems distracted during the briefing. He confides to Jack later, filling him in about the hotel register. Jack tells him that someone is seeking leverage from his grief and Sloane reveals it's actually his guilt. He explains that he killed Emily using sodium morphate in her wine. The doctor says she was going to die anyway, and this way she didn't suffer. Sloane was promoted when Emily died – he sends Jack to find who would have got the job otherwise, as he'd seem to be a prime suspect. Sloane steps out of the shower and he finds a glass of wine. He phones Security Section, who tell him the surveillance cameras were turned off ten minutes before. Examination of the glass reveals no fingerprints, but the presence of VTX, a calcium-based antidote to substances that can induce a heart attack – like sodium morphate.

Jack Bristow: Jack is visibly uncomfortable at the opening of Francie's restaurant, but betrays no emotion when Sloane confesses to killing Emily. Jack sees on the daily report that Vaughn saw Manolo DeSouza. Jack was working on Project Christmas for at least ten years and the whole time he was married to Irina (it's why she's sent to the US; the flashback is set just after she 'died').

Marcus Dixon: Marcus co-ordinates Sydney in Budapest.
Will Tippin: In sixth grade, Will was just anonymous.
Francie: Francie opens her restaurant and the first night it's packed. She invited a hundred people, thinking seventy would turn up, but everyone seems to have come along and brought a friend. People from Will's AA meeting are here, but not spending enough!
Irina Derevko: Irina leaves her earrings behind in her cell and Sydney finds them. Irina was sent to the US with one specific purpose: to steal information on Project Christmas, which Jack was overseeing.
Intelligence: A Joint Intelligence Committee Special Session is set up to assess Irina's case, headed by Senator Douglas. They press charges against Irina and will press for the death penalty.

The Triad is a loose coalition of organised crime. They've specialised in drugs and prostitution in the past, but have moved into arms sales in the last few years. Nils Hador, the 'Austrian Connection' is a Triad member who has been selling intelligence to SD-6. His last report was that the Triad had sixteen 'next-generation weapons' in Budapest. When Sydney investigates, she discovers sixteen blindfolded children sitting at desks field-stripping pistols. Agents need proficiency with numbers, 3D thinking and problem-solving abilities. All these talents are obvious at an early age. The Triad has bought the organisation that administers school tests across the EU and is identifying children with the necessary skills. Twenty-eight children passed this year and sixteen took up the offer of an 'achievement course' in Budapest. The children's memories were tampered with so they remembered having a great time. The programme is run by Valery Kholokov, who ran KGB psych-ops. The CIA believed he was dead but he is based in Buenos Aires. There is a rumour, never proved, that the KGB did something similar to the Triad plan in the 80s.
Office Politics: As Jack was proved right about Irina, Devlin has now given him operational control of missions against SD-6.

Breaking the Code: The code for the computer room in Budapest is 82402. Sydney sends the CIA data about the weapons via Port 47. Sydney and the CIA use the 'mountaineer' and 'boot camp' callsigns. Location letters: V, A, P and S.
Plot Devices: Marshall gives Sydney a lipgloss container that not only acts as a (pistachio-flavoured) lip salve, but also contains three mini-cameras that can be fired using compressed air to stick into walls and ceilings. When Marshall demonstrates it, he notices (for the first time?) how large his chin is. In Budapest, Sydney carries a lockpick and a retractable truncheon. In Buenos Aires, she uses a tranquilliser gun and a compressed air springboard which hurls her over the perimeter wall of Kholokov's house.
Action: Sydney gets into Kholokov's house, shooting guards and cutting the power. The CIA team storm the building. She then fights Kholokov, who carries a taser. She pushes him into a pool and he's knocked out by the electric shock.
Undercover: In Budapest, Sydney is disguised as an unnamed American student who's researching her family's genealogy. She has a short blond wig, glasses, a brown jacket and sweater.
Reality Checks: Vaughn says that every first grader in the EU gets a standardised intelligence test. They don't.
Trivia: Lena Olin is credited but doesn't appear.
Music: 'This World' by Zero 7, 'Brimful Of Asha' by Cornershop, 'Alone' by Thicke, 'Canzone del Salce – Ave Maria' by Verdi, 'The Golden Age' by Beck and 'River' by Joni Mitchell.
Injuries: Vaughn reports that Weiss is feeling rough but is OK (after **23,** 'The Enemy Walks In') and will be back next month.
The Big Picture: Jack is revealed as perhaps even more callous than he's been before: his lecture to Vaughn about how morality is a weakness, listening impassively as Sloane tells him he poisoned his own wife and, of course, the lifetime of lies he's told Sydney. Just what is he up to? How

can being sentenced to death be part of Irina's plan and how will she survive? Who's terrorising Sloane?

Debrief: 'Evil must be eliminated, by every means.' A wonderful reversal – from the closest Jack and Sydney have ever been, to the furthest apart. This has a couple of fantastic images – or, rather, just the one, repeated – a child field-stripping a pistol. The first time it's shocking enough, but then we see Sydney do it. Expert storytelling: we see how evil Kholokov is, then learn that Jack was doing the same thing decades ago – to his own daughter.

28
Salvation

Production: #E657

1st US Transmission Date: 10 November 2002
1st UK Transmission Date: 7 April 2003

Writers: Roberto Orci and Alex Kurtzman-Counter
Director: Perry Lang
Guest Cast: James Handy (Devlin), Stephen Markle (Senator Douglas), Austin Tichenor (Dr Nicholas), Amy Irving (Emily Sloane), Daniel Faltus (Jan Spinnaker), Kevin Sutherland (Agent), Hope Allen (Waitress), Glenda Morgan Brown (Flight Attendant), John Patrick Clerkin (Priest), Timothy DeHaas (Doctor #2), Ira Heiden (CIA Techie), Mette Holt (Nurse), John Koyama (Patient Zero), Alex Morris (Homeless Vet), Cliff Olin (Cliff), Robert Martin Robinson (Doctor #1)

Briefing: Sloane thinks Sark is developing a virus and Sydney and Jack are sent to Geneva to investigate. Jack tells Sydney he gave her Project Christmas training so she'd never be a victim. Irina's trial starts, she pleads guilty and is given the death penalty. Sydney writes a letter to Devlin to tell him about Jack framing her mother. Vaughn realises that the KGB may have recruited sleeper agents in the US, and hires Will to investigate. Jack and Sydney talk – she says he must associate her with failure. They get the intelligence they need from Geneva. Back in LA, Jack suggests Sloane exhume Emily – he does, and the coffin is empty. Sydney and Vaughn are suspected of having the virus but are quickly cleared. Jack is sent to prison. Sydney lies to Senator Douglas to release both her parents. Vaughn discovers his fingernails are bleeding.

OMG: Sloane sees Emily and chases her into a church.

Mission: SD-6 send Jack and Sydney to Geneva to recover a sample of the virus and to download any data on the victims. The mission is a total success.

Countermission: Jack and Sydney are to pass some of the sample and a copy of the data to the CIA.

Destinations: Geneva (Switzerland), Los Angeles (USA), Washington DC (USA).

Timescale: It's five weeks since Vaughn and Sydney were in Taipei. Irina is sentenced to be executed in three days early on in the episode and is due to die at 08.00 the morning the episode ends. Will has earned a 30-day sobriety pin from the AA.

Transcripts: Sydney (to Jack): 'It's true, isn't it? If Mom hadn't fooled you, if you hadn't been so gullible, I never would have been born.'

Jack (on Sydney): 'I see only the promise of my redemption . . . I love her more than I could ever say.'

Irina Derevko: Irina is charged with 86 counts of espionage and the murder of twelve US agents. She pleads guilty to all charges and is swiftly given the death penalty. She waives her right to appeal so she'll die by lethal injection in three days' time.

Sydney Bristow: Sydney wants to see her mother's trial and Vaughn arranges a video link. She writes a letter to Devlin outlining how Jack framed her and passes it to the CIA via the homeless vet dead-drop. Jack hands her back the letter. She angrily speculates that he sees her as his greatest mistake and wishes that she'd never been born. She doesn't believe a word he says. At the hospital, she's shocked when Patient Zero calls her 'Irina'. She seems deliberately to fire live rounds over the guards' heads, rather than kill them. She reports her father to Devlin face to face and he says that Jack has already confessed.

She and Vaughn are placed in isolation (together) while bloodtests are done to see if they have the virus. She talks in her sleep, saying 'don't frost the pie'. Sydney is about to tell Vaughn something important, but the doctor comes in to tell her she is clear. Sydney cries when she sees her father testify. Later, Vaughn and Sydney meet covertly in a bar to celebrate his being given the all clear.

Sydney flies to Washington, poses as Senator Douglas's chaffeur and tries to get him to release her parents. She says that she and Jack are the only two people that know that a Senator is on the Alliance payroll and has taken $6.3 million in bribes. If Jack is imprisoned, she'll have to make the inquiry more public and formal. Both Jack and Irina are freed by the morning.

Jack Bristow: Jack tells Sydney he used Project Christmas techniques because he felt she needed to be as strong as she could be, to think strategically and to see through people's lives. His original plan was to recruit Sydney to the CIA when she had graduated. It is his greatest regret that Sloane got to her first. He calculates that Irina pleaded guilty so that Sydney won't have to see the trial, where her crimes will be outlined and graphic evidence presented. Sydney would lose all sympathy for her mother if she saw that. He hands back her letter to Devlin and urges her to reconsider. He seems disconcerted by Sydney's analysis of him. He spent ten years with Irina and another twenty analysing how she had tricked him.

Testifying before Senator Douglas's inquiry, Jack says Irina will prove she's a threat as soon as she's ready. He refuses to reveal the reasons for framing her and denies he confessed because he knew Sydney was about to incriminate him. But, when pressed, he says that he's confessed because he wants Sydney to know he loves her and that, when he looks at her, he sees only the promise of his redemption. Jack cries, knowing Sydney will be watching – and surely this theatrical performance is exactly what he's just accused Irina of? Senator Douglas sends Jack to jail, telling Sydney that his intentions are irrelevant – he's lied and manipulated. Sydney lies to get him freed.

Jack has more fun with morphine. This time he ups Patient Zero's dose.

Will Tippin: Will is running out of money and is thinking of selling his car. Sydney offers him money, but he refuses. He contacts Vaughn and asks him for a job. Vaughn has to break it to him that he can't work for the CIA because he has a criminal record – one, of course, that's fabricated. Instead Vaughn uses his discretionary fund to pay Will to look into the standardised tests, to see if any of the Project Christmas questions appear on them. At this stage, he simply thinks he's comparing IQ tests.

Arvin Sloane: Sloane tells Jack he killed Emily to end her suffering. Jack sees two possible motives for Sloane's tormentors. Either Emily guessed Sloane would kill her and took countermeasures or, more likely, someone wants Sloane to believe she's alive. Sloane realises that the Alliance would see Emily surviving as a betrayal and they'll think the whole of SD-6 is rogue. Jack and Sloane are returning from a chamber of commerce lunch when Sloane sees Emily in the street. He chases after her into a church – where he recoils from the crucifix! Jack saw a woman, but didn't think it was Emily. He suggests Sloane has Post Traumatic Stress Disorder and that going into a church betrays an unconscious desire to confess. Jack suggests there's one obvious way to check if Emily's dead. That night, Sloane and a team exhume the coffin – which is empty.

Francie Calfo: Francie hires a young man, Cliff, to dress as a hamburger and pass out leaflets advertising her restaurant. He gets $12 an hour.

Michael Vaughn: Sydney asks Vaughn to tell her a joke and he tells her a very bad joke about a grasshopper. He watches Sydney sleep as they spend time in isolation together. By accident or design, he stays out of Jack's way during this episode. At the end, he's shaving when he discovers his fingers are bleeding – he has the virus.

Intelligence: Richter was exposed to Khasinau's virus, which was contained in the 'fluid' from the Mueller device. A bloodtest shows he has 1,000 per cent of the antibodies he ought to have. The virus breaks down the bonds between cells, liquefying its victims. Sark charters a medically equipped 727 and takes victims to his Geneva hospital. One of these victims, Patient Zero, is dying. He's grey-faced, bleeding from his eyes and fingernails. He is still loyal to Irina, even though she deliberately infected him to test the virus. The first symptom of the virus is haemorrhaging from the fingernails. Sydney and Vaughn may have become infected in Taipei. Sloane describes Sark as a key player in the world of organised crime. One of his business fronts is a hospital in Geneva, St Albans, which has a worldwide reputation for discretion and security.

The CIA now know for certain (presumably after interrogating Kholokov, although he's not mentioned) that the KGB developed their own version of Project Christmas and used it to train European and possibly American sleeper agents. Vaughn thinks the questions look like ones on tests given to first graders and wants to check US standardised tests for evidence that the KGB manipulated them, but Devlin says they can't spare any men at the moment – particularly as the KGB no longer exists.

Office Politics: Devlin is Deputy Director of the CIA.

Breaking the Code: Jack's callsign is 'Blackbird'. The helicopter that rescues them is 'Eagle Eye'. The extraction point is LZ-Bravo. Location letters: G, N and O.

Plot Devices: Marshall gives Jack a satchel that contains halothane gas – when he and Sydney are being anaesthetised, he'll release the gas and it'll be the doctors and nurses who are knocked out instead. So that they aren't knocked out, they take an anti-anaesthetic laced with caffeine. Sydney and Jack carry tranquilliser guns that carry four darts and knock out victims for fifteen minutes. Jack mixes iodine and ammonia in a centrifuge to create an explosive diversion at the hospital. VTX counteracts the effect of sodium morphate.

Action: A terrific fight in the hospital – Jack and Sydney punching their way past seven armed guards, then Sydney holding off the reinforcements while Jack hotwires a lift. They escape via helicopter.

Undercover: Jack and Sydney go to the hospital, Jack as a Texan Mr Hallison and Sydney as his daughter Nerry. The cover story is that he needs a kidney transplant and his daughter is donating one of hers. They change into hospital gowns and masks once they have knocked out the doctors. In Washington DC, Sydney dresses as a chauffeur to get to Senator Douglas.

Reality Checks: Mixing iodine and ammonia does result in an explosive reaction – but not the devastating blast Jack manages to create with a couple of testtubes' worth.

Background Checks: The young man dressed as a hamburger is played by producer Ken Olin's son, Cliff.

Music: 'A Place Called Home' by Kim Richey, 'Blister in the Sun' by Violent Femmes, 'Go' by Andy Hunter and 'Violent Rain' by Gus.

The Big Picture: What's going on with Project Christmas, the KGB version and the new Triad version? How are they linked?

Debrief: 'Ask yourself if that is a person worth saving.' An extremely bleak episode, with Irina due to die, Sloane exhuming his wife and wiping mud from the coffin with his bare hands, Will running out of money, Jack plumbing new depths of coldness, even Sydney lying to a Senator to get two people off the hook despite the fact they're plainly guilty. The last shot's of Vaughn bleeding from his fingernails. There's humour here, but it's black humour – Sydney and Jack are forced to play the loving father and daughter. A very tense, dark episode where everyone's lying to each other and to themselves.

29
The Counteragent

Production: #E658

1st US Transmission Date: 17 November 2002
1st UK Transmission Date: 21 April 2003

Writer: John Eisendrath
Director: Dan Attias
Guest Cast: Terry O'Quinn (Kendall), Austin Tichenor (Dr Nicholas), Petra Wright (Alice), Chris Ellis (Chapman), Victor McKay (Rudman), Stephen Davies (Sark Associate), Stephen Mendillo (Henry Fields),

Jim Hanna (Claus Richter), Michelle Arthur (Abigail), Reamy Hall (Nurse #2), Don Took (Gray), Ivan Borodin (Lab Technician), Peggy Goss (Attending Nurse), Joel Guggenheim (Agent On Call), Mak Takano (Ryokan Guard)

Briefing: Vaughn goes to see Irina looking for an antidote to the virus. She tells Sydney that she'll find it in Paldiski. Vaughn has three days to live. Sydney is captured in Paldiski by Sark. He does a deal: she can have the antidote if she delivers Sloane to him, so Sark can kill him. Sydney agonises, but does as Sark wants in Japan, posing as a geisha (see **Sloane**). Sark drives off with an unconscious Sloane and the next day he turns up at SD-6 with Sloane, the two having formed a 'strategic alliance'. Vaughn is cured. Sydney leaves before Vaughn can say something important to her.

Will finds anomalies in the US testing system.

OMG: Jack kills a prisoner with a blowtorch, then in his next scene lectures Sydney on the ethics of murder.

Mission: Sloane forms an alliance with Sark, bringing him into SD-6.

Countermission: The CIA send Sydney to Paldiski to get an antidote for Vaughn. She is captured. Sark gives Sydney a mission – she's to go to Japan and knock Sloane out, before delivering him to Sark. Kendall refuses to sanction this, but Jack agrees to help her carry it out.

Destinations: Paldiski (Estonia), Tokyo (Japan), Los Angeles (USA).

Timescale: Vaughn has three days to live at the start of the episode and has been unconscious for forty hours when Sydney returns from Japan with the antidote.

Michael Vaughn: Vaughn has the virus. Before handing himself in to the doctors, he goes to see Irina. Irina will only speak to Sydney, but Vaughn insists he doesn't have much time. She asks him how he feels about her daughter and whether he loves her – she doesn't see them together casually, so can't read their body language. Vaughn says he will tell her when he's cured. He collapses on the way out and is taken to a US Naval Military Centre where he's placed in an oxygen tent. As Sydney leaves, she meets Alice, a pretty blonde woman who introduces herself as

Vaughn's girlfriend. After he takes the antidote, he recovers quickly. He can already walk with some difficulty and is able to return to work. He goes to Irina and tells her he wants Sydney to have a normal life. He then sees Sydney, who puts on a brave face about Alice, then leaves. Vaughn cuts Kendall off to follow her, but she's vanished before he can talk to her.

Irina Derevko: Irina says she doesn't save Vaughn for his sake – the implication being it's for Sydney's benefit.

Sydney Bristow: In Paldiski, Sydney is ordered to abort the mission when the CIA realise that using the serum generator has set off an alarm. Sydney refuses and gets an antidote but is cornered by Sark, who sets off sprinklers containing a corrosive decontaminant (ammonia fluorochloride). Sydney agrees to help him get Sloane in return for the antidote. Sark says he and Sydney are destined to work together. Sydney is troubled at having to deliver Sloane to Sark so that he can kill him. In the event, Sark intends to do a deal with him, not kill him. She is shocked to see Sloane at work when she goes there and to see Sark with him on good terms. Sloane asks her to debrief Sark to learn what he knows about Irina.

Sydney hugs Vaughn when he returns to work and puts on a brave face about Alice. She speaks Japanese.

Will Tippin: Sydney tells Will the background on Project Christmas. He meets Abigail, who tells him the spatial awareness questions don't appear on the 1982 test she's found. Francie sees the 1982 test, and notices a discrepancy: it mentions the invasion of Grenada – which happened in 1983. Will visits the author of the original tests, who produces a master copy of the 1982 test. The official is shocked to discover there are spatial reasoning questions on the paper that he didn't put there.

Arvin Sloane: Sloane tells Jack about Emily's empty coffin; he believes Emily is alive. He told Christophe that someone is trying to discredit him and he senses that Christophe is looking for Sloane to make a mistake. He is worried he's been distracted and he needs SD-6 to score a big victory to demonstrate that he's loyal and competent. He wants to find the antidote to the virus and he and Jack torture Richter to reveal Irina's base of operations, until he says one word: 'Smila'. Sloane sends agents to Smila in the Ukraine, but they find nothing. Richter laughs – it's his wife's name. Sloane orders Jack to kill him.

Sloane speaks Japanese – and doesn't recognise Sydney in her geisha outfit. He tells her – in English – that he saw a man killed in cold blood yesterday and the man's dying thought was for his wife. Sloane seems troubled by this and says he loved his wife. Sydney tranquillises him before he says any more and gets him to Sark's ambulance.

Presenting Sark to the Alliance as an ally boosts Sloane's standing, which Vaughn now says 'has never been higher'.

Jack Bristow: Jack covers for Sydney with Sloane, saying she's on a reconnaissance mission in Armenia. He tortures Richter with a blowtorch and kills him on Sloane's orders. Shortly afterwards, when Sydney is faced with having to deliver Sloane to Sark and being responsible for his murder, Jack – with a perfect poker face – thinks it's appalling, and notes she never had to do anything like this until her mother reappeared. Jack is by Vaughn's bedside when he recovers.

Francie Calfo: Francie had an uncle involved in the 1983 invasion of Grenada and remembers listening to the news in between Duran Duran records.

Intelligence: The standardised tests from 1982 are missing and the ones on file don't have any of the Project Christmas questions on them. The ones on file have clearly been planted, though – the question on the invasion of Grenada, which didn't happen until the following year, gives it away. The original master copy does have the spatial awareness questions. The test was given to five million students in 33 states.

The virus isn't airborne and, once Vaughn starts bleeding from his fingernails, even in hospital, he has about three days to live. (We can infer an incubation period of five weeks. It's clearly not very contagious, as apparently no one Vaughn's been in contact with since Taipei is tested.) The antidote is found in a former nuclear testing facility in Paldiski, Estonia. Each person has to have an antidote tailored individually for them in a unique serum generator and a blood sample is needed for this.

Sark meets Sloane and (offscreen) they form an alliance to hunt for Irina. Sark also tells Sydney he's going to help SD-6 investigate the Rambaldi mystery. Sark has told Sloane that he foiled an assassination attempt on him – and now he has some control over Sydney, because she betrayed Sloane. He gave a piece of paper with a second piece of information on it to Sloane that confirmed his sincerity, but won't admit what it said.

Office Politics: Sydney disobeys two direct orders from Kendall in order to save Vaughn – she doesn't abort the mission in Paldiski and she goes to Japan to deliver Sloane to Sark.

Breaking the Code: Sydney uses her 'mountaineer' callsign. The passcode to the room with the serum generator is 26647729. The reference for the 1982 test is FYB 55/L. Sark's briefcase code is 10-11-92. Location letters: K and A.

Plot Devices: Sydney has a bug-killing device in her lipstick (presumably much the same as the one Jack has in his pen). In Paldiski, she wears underwater propulsion boots that propel her along at five knots. She carries a tranquilliser gun and a palmtop computer that has a satellite link.

When Jack goes to see Marshall, he's examining a polar bear skin, because polar bears don't show up on infrared scans.

Sark's briefcase containing the antidote has a remote detonator if it's tampered with or stolen.

Action: Sydney fights her way past some guards in Paldiski. In Japan, she knocks out two guards and manages some acrobatics while dressed as a geisha.

Undercover: Sydney tells Alice she's Rita Stevens and that she works with Vaughn. She gets into the Paldiski base in a wetsuit, before quickly changing into a yellow HazMat suit. In Japan she disguises herself as a geisha in a pink kimono and facepaint.

Music: 'Slumber My Darling' by Yo-Yo Ma (featuring Alison Krauss), 'I Grieve' by Peter Gabriel, 'I Shall Believe' by Sheryl Crow and 'Home' by Debbie Weisberg.

Injuries: Vaughn is very sick and in an oxygen tent from exposure to the virus. He has three days to live without an antidote and he is already very weak. Sydney goes to get a blood sample, but while she's there he starts bleeding internally. He recovers when he gets the antidote, but needs to spend some time in a wheelchair. Richter is also suffering from the virus, but he's killed by Jack – with a blowtorch.

The Big Picture: Sloane and Sark now have a strategic alliance. This brings Sloane a number of advantages – Sark can help with the hunt for Irina and with an analysis of her organisation; he knows at least something about Rambaldi and it increases Sloane's status with the Alliance. He realises that SD-6 have been suffering a number of setbacks recently, but blames himself for being distracted. The Emily blackmail continues. The standardised test story bubbles away – someone has clearly interfered with the tests, but who? As ever, the loyalties and motives of Jack, Sloane, Sark and Irina are unknown.

Debrief: 'I didn't do it for you.' A cleverly constructed story of ethics, showing Sydney disobeying orders from Vaughn, the very moment she discovers he's going out with someone else. This is contrasted with Jack, Sloane, Sark and Irina, who are mired in a complex web of mutual mistrust, means justifying the ends, cold-blooded murder and blackmail.

30
Passage I

Production #E658

1st US Transmission Date: 1 December 2002
1st UK Transmission Date: 28 April 2003

Writers: Debra J Fisher and Erica Messer
Director: Ken Olin
Guest Cast: Terry O'Quinn (Kendall),
Pasha D Lychnikoff (Zoran Sokolov), Shishir Kurup (Saeed Akhtar),

Kiran Rao (Lead Soldier), Chayton Arvin (Soldier),
Rahul Gupta (Passport Officer), Keith Lal (Porter),
KT Thangavelu (Woman), Richard Whiten (Security Station Agent)

Briefing: It's Sark's first day at SD-6, and he and Sloane are concerned that communications codes from the Uzbeki Army are being offered for sale. Irina is extremely worried at the news. Sydney and Dixon retrieve the codes.

Will has news about Project Christmas for Vaughn, who has to tell him that he's no longer needed as a researcher (see **Will Tippin**).

Kendall has learned that the codes are for six missing portable nuclear weapons. Jack, Sydney and Irina must go to Kashmir, where the PRF have the nuclear weapons. They get into Kashmir, are ambushed by the PRF who they wipe out, but they lose their jeep. They'll have to walk twenty miles through hostile territory.

OMG: Irina kisses Jack, the perfect loving wife; the three Bristows stand together, blasting away at a common enemy.

Mission: Sydney and Dixon go to Uzbekistan to buy the communications codes from Sokolov (see **Office Politics**) with a case full of cash. The briefcase with the codes is booby-trapped and they need the fingerprints of a colonel in the Uzbeki Army to open it or it will self-destruct. Sokolov has killed the colonel and they must go to the morgue to retrieve the fingerprints. Despite this complication, the mission is a success. The CIA send Sydney, Jack and Irina to infiltrate the People's Revolutionary Front (PRF) base in Azad and neutralise the nuclear weapons with Jack in operational control. They fly from Van Nuys to India, then take a sleeper train to the border with Kashmir.

Countermission: In Uzbekistan, Sydney is to dead-drop a copy of the codes, so the CIA can work out what they're really being used for. The countermission is a success.

Destinations: Los Angeles (USA), Uzbekistan, New Delhi (India), Kashmir.

Timescale: It's two months since Irina handed herself over to the CIA and she's spent 36 nights in her cell. It's two

weeks since she was nearly executed. Sark handed himself over to Sloane 'last week' according to Sark, 'two days ago' according to Jack. Vaughn first met Sydney on 1 October (2001, presumably – the first episode was broadcast on 30 September 2001). It's a nine-hour trek from the Bristows' entry point into Kashmir to the PRF stronghold.
Transcripts: Marshall (to Sark): 'Hello. Welcome. Don't kill me.'
Michael Vaughn: Vaughn's father gave him a watch which he told him he could set his heart by. It stopped the day he met Sydney. He has trouble sleeping when she's in the field.
Sydney Bristow: As Sydney is about to reply to Vaughn, their pagers go off and they have to return to the CIA. After handing the codes to SD-6, Sydney feels guilty. En route to India, Irina asks Sydney about Vaughn, who she insists is just a colleague. Irina thinks that she is used to taking risks for her country, but needs to take risks for her own happiness. Jack counters that Irina is probably not the best person to give out relationship advice. Sydney finds herself arbitrating between her parents – she tells Irina to stop baiting Jack and him not to be such an easy target.

They have to make a parachute jump, but Jack and Irina squabble about what order they should jump in. Sydney settles it by jumping first.
Marcus Dixon: Dixon strongly objects to working with Sark and with Sark being given immunity. He calls him a terrorist. Dixon can speak Uzbek.
Will Tippin: Will has been researching Project Christmas and has just discovered that some of the suspect questions were integrated into the 1982 tests, which were taken by five million children. Vaughn has to tell Will to abandon his research, as the FBI are now dealing with the case. Devlin thinks Will is a security risk and Vaughn gives him a payoff of $700. The FBI have found nothing, but Will discovers that 40 of the children taking the test scored 100 per cent. Will isn't happy to learn from Sydney that Sark (who abducted and tortured him) is now working alongside her at SD-6.
Arvin Sloane: After Sark points out how pathetic the SD-6 employees are for not realising they're working for the

enemy, Sloane is angry at him for insulting his people. Sark is worried about Sydney, but Sloane insists that she believes what he tells her. Sark advises him not to tell Jack what the codes are really for and he agrees. Sloane receives a call about his wife, which he records. The anonymous caller tells him they want SD-6 investment details or they'll tell the Alliance he failed to kill her. Later, he gets a neatly wrapped package that is checked out by Security Section and handed to him. It's a little leather case containing Emily's ring finger and he is visibly shocked.

Irina Derevko: Irina says that she didn't tell Sark about Sydney being a double agent. When Irina hears that the Uzbekistan communications codes are being traded, she looks worried and asks to be let out for 48 hours under guard with a tracking device. She refuses to explain why, reminding Jack that it's not long since the US government was going to have her killed. She tells them that everything they have worked for will be lost unless she takes care of this. It transpires that Irina knows about the nuclear weapons and where they are and that's why she's so worried. All she initially wants to discuss the matter is a pillow and blankets for her bed. Irina explains that she wanted to go to the PRF's base in Uzbekistan, because that's where the nuclear weapons are. Kendall reminds her that her immunity from prosecution (and, although he doesn't say it, execution) is dependent on her full co-operation. Irina is fitted with an explosive necklace (see **Plot Devices**), and seems almost to enjoy Jack putting it on her. When she poses as Jack's wife in India, a railway official compliments her on her necklace and Irina tells him it's a present from her husband and gives Jack a long, lingering kiss.

Jack Bristow: Jack is worried Sark might have told Sloane that he and Sydney are double agents. When Kendall asks Jack's opinion about letting Irina out for 48 hours, he says he's not objective when it comes to Irina, but agrees with Sydney that they should. She accuses him of playing mind games – planting the idea that his judgement is faulty before explaining what his judgement is. However, he's got his way and Irina won't be released. Jack realises Sloane is keeping him in the dark about the codes. He is understandably nervous about letting Irina get her hands on six nuclear weapons and won't let her carry a gun on the mission to India. When Jack and Irina share a sleeper compartment in the train, Irina strips down to her underwear and Jack finds himself staring, before turning away.

Mr Sark: Will describes Sark as 'British'. Although Sark has a British accent, he also uses American pronunciations ('dat-ta', rather than 'day-ta', for example).

Intelligence: An escalation in the Pakistan/India dispute over Kashmir means the border is sealed. Jack's contact in Pakistan is an old colleague, Saeed Akhtar. Saeed doesn't know Irina, but knows Sydney by reputation.

Office Politics: Sydney warns Sark that if he tells Sloane she's a double agent, she'll tell him that Sark was planning to kill him in Japan. He reminds her that he can't expose her without exposing himself. Sloane says that Security Section are constantly following Sark to make sure he's not a double agent. Sark deals with a man called Sokolov, who sells him intelligence data. He offered Sark communications codes from Uzbekistan showing the movements of ground forces, but Sark had little use for them and Sokolov plans to sell them to rebels in Tajikistan instead.

Home Front: Sydney needs to postpone a day at the spa with Francie, but promises to go next week.

Lies: Jack sets up a cover story to explain to Sloane where he and Sydney are while they are in India (what this is is never made clear).

Breaking the code: The dead Uzbeki colonel has the code C16 on his tag. Location letters: A and W.

Plot devices: Sydney has a pocket fingerprint scanner in Uzbekistan – presumably either supplied by Sokolov or SD-6 standard issue, as retrieving fingerprints wasn't part of her original mission. Irina is fitted with a necklace which contains C4 explosive and a tracking device. It's triggered by removing it or by a remote trigger on Jack's wristwatch. It can also be deactivated from the wristwatch (see **Action**).

Sydney has a device to locate their cases in the luggage compartment of the train. She also has a compass/GPS device in her wristwatch. Saeed gets them a radiation detector, explosives, weapons and a jeep.
Action: Sydney starts the day with a car chase, pitting her Toyota SUV against Sark's Mercedes. He yields and the two talk. Sydney has a fight in the morgue when she's discovered. When she makes her escape, Dixon almost shoots her – and she blows their cover somewhat by shouting in English not to shoot, using Dixon's name! To get into Pakistan, Sydney, Irina and Jack parachute off a bridge. The Bristows are ambushed and Saaed is shot dead. Their attackers are the PRF, who know the Bristows are CIA and looking for them. Jack deactivates the necklace and Irina throws it, destroying the jeep and causing enough of a distraction to let the Bristows take the upper hand. The three of them grab guns from their attackers and wipe out the ambushing party.
Undercover: Sydney and Dixon pose as Sark's employees for the Uzbekistan mission. Sydney wears a black outfit and has long brown hair. To infiltrate the morgue, she poses as a dead medic in the Uzbekistan Army, complete with uniform, body bag and fake bullet hole in the forehead. Dixon poses as another medic. In India, the Bristows pose as a family of American tourists, the Godsons. Jack has a moustache, Irina has blonde hair and Sydney is their gum-chewing daughter in high school. They change into black combat gear, with parachutes. Once inside Pakistan, they pose as international aid workers.
Reality Checks: Kashmir is a disputed region between India and Pakistan. It's specified that the PRF stronghold is in the Pakistani-administered Azad region of Kashmir.
Music: 'Bad Moon Rising' by Creedence Clearwater Revival, 'Almost Ran' by Josh Canova and 'Walk On' by U2.
Injuries: Sydney gets 'a scratch' during the fight with the PRF – presumably from a bullet.
The Big Picture: Sark knows that Sydney was willing to kill Sloane – he doesn't know (as far as it's clear) that she is a double agent. Irina says she didn't tell him. The People's

Revolutionary Front are 'mercenaries' with a base in a former prison in Azad. Irina knows the organisation and has had dealings with it, as has Sark. What is the true nature of Sark and Sloane's alliance? As ever, Sark's motives are unclear, as is his current connection to Irina. Who tipped off the PRF that the CIA were coming?

Debrief: 'Mom, I need your help.' The first half of *Alias: The Movie*? An expert piece of storytelling that combines big, high-stakes action with silly family squabbling. It's an episode where good stuff just keeps falling over itself to get on to the screen, but events are made to seem almost straightforward here. The show never lets you forget just how momentous it is to see the three Bristows on screen at the same time, all working to the same purpose.

31
Passage II

Production: #E659

1st US Transmission: 8 December 2002
1st UK Transmission Date: 5 May 2003

Writer: Crystal Nix Hines
Director: Ken Olin
Guest Cast: Terry O'Quinn (Kendall), Derek De Lint (Gerard Cuvee), James Lesure (CIA Agent Craig Blair), Wolf Muser (Ramon Veloso), Marshall Manesh (Hari Singh), Iqbal Theba (Arshad), Joseph Ruskin (Alain Christophe), Ira Heiden (Rick), Andy Gatjen (Aide), PD Mani (PRF Guard)

Briefing: The CIA, monitoring the Bristows, know that the necklace has been detonated, but nothing else. Kendall gets intelligence that the PRF's nuclear weapons are being prepped. The Bristows take a train to Srinagar, where Jack meets an old contact, Singh, who lends them a truck, but it breaks down ten miles from the stronghold. Irina's knowledge means they can get into the base. She leaves them for a moment – and returns with Cuvee, who she's clearly very friendly with. They lock up Sydney and Jack and Irina taunts her husband but, once she's alone with him, Irina gives him the key to his cell. Vaughn is sent to India as the Indians prepare an airstrike on the stronghold. Jack and Sydney watch as Cuvee and Irina reveal what they're using the plutonium for – to power a Rambaldi artefact. The artefact cracks open to reveal a flower. As the airstrikes start, Irina punches Cuvee and the three Bristows retrieve the flower and are evacuated by Vaughn, who arrives by helicopter. They arrive safely back in LA.

Sloane pays his blackmailer – who disappears, leaving behind photos that show Emily is dead.

OMG: Jack in his turban; Irina and Cuvee walk in, hand in hand.

Mission: As in **30,** 'Passage I', the Bristows are to infiltrate the PRF stronghold in the Azad region of Kashmir. Following the ambush, they no longer have their equipment or the element of surprise. The Bristows recover the cores of the warheads and the flower from the Rambaldi artefact.

Destinations: New Delhi (India), Srinagar (Jammu and Kashmir), Los Angeles (USA), London (UK).

Timescale: Sydney was four at the time of the Bristow family house fire. It's nineteen years since Irina was at the PRF stronghold.

Transcripts: Singh (to Jack and his family, on the need for disguise): 'First of all you need to be looking not like you.'

Jack Bristow: Jack has a contact, Hari Singh, who gets them clothing and a few other supplies. He tells Sydney that Jack always brags about her. It's two years since Singh's supplier, Sirath, died of a heart attack.

Jack and Irina reminisce about married life, particularly when 'toaster' Jack was making toast; the two of them got drunk and amorous, forgot about the toast and there was a house fire so serious they all had to move out to a hotel. Jack smiles and looks fondly at Irina. However, for the truck ride to the stronghold, he decides that the PRF will be looking out for three people and hides Irina in a plastic grain barrel on the back of the truck. This seems at least partially motivated out of sadism – Sydney isn't even sure her mother will be able to breathe. It's a five-hour trek, in burning heat. Jack does give Irina a gun as they head through the minefield surrounding the stronghold, however, and won't leave without her, even though that means staying as the airstrikes begin.

Sydney Bristow: Sydney had forgotten the house fire, but remembers that the hotel they moved to served sundaes. Irina asks about Sydney's education. She replies she's 'supposedly' writing her dissertation. Once again, she finds herself arbitrating between her parents. She assigns Jack operational command until they get to the base, when Irina will be in charge. There's a further debate once they are inside the stronghold – Jack doesn't want to let Irina out of his sight, but they don't have time: they need to deactivate the alarms and access the computers. Sydney speaks Urdu.

Irina Derevko: Irina can remember the precise layout of the minefield and the sewage system, even though it's nineteen years since she was last there. She reveals she wasn't in charge of the facility, but was a prisoner here.

Irina leaves Jack and Sydney, apparently to deactivate the security system. She seems to do this – then walks in arm in arm with Cuvee, and Jack and Sydney are locked up. It transpires that Cuvee was her supervisor at the KGB, the man who sent her to the US looking for a CIA agent to seduce. There were a number of candidates, but Jack had the most potential because he had a big ego. Irina does stop Cuvee from killing Jack, though. Irina tells Cuvee she wants to know who Sark is working for now. Cuvee seems particularly wary of Sark. Once Cuvee has gone, Irina tells Jack she's still working with him. She pistol whips Jack and leaves. He quickly recovers and finds he has a key in his hand.

As the airstrikes hit, Irina punches Cuvee and makes her escape. On her return to custody, she finds blankets and pillows on her bed. She tells Sydney she shot her in Taipei because Cuvee was in the next room, watching to make sure where Irina's loyalties lay. She lets Sydney escape.

Arvin Sloane: Sloane is contacted by the blackmailer, who now wants $100 million in bearer bonds, or he'll contact the Alliance to tell them Emily is alive. In London, Sloane tells the Alliance that he failed to kill Emily. As only Alliance leaders know he was meant to murder his wife and he doesn't suspect any of them, there must be a security breach at the highest level of the organisation. He suggests they pay the blackmailer and track him down. If Emily is still alive, he will have to kill her. Sloane drops a briefcase containing the bonds on a park bench and picks up an envelope which contains photos of Emily, shot through the head.

Michael Vaughn: Vaughn was stationed in India for two years and Kendall sends him there to buy some time for the Bristows. He knows General Arshad, who tells him he looks like his father and lends Vaughn a helicopter to get the Bristows out of the stronghold before the airstrikes.

Intelligence: Jack describes the PRF stronghold as a Class A target. It has biometric sensors, infrared detectors and fibre-optic surveillance. The Indian airforce, aware that the nuclear weapons are being prepped, is preparing for airstrikes within 24 hours.

Home Front: Sydney plays Will and Francie at crazy golf when she gets back from Kashmir (neither of her friends get any dialogue in the episode). From a distance, Vaughn watches them enjoy themselves.

Lies: Irina's loyalties are so complex that she's now at least a quintuple agent – she double-crosses Cuvee by double-crossing the CIA by saying she's working for Cuvee but she's really working with the CIA, albeit for her own purposes.

Breaking the Code: The activation code for the artefact is AC-7-1-10.

Plot Devices: Singh supplies the Bristows with a truck, but – as Irina suspected – it's not suitable for the journey to Kashmir and the filter clogs. The minefield surrounding the PRF stronghold consists of American M26 mines (which both Jack and Irina can defuse).

Marshall places an invisible liquid tracer on the bonds Sloane hands over to the blackmailer; the blackmailer manages to deactivate it within seconds.

Cuvee isn't using the nuclear weapons as arms, but to power a big, computer-controlled refrigeration machine that activates a Rambaldi artefact capable of self-sustaining cell regeneration – 'proof of endless life'. The device cracks open to reveal, bafflingly, a small yellow flower.

The CIA analyse the flower and discover it's between four and six hundred years old.

Action: The Indian airforce launch airstrikes on the PRF stronghold with a couple of waves of missile attacks. The Bristows barely get out in time.

Undercover: Singh kits out the Bristows. Sydney gets a blue sari with silver accessories, Irina a dark red sari and Jack a turban and beard. Once at the stronghold, they switch to their combat gear. In the stronghold, Sydney dresses in a burka and poses as a worker at the complex.

Reality Checks: You can't fool an IR sensor by raising the temperature of the room – even if you could, it wouldn't fool the motion sensors that come as standard on even household burglar alarm kits.

Music: 'Emotional Rescue' by The Rolling Stones.

Injuries: Irina treats Sydney's 'scratch' using cuminum. Jack is lucky: he's shot, but it hits his vest. The impact knocks him over on to a mine, but it doesn't go off. Later, though, he's whacked over the head with a pistol by Irina.

The Big Picture: It looks like Irina isn't in league with Cuvee – she has every opportunity to betray Jack and Sydney, the US and the CIA, but chooses to free Jack and leave Cuvee to the mercy of the airstrikes. It's not made clear if Cuvee survived them. However, Irina is clearly up to something. She realises what Cuvee is planning and prevents him from doing it. Cuvee's Rambaldi artefact is even more baffling than usual. It's got something to do with eternal life; it has a power source so arcane that six plutonium cores are needed, and it can preserve (or rejuvenate) flowers. What is it and why is Irina so worried? Taking them at their word, neither Irina nor Cuvee know what has happened to Sark or what he's planning. Added to the usual question of who is blackmailing Sloane, we can also ask how they deactivated the tracer so quickly, whether Sloane really believes (as he claims) that it isn't someone from the Alliance and whether Emily is really dead this time.

Debrief: It's what passes as a straightforward episode of *Alias* – no balancing of work and home life for Sydney, no countermission, Sydney's not even working for SD-6. But it's jam-packed with everything from comedy scenes, character moments, jaw-dropping double-crosses and big action sequences. As with the first part, the three Bristows working with (and against) each other is endlessly entertaining – if the three of them ever teamed up, they could take over the world.

32
The Abduction

Production #E660

1st US Transmission Date: 15 December 2002
1st UK Transmission Date: 12 May 2003

Writers: Alex Kurtzman-Counter and Roberto Orci
Director: Nelson McCormick
Guest Cast: Faye Dunaway (Ariana Kane), Petra Wright (Alice), Ric Young (Suit and Glasses), John Balma (Thatcher Powell), Charles Constant (Data Clerk), Don Took (Agent Grey), Kenny Gould, Paul Anthony Scott (Guards)

Briefing: Sydney and Sark go on a mission to Paris to get an ECHELON computer terminal. Sydney sabotages the operation, but there's another way into the system and SD-6 send her to London with Marshall. Jack is investigator Ariana Kane's prime suspect as Sloane's blackmailer. Unable to sabotage the SD-6 mission without revealing the organisation's true nature to Marshall, the CIA plan to extract him from SD-6. On his return to LA, though, he's abducted by Suit and Glasses before they get the chance.
OMG: Marshall goes on his first field mission.
Mission: SD-6 send Sydney and Sark on a joint mission to Paris to recover a computer terminal that allows Cuvee access to ECHELON. There is another way into ECHELON, via a backup terminal in London. Only Marshall can crack the codes, so he's to go with Sydney. They'll steal an access key

from Thatcher Powell, a Cuvee associate who'll be at a symphony, then crack the code on site. Although Marshall is shot with a tranquilliser dart, the mission's a complete success. However, Marshall is abducted before he can be debriefed.
Countermission: Sydney is to wipe the hard drive of Cuvee's computer terminal, blaming it on a booby-trap. This countermission is a total success.

Unable – as Sydney points out – to create a fake Marshall, the CIA decide to bring him in after the London mission. Sydney is to proceed as per the SD-6 mission and tell Sloane the truth – that the last she saw of him was at LAX. This fails when Marshall is kidnapped by Suit and Glasses before the CIA can get to him.

Destinations: Los Angeles (USA), Paris (France), London (United Kingdom).

Timescale: Jack tells Ariane that he's known Sloane for thirty years.

Transcripts: Ariana (after Jack's just admitted he should be her prime suspect): 'It's the only thing you can say to diminish your viability as a suspect.' Jack: '. . . your obvious awareness of game theory would invalidate my approach, therefore the best course of action for me . . . is simply to tell the truth.'

Sydney (coming up with a statement that should be the Bristow family motto): 'It's a gesture of love to deceive people I care about.'

Sydney Bristow: Sydney tells Will that going on the mission to Kashmir, where she and both her parents worked as a team, was comforting (this is intercut with footage of them standing in a row blasting away with their sub-machine-guns). Will deadpans that he and his parents went through the same thing. She tells him later that she doesn't like lying to Francie, but it protects her (see **Transcripts**). Sydney's maths skills are above average, but not enough to do advanced calculus in her head. When Vaughn tells her the CIA are going to put Marshall in protective custody, her first thought is that SD-6 is his life and he'll be terribly hurt; the second is to make sure they also protect his mother.

Michael Vaughn: Sydney notices Vaughn's suit, which he's wearing because he's come from the funeral of Alice's father, and she sends her sympathies. Vaughn wants to talk about meeting Sydney in the bar, see **31**, 'Passage II'. She asks him if he saw the security camera – they can't be seen together – but an agent has already recovered the tape.
Will Tippin: Will takes the CIA allegiance test, with a view to working as Vaughn's researcher. It's a psychological test, not a general knowledge one. Vaughn advises him not to lie, because he'll be disqualified if they catch him out. One question asks whether you'd rather kill your father, mother or yourself. Sydney explains to him afterwards that it's used to determine your loyalty and feelings towards authority (although you wonder what Sydney put and whether her answer now would be different). It's not explained why his criminal record previously prevented him from getting a CIA job in **28**, 'Salvation', but doesn't now. (Presumably Will's criminal record prevented him from working for a CIA front company, which would have to maintain an appearance of respectability, but this isn't an obstacle for secret work.)
Arvin Sloane: Sloane brings in Ariana Kane from Alliance Counterintelligence to find the blackmailer. She had previously plugged a leak at SD-9.
Jack Bristow: Ariana suspects that Jack is hiding something and is aware that he is a first-class strategist. He counters this by telling her that, in her position, he'd suspect himself (see **Transcripts**). Jack tells Ariana that he's known Sloane for thirty years, from when they were both in the CIA. They became disillusioned with a government they thought was corrupt. He says they both believe the Alliance will achieve its aim of global dominance. Ariana asks Jack about his 'intimate contacts' in the last ten years, but he refuses to answer, gets angry and Ariana approves of his fighting spirit.
Irina Derevko: Alone in her cell, Irina demonstrates she has the focus and ability to catch flies in mid air – by the wing. At Sydney's request, Kendall lets her out on to the roof to see open air twice a week, for fifteen minutes. She's

surrounded by armed guards and no one – not even Sydney – is allowed to touch her.

Irina was eighteen when she was recruited by the KGB. She was proud to serve her country, as it made her feel empowered, but now says she was a fool to imagine that any ideology was more important than her daughter. Sark tells Sydney that he's learned a lot from Irina and in some ways thinks of her as his mother.

Jack visits Irina. He knows that she had the chance to betray the CIA in Kashmir and didn't. Jack's decided that her strategy is therefore long term and suspects she and Sark are co-ordinating their efforts to infiltrate the CIA and SD-6. He offers Irina a move to a private residence on Puget Sound, as long as she confesses to what she's really up to. She counters by noting that, technically, they are probably still married. This rattles him and he confirms to Irina at the end of the episode that, as the marriage was never annulled, this is the case. Irina claims that, as she's telling the truth, she can't confess anything to Jack so has to decline his offer. She would have turned him down straight away, but wondered if she might gain some advantage by coming up with a convincing lie.

Intelligence: Cuvee and his People's Revolutionary Front are on the NSA watchlist. Sark has been dealing with Cuvee for several years. The Alliance want access to the US government's ECHELON surveillance software, hoping to use it to blackmail and extort governments and companies.

Office Politics: Sloane is angry with Sark – the SD-6 Kashmir operation (which isn't shown) was a failure, as they only found the remains of the prison. He has Sark strapped to a chair and threatens to use an old Khmer Rouge torture technique on him: putting a glass ball in his mouth and smashing it. Sark talks, saying his motivation is simply to 'combine his efforts' with SD-6, but his contact Cuvee didn't foresee the airstrike. Sark specifies that it was the Indian Western Command that attacked the PRF stronghold. He also confirms that the Rambaldi artefact was destroyed. Sark provides technical details of the back-up ECHELON terminal in London. Cuvee uses the front organisation 'Jennings Aerospace' (oddly, the same company Jack claimed to work for back in the episode **1**, 'Truth Be Told').

Marshall asks Sydney to take snapshots of Paris. His mother thinks he works in IT, travelling the world, so he gets people to take photos, then digitally superimposes a picture of himself. Marshall has a photographic memory and can solve polymorphic algorithms in his head. Sark quickly gives him enough training to qualify as a field graded agent. It's the first time he's flown and he settles his nerves by hacking into the plane's computer to make sure the pilots remember everything, sewing a parachute into his jacket (he's not forgotten Sydney – it has a tandem sling) and memorising the FAA flight ops manual of the 747 when he couldn't sleep. Marshall says that Bach is his favourite composer, and he certainly seems to appreciate the concert. He is shot with a tranquilliser dart, but doesn't get a full dose. He just has time to praise British anti-gun legislation before he begins to get drowsy. He sleepily tells Sydney he loves her and almost dozes off at the keyboard – until she kisses him, full on the mouth. From then, he's wide awake and completes his task with ease. Vaughn hopes that, after he's been debriefed, Marshall will come to work with the CIA.

Home Front: Francie wonders if there's something up between Sydney and Will, as they always clam up when she arrives. Sydney has bought Francie a season ticket to the Hollywood Bowl for her birthday.

Breaking the Code: The entry code to the 'Jennings Aerospace' terminal room is 86119.

Plot Devices: In Paris Sydney has a laptop that can control traffic lights, as well as a device that can blow a hole in the roof of an armoured truck before pumping it full of tear gas. Sark has a simple tear-gas gun (further evidence that Marshall only gives the cool stuff to Sydney?). In London, Marshall supplies himself and Sydney with the parachute in his jacket (see **Intelligence**) and a scopolamine tablet to make Thatcher Powell go to sleep.

Action: In Paris, Sydney blows a hole in an armoured car, slides down a rope to get into it and then chases a man over the tops of cars before leaping off one and scissor-kicking him before she hits the ground. Sydney knocks out two guards armed with tranquilliser guns in London while wearing a full-length gown.

Reality Checks: ECHELON really does exist and it really is the software behind the American NSA's surveillance system (less-informed sources often state that it's the name of the system). Royal Hall, the supposed location of the London Philharmonic, doesn't exist (there's a Royal Albert Hall and a Royal Festival Hall), and they're an orchestra, not a quartet. British law prevents security guards from using firearms – but those same laws also ban them from carrying tranquilliser guns, as shown here.

Background Checks: Faye Dunaway is best known for *Bonnie and Clyde* and the original *Thomas Crown Affair*.

Trivia: The pre-credits sequence for this episode lasts eighteen minutes – with the first adverts coming after the credits. This does make for a short Act II and Act III.

Injuries: Irina asks how Jack's injuries are healing – which is a little odd, as he wasn't wounded (beyond mild bruises) on the mission.

Undercover: In Paris, Sydney dresses in the overalls and hard hat of a road surveyor, before losing the hard hat and gaining a gas mask when she storms the truck. Sark disguises himself as a gendarme. Sydney once again calls herself 'Rita' when she meets Vaughn's girlfriend, Alice (see **29,** 'The Counteragent'). In London, Sydney's alias is an unnamed married woman at the symphony and Marie Robinson of Jennings Aerospace at the server building. She dusts off the faultless English accent last heard in Sri Lanka, see **25,** 'Cipher', and wears a low-cut, floor-length black evening gown. Marshall wears a tuxedo and poses as Sydney's husband at the concert and her business associate Frederick Fields at the server building. He adopts an English accent, seemingly culled from watching a lot of PBS ('Cheerio!'). In the server building he distracts the guards by gabbling in a language that Sydney doesn't understand –

a series first. He explains that it's Ewok, 'official language of the indigenous creatures on the planet Endor'.
Reference Points: The Ewoks appeared in *Return of the Jedi*. You knew that already!
Music: 'The Wreckoning' by Boomkat, 'Beauty of The Rain' by Dar Williams, 'Don't Try This At Home' by Chumbawamba and 'Sleepers, Awake' by JS Bach (a terrific in-joke – it's playing as Thatcher Powell and Marshall doze at the concert).
The Big Picture: Cuvee survived the airstrikes in Kashmir and is in contact with Sark. He believes Sark tipped off the Indian authorities.
Debrief: 'Yub-nub!' The series has always been funny, but it's usually been surreal or deadpan humour. Marshall's mission is the first out and out comedy sequence and it's a huge success, with Jennifer Garner matching Kevin Weisman beat for beat as he displays impeccable comic timing. Once again, it's tempered with moments that really tug at the heartstrings – Marshall's happiness at being one of the good guys moments before the CIA plan to pull him into custody and the sheer horror as he's abducted by someone else. Meanwhile, in a subplot, Victor Garber is crossing swords with Faye Dunaway. Beautifully written, directed and acted, this is the sort of episode that not only wins awards, but also makes the other nominees wonder if they should even bother showing up.

33
A Higher Echelon

Production: #E661

1st US Transmission Date: 5 January 2003
1st UK Transmission Date: 19 May 2003

Writer: John Eisendrath
Director: Guy Norman Bee
Guest Cast: Faye Dunaway (Ariana Kane), Terry O'Quinn (Kendall), Ric Young (Suit and Glasses), James Lesure (Craig Blair),

Ira Heiden (Rick McCarthy),
Elizabeth Penn Payne (CIA Print Technician),
John Christopher Storey (CIA Video Technician),
Mark Humphrey (SD-6 Technician),
Nelson Mashita (SD-6 Optech Agent), George Tovar (Waiter),
Shawn Michael Patrick (SD-6 Forensic Expert)

Briefing: Marshall is tortured by Suit and Glasses, who wants to know how to access ECHELON. He cracks when his mother is threatened and sets to work. Sloane sends Sydney and Dixon to Vietnam to recover some of the ECHELON data that was lost in transit. Irina wants access to the system, but Kendall refuses. The data Sydney recovers has a security system and the CIA are helpless. They give Irina access to counteract this. Ariana Kane revokes Jack's security clearance, forcing him to fake alibis to cover his work against SD-6. Marshall signals SD-6 from his computer and Sydney and Dixon rescue him. Jack runs from Ariana when she realises he's faked some evidence. He confides in Sloane, who contacts Kane the moment Jack leaves.

Vaughn tells Will he's now a CIA analyst.

Mission: Sydney and Dixon are sent to Vietnam to recover the hard drive with the ECHELON data packet on it. The mission is a success.

Countermission: Sydney is to replace the hard drive with an identical one with corrupted data. Dixon gets to the original hard drive first and takes it back to SD-6. The countermission is a failure.

Destinations: Ho Chi Minh City (Vietnam), Los Angeles (USA), Mexico City (Mexico).

Timescale: Sydney has worked with Vaughn for almost a year.

Transcripts: Ariana Kane (to Jack): 'There are no protections here, no civil rights, no reasonable doubt.'

Marshall: 'Hi, my name is Marshall J Flinkman and I'm here to rescue you!'

Dixon: 'I speak nine languages and techno's not one of them.'

Sydney Bristow: Sydney sketches in the workings of ECHELON to Will (and the audience). Will is worried about the Big Brother aspects of the technology, but Sydney blithely states that the NSA don't abuse the system, but use it to fight terrorists. Sydney (unaware he was kidnapped) is relieved Marshall got back from his mission to London. She tells Francie she's got a crush on a guy at work, Michael, but that the bank have a policy against the staff fraternising. Sydney can speak and read Vietnamese.

Jack Bristow: Jack finds his security clearance has been revoked. Kane says he has no alibi for the key dates of the Emily kidnap saga so he heads back to the CIA to manufacture evidence he was in Taipei, Istanbul and Azerbaijan on the dates Kane has given him (he later says Karachi, Istanbul and Taipei). Kane has located the gun Jack checked out the day Emily died and there's brain matter on it. This is one of the few examples of the show getting confused by its own convoluted continuity – it's right that Jack shot Haladki the day Emily died. Both events took place in episode **22,** 'Almost Thirty Years'. However, that was the first time Emily 'died', and Emily was poisoned, not shot. Emily 'died' again as part of the blackmailer's scheme, but this time she was shot. But that was about two months later, see **31,** 'Passage II'. Vaughn is shocked by the revelation Jack shot Haladki, who Jack says was loyal to Irina, and he didn't report to avoid drawing attention to the operation.

Ariana meets Jack over lunch, with two Security Section teams watching (although they don't spot the CIA monitoring them, or notice the waiter's an agent, passing things to Jack). Jack manages to convince Ariana with his alibi – until the ink on the fake SIM card rubs off. She sends Security Section after him, but he manages to evade them by jumping into the CIA van. Jack goes to Sloane's house – he's being framed. Ariana needs to blame someone, so she's blaming him. He's going to find out who's really blackmailing Sloane. Sloane agrees, but the moment Jack's gone, he phones Ariana.

Marcus Dixon: Dixon briefs Sydney on the Optech, in Marshall's absence. He accompanies her to Vietnam, doing his usual business with laptops and security cameras. It's Dixon who realises that anyone able to hack into SD-6 would be able to hide their IP address – it's Marshall, signalling them. He and Sydney volunteer to rescue Marshall. He uses cover as a DJ to mask the sound of Sydney entering the neighbouring building, then locks down its lifts.

Will Tippin: Will isn't reassured by Sydney's assurances that the US government wouldn't abuse the ECHELON system. Will passed his CIA psychological test. Vaughn gives him a cover – he'll be working for *Trade Roads* travel magazine, a CIA front organisation. He'll really be a desk-trained analyst. He warns Vaughn to respect Sydney.

Arvin Sloane: When he's with Jack, Sloane is unconcerned at the loss of Marshall – the security breach is easily patched by changing his access codes. SD-4 are sending him a replacement head of Optech. Publically, he says his thoughts and prayers are with him. Even when Marshall is located, he's more interested in ECHELON than recovering him, but does allow Sydney and Dixon to rescue him. He's all smiles when Marshall returns. Sloane telephones Alain (see **15,** 'Page 47') to announce he has access to ECHELON, but, as he does so, his technical people have to report that there's a problem and he's been blocked.

Michael Vaughn: Vaughn listens in and discovers Jack killed Haladki.

Irina Derevko: Irina warns about the 'quicksand' virus, and asks for unlimited, supervised access to the CIA computers. Jack thinks she should get it, otherwise SD-6 will gain access to ECHELON, but Kendall refuses. He relents, but asks Irina how he knows she won't contact her associates. She replies that he doesn't. She can hack the Russian SOUD system (see **Intelligence**) because she has the access code. She spends at least twelve hours at the computer and finds a gap in the system. She takes her coffee black, no sugar.

Marshall Flinkmann: Marshall swears on his mother's grave that he can't access ECHELON, clarifying that, though she's still alive, she has picked out a plot. Suit and

Glasses uses Marshall's mother as leverage, threatening her. Marshall says that he can recreate the code using his photographic memory. He thought he had the world's largest collection of PEZ dispensers (see **Reality Checks**) but, when he wrote to the *Guinness Book of World Records*, it turned out it was only the second: a nine-year-old girl in Australia beat him. He pings SD-6 – bombarding the server with messages. He claims he's simply downloading Sammy Hager MP3s to work to. He reveals his handiwork to Suit and Glasses – it's not the code to ECHELON, it's a game of Pong. He's defiant, knowing he's going to die, but Sydney rescues him. To escape, he uses the parachute sewn into his jacket (it's not the same jacket as before, but he's got one in this one, too).

Suit and Glasses: Following his injection by Will in **22**, 'Almost Thirty Years', Suit and Glasses has proven to be the 'one-in-five' – he is paralysed, confined to a wheelchair.

Intelligence: ECHELON is software that monitors every phone call, fax and email in every major language in the world for certain key words and phrases. It works by access to a communications satellite. The Russians have an equivalent, SOUD. The ECHELON email was broken up into several data packets and some weren't received properly at SD-6. It will take six months even to attempt to reconstruct it. One package is on a hard drive on a server in Ho Chi Minh City. There is a virus, 'quicksand', that anyone trying to trace Cuvee will encounter. It shuts down the CIA's computers. Cuvee used access to the system to locate and destroy a US military lab in Dresden. On tracing the plates of the rented SUV that Marshall was bundled into, the CIA discover 'Charles Williamson', who's a match for a Cuvee associate.

Office Politics: A four-man CIA team is sent to a safehouse in London to look for Marshall, but it was a booby-trap and they are all killed. The search is called off as too risky. Marshall's title is Tech Ops Officer, SD-6.

Home Front: Will and Francie spend time at the restaurant combining half-empty tomato ketchup bottles to make full ones. Francie is worried that Sydney is doing too much travelling and thinks it's unfair she can't date her co-worker. She's worried that she has done nothing but work since Danny died.

Breaking the Code: The server room is 206 and the hard drive with the incriminating data has the serial number 65733PY12. It's being repaired in room 147. Suit and Glasses is keeping Marshall on the 47th floor. Location letters: M, G and O.

Plot Devices: The CIA quickly manufacture evidence to give Jack an alibi. This involves him putting fingerprints on documents, doctoring phone and credit card records and even filming him in front of a greenscreen and dropping the footage on to hotel surveillance tapes. SD-6 supply a projector that strobes in a sequence that sends people to sleep in seconds. Sydney can protect herself by wearing special glasses. Jack's standard issue SD-6 pistol is a 19 Compact (a Glock).

Action: Sydney kicks ass when she rescues Marshall. She may, or may not, have killed Suit and Glasses with a kick to the chest.

Undercover: Sydney arrives in Vietnam as a microsatellite expert, Nina Bails of Tech-Sky Industries. She wears her hair up in a bun, with a chopstick-style grip. Dixon quickly adopts the identity of Roderick Milton, her nerdy colleague. In Mexico City, Sydney wears a red track suit, beret and cut-off gloves – clubbing gear, apparently. Dixon is a techno DJ with dreadlocks. His act isn't terribly convincing, as Sydney points out.

Reality Checks: SOUD doesn't officially exist. There's some debate about what it stands for. It's either the Integrated Information Assessment System or the Operational and Institutional Information System. It's thought it was set up in 1977 and that it's run by FAPSI, but information is sparse – it's never been referred to in the Russian press and is only cited, in passing, in one Russian book on intelligence organisations. Its exact capabilities and technological sophistication are the subject of speculation (and conspiracy theory). People do indeed collect PEZ sweet dispensers.

Music: 'Serious JuJu' by Sammy Hagar, 'Noche De Toxinas' by Kinky, 'Weapon' by Matthew Good Band and 'All I Wanna Do' by Jude.
Injuries: Marshall's mouth is prised open and Suit and Glasses pours resin into his mouth. This is one half of an epoxy binary compound. If Marshall swallowed the hardener, the resin would solidfy and suffocate him.
The Big Picture: The CIA shut down SD-6's access to ECHELON, but what has Irina done with all that time at the computer? How will the CIA react to Haladki's death?
Debrief: 'Are you ready to party?' We're reminded that Sloane's a nasty piece of work as he callously writes off Marshall. The episode isn't the barnstormer of the last few, but it's a more than satisfying hour of television, with some wonderful stuff in the Jack subplot and a lovely moment of triumph and bravery from Marshall.

34
The Getaway

Production #E662

1st US Transmission Date: 12 January 2003
1st UK Transmission Date: 26 May 2003

Writer: Jeff Pinkner
Director: Lawrence Trilling
Guest Cast: Faye Dunaway (Ariana Kane), Terry O'Quinn (Kendall), Greg Grunberg (Agent Weiss), Ira Heiden (CIA Agent Rick McCarthy), Doug Kruse (Patton Birch), Don Took (Agent Grey), Phillipe Simon (Claude Rousseau), Courtney Gains (Holden), Kevin Sutherland (CIA Agent Blake), Roger Ranny (Black Sweater), Sonny Suroweic (Leather Jacket), Laurent Alexandre (Airport Security Guard)

Briefing: Jack meets a contact at a cinema but he's been murdered. Agents try to arrest Jack, but he escapes and Sydney is waiting in a getaway car. Sydney goes in to work at SD-6 as normal and Sloane sends her and Dixon to Nice to steal an experimental gyroscope that's being moved to Berlin. While she waits for the CIA to duplicate the gyroscope, she agrees to go to dinner with Vaughn. They flirt, but they've been spotted and Alliance Security attack them. Sydney has to get back to SD-6 quickly and hand over the real gyroscope. Meanwhile, Jack and Irina have discovered evidence that Kane is behind the blackmail of Sloane. As Jack goes for proof, he's caught by Kane, who injects him with a truth drug. Just as he's about to tell her the truth, Sloane has her dragged away. He then goes off and acquires something to block the Alliance tracking device. He heads for the Philippines. Emily is there and he tells her they are free.

OMG: Sloane did it!

Mission: Sydney's mission is to intercept the gyroscope en route to Berlin and bring it back to SD-6. She succeeds.

Countermission: Sydney is to give the gyroscope to the CIA, who will reproduce a fake one for her to give to SD-6. After the fight with Alliance Security in Nice, she has to take the real gyroscope back to SD-6. But she later manages to switch it for the fake.

Destinations: Los Angeles (USA), Nice (France), The Philippines.

Timescale: It is 'several months' since Emily 'died'. Sloane became an Alliance partner 'this past summer' and was injected with the tracking device 89 days ago. It's three months since Dixon reported Sydney to Sloane and since Weiss was shot. It's two weeks since Vaughn knew that Jack was being investigated. Briault's visits to Peru were 'last February', '2001 November' and '2001 September', suggesting this is 2002.

Transcripts: Sydney (echoing Jack in **1,** 'Truth Be Told'): 'Dad, get in!'

Sydney (weighing up whether to sleep with Vaughn): 'There are clearly issues.' (She pauses for eleven seconds.) 'OK.'

Sloane (to Emily): 'We did it. We're free.'

Sydney Bristow: After rescuing her father, she returns to work as normal. She hates the way that Sloane 'wraps himself in the flag', telling Marshall and Dixon that he's fighting for America. Sydney is also angry with Vaughn for not telling her that her father was being investigated. He says she didn't need to know and she links it with him not telling her about Alice. It's clear she had trusted him completely and feels betrayed. However, she goes to dinner with him. After the meal, the owner suggests they spend the night at his inn. They consider whether to accept the offer. Sydney thinks there are issues, but agrees. Before they can do anything, Alliance Security attack them. She's very guilty – she has no time to get the duplicate gyroscope and she has to hand the real one to SD-6. But, once Kane is dragged off, she knows that no one will look for her missing men in Nice and swaps the real gyroscope for the fake. Sydney speaks French.

Marcus Dixon: Dixon accompanies Sydney to Nice and travels back separately.

Michael Vaughn: Vaughn asks Sydney out to dinner. She's worried that the Alliance will spot them, but (in an in-joke) he replies that they are far more likely to be spotted back home in LA. Another good in-joke is that the owner of the restaurant compliments Vaughn that he can 'speak French almost as well as I do' (Michael Vartan, the actor, is French). Vaughn keeps a radio link open to Weiss, who can't believe how lame his chat-up techniques and small talk are. Vaughn turns off the radio link, which means that when Weiss discovers Vaughn's Department of Motor Vehicles record has been hacked, he can't warn them. According to his DMV record, Vaughn's middle initial is C. Weiss tries to talk Vaughn out of giving the real reason the mission failed in his report and even offers to take the blame himself. Vaughn does agree to consult Sydney, because it reflects badly on her. When he meets her to discuss it, they rationalise that if he was to report the incident, he'd be removed as her case officer and they do good work together. They agree to leave it off the report.

Arvin Sloane: Sloane speculates that the investigation into Jack was initiated because someone wants revenge for his murder of Jean Briault (**16,** 'The Prophecy'). Sloane keeps out of the way for much of the episode, apparently happy to let Jack and Kane cancel each other out. He saves Jack however. Sloane visits a lab, paying £10 million in cash for a device that jams the signal from the device in his neck and replaces it with a convincing fake. Sloane is delighted, then shoots the man who made the device. He then flies to the Philippines and goes to a secluded beach house. The door opens and Sloane says he did it and they are free . . . Emily steps out and embraces him, and she's missing her finger.

Jack Bristow: Jack tells Sydney that SD-6 are investigating him. Sloane emails him to suggest that it might have something to do with the death of Briault. Jack goes to Irina and brainstorms with her, trying to follow the lead. He goes to SD-6 to access Kane's bank account to see if the $100 million Sloane paid ended up in the account, but discovers the account is empty just as Kane arrives. He's shot with a tranquilliser dart. He wakes up in the 'conversation room', where Kane tells him she's taking him to London. She suspects Sydney is involved and is waiting for her to return from France. She injects Jack with sodium pentathol – in a few minutes, he'll tell her the truth. But Sloane arrives and drags Kane away. Jack had managed to send an email moments before he was caught. While the account balance is zero now, $100 million had recently left the account. Sloane points out that Kane might not be the blackmailer, as she was the perfect person to frame. Jack notes it's an interesting theory.

Irina Derevko: Irina discovers that Briault made undeclared visits to Peru, and suggests they look at hotel records. When she was in the KGB, she always met her contacts at a hotel. They find footage of Kane and Briault, and discover that Briault opened a bank account in Monaco.

Francie Calfo: Sydney tells Francie that there's no point fantasising about 'Michael from the bank', and Francie takes her for cocktails to commiserate. Francie mentions that she's getting a health test for insurance (this is only a casual reference, but in retrospect it could be the time her DNA was sampled for Project Helix – **36,** 'Double Agent').

Marshall Flinkman: Marshall likens his kidnap experiences to his terrible third grade with its 'lunch money thing'. To thank everyone for rescuing him, he buys Sydney an enormous bunch of flowers, Dixon some cologne and he's bought a tie for Sloane (which he isn't wearing).

Intelligence: Alliance counterintelligence come for Jack. There is a prototype quantum gyroscope and the prototype is being sent to Berlin using Triad courier Carl Shatz. The nearest Alliance cell to Nice is in Geneva. Infosec at the CIA detect Vaughn's DMV licence being tapped.

Office Politics: Weiss returns to work after being shot in Barcelona (see **23**, 'The Enemy Walks In'). He didn't have a near-death experience, but simply saw darkness and now thinks he (and Vaughn) should live for the moment. His dog is called Alan. Ariana Kane realises that Jack and Sydney are in league, but she isn't sure if they are blackmailing Sloane or involved with something more long term. Jack proves that Kane was the blackmailer.

Breaking the Code: Sydney uses the 'mountaineer' code in LA. Dixon collects 47 euros while posing as a priest at Nice Airport. Vaughn has the callsign 'Boy Scout'. He earned this when he forgot his field manual during training. His instructor warned him to 'be prepared'. The CIA station in Nice is 'Baseops'. The number of the bank account Kane opened was 4783479599321. Location letters: C and H.

Plot Devices: The quantum gyroscope missile guidance system can be fitted to old missiles, like 70s-style SCUDs, to make them a precision weapon as dangerous as a cruise missile. The device the Alliance injected into Sloane's neck relays his conversations and vital signs to the Alliance. It tracks his heart and breathing patterns. Marshall has created the Artful Dodger – a device fixed to a ring that can cut through anything. He slices his tie in half to demonstrate it. It allows Sydney to remove the gyroscope from Shatz's pocket. He gives Dixon a collecting tin that has a switch underneath that can control the metal detector at the airport, delaying Sydney so that she can bump into Shatz. The CIA can duplicate the gyroscope in two hours. Sloane buys a device that cracks the algorithm of the Alliance tracking device in his neck. It blocks the real signal, sending fake ambient noises.

Action: Jack's brutal when the agents come for him, shooting one with his own gun, before apparently beating another to death. This segues well into a fantastic car chase, with Sydney at the wheel. She's guided by the CIA, the chase ending when she drives her car into a waiting CIA removal truck. Sydney and Vaughn are attacked by Alliance Security in a Nice restaurant. This time, Vaughn does most of the work. He has a concealed knife, which he uses to kill one man, then takes his gun and kills another two.

Undercover: At Nice Airport, Dixon plays a French priest, collecting for children. He wears shades and carries a collecting tin. Sydney poses as an American punkette with a purple spiky wig and eyelashes, yellow fishnets, a leather dog collar, tattoos and she strips down to a PVC bra.

Trivia: Sydney's suddenly driving a Ford Focus – it's obvious because it keeps zooming in on the logo. Amy Irving is not credited on screen for her appearance as Emily Sloane in this episode.

Music: 'Hella Good' by No Doubt, 'Guess I'm Doing Fine' by Beck and 'Salut Demeure' by Charles-Francois Gounod.

Injuries: Jack is tranquillised and drugged.

The Big Picture: Kane is dragged off and there's evidence that she's the blackmailer. But is she really? Irina led Jack to Peru and to the hotel footage – what did she know already? Does Sloane really just want to be left alone with Emily, to live in a beach hut?

Debrief: 'Your life is complicated, Sydney. Forgive me for trying to make it any easier.' Only *Alias* could tell a story where it's a surprise that a woman we're pretty sure is alive is alive, and that the bad guy is behind it all. If there's one criticism, it's that Vaughn and Sydney's relationship is all over the place in this episode, with Sydney jealous of Alice one minute and agreeing to sleep with Vaughn the next. It's obvious that Weiss spurs Vaughn on, but not what motivates Sydney. Despite that, the scenes between Vartan and Garner are excellent stuff and it's great to see Weiss again. The tension in this episode is extraordinary –

they're building to something big, but what? Jack being exposed? Vaughn and Sydney sleeping together? The last shot is so deliciously evil – you find yourself sympathising with Sloane for just wanting to be with his wife, then you're reminded of the price of getting here, and that it's Emily who paid it.

35
Phase One

Production #E663

1st US Transmission Date: 26 January 2003
1st UK Transmission Date: 2 June 2003

Writer: JJ Abrams
Director: Jack Bender
Guest Cast: Rutger Hauer (Geiger), Terry O'Quinn (Kendall), Jean Pierre Bergeron (Macor), Angus Scrimm (McCullough), Greg Grunberg (Weiss), Elizabeth Penn Payne (Techie #1), Ira Heiden (Techie #2), Kevin Sutherland (Techie #3), Mark Golasso (Medic), Lyle Kilpatrick (Police Officer), Alex Morris (Homeless Vet)

Briefing: Sydney, posing as a call girl, impresses the repulsive Giles Macor. They are on a 747 and she gets him alone, then throttles him until he reveals where Server 47 is hidden. She accesses it, but as she's about to escape, she's attacked.

Twenty-four hours earlier in the CIA operations centre, there's a briefing: Sloane has been replaced as head of SD-6 by Geiger, an unknown quantity. Sydney meets Geiger and its clear that he's on a witchhunt. She discovers Sloane had access to a Server 47 and is sent to the 747, which she escapes from, destroying it. The files she's downloaded contain complete information on the Alliance, but the CIA are cautious. They have to move fast – Jack goes to SD-6 to confirm the intelligence, but is captured. Sydney is called in, but realises it's a trap. She meets Dixon, reveals the truth about SD-6 and he returns to work to discover that the code she's given him gives him access to the Alliance database. The CIA launch an attack, wiping out SD-6, as all the other cells are brought down. Sydney rescues Jack and kills Geiger. As they stand in the ruins of SD-6, Sydney and Vaughn kiss. It's all over, except . . .

Sark phones Sloane to tell him that everything went according to plan and Phase One is complete. Sloane tells him to move to Phase Two. Sark confirms that Francie has been killed and replaced with a double.

OMG: Where to start . . . Sydney in lingerie? The plane going down? Geiger finding the email that outs Jack and Sydney? Dixon's life crashing down around his ears? Jack being tortured? SD-6 being stormed? Sydney and Vaughn kissing? The revelation that this was what Sloane planned? That there's a Phase Two? Or the last shot, with Francie as dead as can be – this is an extraordinary episode.

Mission: Sloane has been missing for five days and has been replaced by Anthony Geiger.

Countermission: The CIA have no information on Geiger. Jack and Sydney go to the CIA to gain Geiger's trust. Sydney is sent to replace Macor's latest call girl. She's to locate Server 47 and transmit its contents to the CIA. This mission is a success – more than the CIA could hope for.

Jack is sent to SD-6 to discover if the security code that's been used there matches the one given in the data they downloaded from Server 47. If it matches, then the intelligence is correct and they can move against the Alliance. Jack is captured by Geiger. Sydney realises she can't go in, so she contacts Dixon, who discovers that the code is genuine and emails confirmation to the CIA. There's a simultaneous strike on every Alliance facility on the planet, wiping out the entire organisation.

Destinations: Sydney boards the Alliance 747 in Barcelona, but this is not shown. The 747 explodes Over The Atlantic (but when Sydney parachutes, it's over dry land, close to a city, in fact – one wonders where the plane crashed), Los Angeles (US) and the Philippines.

Timescale: Francie's restaurant is in profit after only six months. The CIA brief Sydney about Geiger 24 hours before she downs the 747. She flies back from Spain to LA. The CIA launch their attack on all Alliance facilities at 22.00, LA time. Jack and Sydney worked out a code last year to use if one of them was ever compromised. Jack and Geiger met, briefly, in 1987.

Transcripts: Weiss: 'There's a meeting about National Security. You remember that?'

Geiger (to Jack): 'Your files had so many red flags, I thought I was at a Russian airport.'

Sloane: 'Move on to Phase Two.'

Sydney Bristow: Geiger asks Sydney about Danny, who was killed by Security Section. Sydney says that her fiancé was training to be a paediatric cardiologist. He had (Sydney uses the past tense) a younger brother born with a heart condition. Sydney pushes hard for the CIA to move on the Alliance and can't believe that they even have to think about it. She's devastated when Jack is compromised, but calls Will and warns him to get Francie and leave town, which he promises to do. Sydney heads away from the main group attacking SD-6 to save her father. She shoots Geiger five times in the heart, killing him.

Jack Bristow: Jack is suspicious that the intelligence from Server 47 is too good to be true, but realises the importance of proving its authenticity. He gets to the SD-6 server, but is caught by Geiger, who takes him down to the 'conversation room' to be interrogated. He remembers Geiger from Kanagawa in 1987, when they both had dinner. They both remember 'the woman with the club foot'. This is, of course, exactly the tactic that Irina has been using on him – reminding a captor of happier times. It doesn't work on Geiger and he subjects Jack to electric shocks, openly speculating about what he'll do to Sydney. Jack doesn't break, despite being shocked three times. They both know he won't survive a fourth.

Marcus Dixon: Dixon is uneasy about Geiger. Sydney asks him to meet her by some oilwells just outside LA. She apologises that she doesn't have much time and tells him the truth: SD-6 are part of the Alliance – he's been working for the enemy. Dixon is devastated and doesn't believe her.

She asks him to try the security code. If she's right, he'll see for himself. He does just that and finds himself logging on to the Alliance computer network. He phones his wife to tell her he isn't sure when he'll be home. He's bottling up his anger as he waits for the CIA to attack and refuses Marshall's offer of eating pigs in the blanket. When the CIA attack, he pulls Marshall down to safety. As he's dragged away, Sydney assures him it will all soon be over. He snaps that he never wants to see her again.

Will Tippin: Will and Francie are cooking lobsters. Will tells her that he's got a new job at a travel magazine (his CIA cover). Francie is sure she'll be able to find a new waiter and the two of them end up snogging. At the restaurant, later, Sydney can tell something's up and the two confess that they 'made out'. Sydney claims to be shocked and Will tells her later that it didn't feel weird. She tells them to leave LA. However . . .

Francine Calfo: Francie is killed and replaced with an identical double. (This happens almost a day after Sydney warns Will to get her to safety – she's killed at her restaurant and it's never explained why he's not taken her.)

Arvin Sloane: Sloane is described in a CIA briefing as the Acting Director of SD-6. Geiger, his replacement, discovers an email from Sloane which he edited before sending. The sentence he edited out was: 'Jack and Sydney Bristow are double agents'.

Michael Vaughn: Vaughn tells Sydney that all he wants to do is kiss her, that he is distracted in briefings when she's around. Weiss notices Vaughn has a new aftershave and recommends he never wears it again.

Mr Sark: Sark says he is feeling unstrung and worries that Geiger will uncover his and Sydney's secrets. He knows that Geiger is former German intelligence (he doesn't specify East or West). Geiger told Sark Sloane was a traitor.

Intelligence: There are twelve SD cells, SD-1 to SD-12. The CIA know the location of seven, the rest is speculation. The downloads from Server 47 include the location of every SD cell, along with details of their security systems.

The security codes are changed weekly, so if the CIA are to act on their information, they need to act fast. The code is genuine – the CIA, FSB, BAP, MI5, Shin Bet (see **Reality Checks**) launch a co-ordinated operation, simultaneously attacking all twelve cells, Alliance HQ and the residencies of all the partners. SD-3 is based in the Congo. SD-10, SD-5 and SD-4 are all mentioned explicitly by name. Most SD-6 staff are office workers – the CIA are to concentrate on the Security Section agents. Within minutes, the CIA and their allies are in control of every Alliance facility. No one seems to notice Sark isn't there.
Breaking the Code: Server 47 is housed on a 747. 'Take the surface streets they're doing some work on the freeway' is a code worked out 'last year' between Jack and Sydney if either is compromised. The code to disable the SD-6 security system is SA134564SA. The CIA team enters through the B4 level of SD-6 HQ. Location letters: A and E.
Plot Devices: SD-6 has 46 computer servers – except Geiger's found Server 47. This server links all twelve SD cells with a central Alliance computer network. Jack, Sark and Sydney were completely unaware of its existence, only Sloane knew about it. The Alliance purchased a 747 in 1998 and refitted it to house Server 47 in luxurious surroundings for its operator, Giles Macor. It only lands to refuel and pick up call girls from escort agencies in England and Spain to keep Macor entertained. He has a panic button close to his bed (which Sydney disconnects). Server 47 is accessed on a rotating panel behind a painting. Sydney has a Personal Digital Assistant (PDA) that can connect Server 47 to a terminal on a CIA plane. This link has a range of 5,000 feet. Her earrings contain an audio and video link to the CIA. The CIA have a cargo plane that can match the speed of a 747.
Action: Sydney has a fantastic fight in the 747 with one of Macor's bodyguards. The bodyguard uses a pistol and a knife. Sydney blocks using a chopping board that first appeared in episode **19,** 'Snowman'. When Sydney's beaten the guard, Macor emerges, shooting at her. Sydney grabs the fallen guard's gun and shoots out the window on the plane's door. This depressurises the cabin, sucking out the

guards and Macor, who hits the engine and the plane starts to crash dive. Sydney manages to get to a parachute and jumps to safety. The assault on SD-6 HQ sees a huge firefight, with the CIA versus the SD-6 Security Section.
Undercover: Sydney emerges for Macor wearing black bra and briefs, suspender belt and stockings, carrying a riding crop. He isn't impressed, so she emerges again in red bra and briefs, with a matching split baby doll. She quickly puts on a flight suit. For the attack on SD-6 she wears full combat gear, quickly losing the balaclava the others wear.
Reality Checks: The FSB is the Russian counterintelligence organisation. The BAP is Swiss counterintelligence, the Bundesamt für Polizei. MI5 is the British domestic intelligence agency. Shin Bet is the Israeli equivalent.
Background Checks: Rutger Hauer starred opposite Harrison Ford in *Blade Runner*, but is best known in the UK for a series of Guinness adverts.
Trivia: This episode was shown after the Superbowl in the United States.
Music: 'American Woman' by Lenny Kravitz, 'Hands of Time' by Groove Armada, 'Back in Black' by AC/DC and 'Use Me' by Bill Withers.
Injuries: Jack's drugged and tortured by Geiger, who subjects him to electric shocks in the 'conversation room'.
The Big Picture: Ahem. Well, as Sark says, 'The Alliance is gone.' Even before that, there are some questions. There are still Irina's secrets and the Rambaldi mystery to uncover. Sloane and Sark are working together and Sloane has known for some time that Jack and Sydney are double agents. It is not clear what Phase Two is – it involves Sydney, because they've had her roommate killed and replaced with a double.
Debrief: 'Phase One is complete.' An episode that starts with Sydney parading in skimpy underwear just keeps getting better. This is extraordinary stuff, an action movie with gut-wrenching character moments in between the set pieces. The script, acting, direction and music are all impeccable. The episode that ought to be the last episode of the last season just grabs the viewer from the first

moment and keeps going. It's jam-packed, feeling more like a double episode than fifty minutes. It's incredibly carthartic and a hell of an adrenaline rush. And, at the end, when you think they've just finished the series off and you can't imagine how they're possibly going to top that, Sloane appears. This has all been part of his plan and you realise the series to date has only been the prologue. The last shot is beautifully composed – it seems they've gone a twist too far and Francie's been a double agent all along. You follow the smear of blood, thinking it's going to be Will – then you see the real Francie with a bullet through her forehead. That manages to be the most shocking image in one of the most surprising, energetic, daring, complex, emotionally charged hours of television you're ever going to see.

36
Double Agent

Production: #E664

1st US Transmission Date: 2 February 2003
1st UK Transmission Date: 9 June 2003

Writers: Roberto Orci and Alex Kurtzman-Counter
Director: Ken Olin
Guest Cast: Ethan Hawke (CIA Agent James Lennox), Terry O'Quinn (Kendall), Greg Grunberg (Weiss), Olivia D'Abo (Emma Wallace), Constance Brenneman (Christine Phillips), Ira Heiden (Techie #4), Michael Maestro (Arden Jezek), Michael Yavnieli (Techie #2), Joel Guggenheim (Techie #3), Steve Heinze (Ranking Agent), Bru Miller (Negotiator), Terry Urdang (Techie #5), Erik Betts (Guard #2)

Briefing: James Lennox and Emma Wallace are in bed together in Berlin. When Lennox takes a shower, Wallace checks his laptop and becomes suspicious. Lennox attacks her, then contacts Sloane, who tells him to use her to send a message.

At the CIA, Sydney and the others watch as Wallace is dumped on to a street corner strapped with explosives. After a moment, the explosives are set off, live on TV.

Lennox and Wallace were investigating a man called Markovic, who was working on the mysterious Project Helix, something with terrorist applications. Sydney and Vaughn go to Cayo Concha, to download information on Helix and find Lennox if possible. They do so, but Lennox says he was kidnapped four weeks ago. Why didn't Wallace report him missing? Lennox is put in Federal custody when the CIA analyse the data on Helix and discover it's a device that allows a person to become a duplicate of another. When Weiss spots Lennox on video footage of Berlin, he is arrested on suspicion of being a double. The CIA question him, and decide he's innocent. He and Sydney are sent to Poland to locate and destroy the Helix device. They find it and rig it with explosives, but another man claiming to be Lennox arrives. Sydney is ordered to bring both of them in. Instead, she realises that, without the device, Markovic won't be able to change back to his own appearance. When she produces the detonator, the new arrival tries to stop her and the real Lennox shoots him. Back in Los Angeles, Sydney and Vaughn consummate their relationship – watched by a hidden camera.

Mission (reclassified): With SD-6 and the Alliance destroyed, Sydney has no countermissions. As such, all her missions are now for the CIA. Sydney and Vaughn are sent to Cayo Concha to discover what Helix is and to recover Lennox, if possible. The mission is a complete success. They are then sent to Poland, location of the Helix prototype. They are to download the schematics and then destroy it. This mission is also a complete success.

Destinations: Berlin (Germany), Los Angeles (USA), Cayo Concha (Dominican Republic), Poland.

Timescale: Sydney visits SD-6 the morning after Phase One. Lennox and Wallace have been after Markovic for 'a few months' and Lennox was replaced with a duplicate 'four weeks' ago.

Transcripts: Phillips: 'I have a boyfriend.' Weiss: 'Er . . . me too.'

Sydney Bristow: Sydney returns to the ruins of the SD-6 to check it wasn't all a dream. Today, she can go to work at

the CIA and walk through the front door and Vaughn can give her a lift there. Sydney knew Emma Wallace, but not Lennox. She trusts him because he saved her life in Cayo Concha. She tells him that, despite her training, she can't compartmentalise her thoughts and feelings. She'd rather feel it than not feel anything. She lost her fiancé too, of course, and says that she was glad to know Danny as long as she did. She speaks fluent German. She tells Lennox that her hair is 'usually brown'.
Michael Vaughn: Vaughn tells Sydney he has split up with Alice. He sees Sydney's house for the first time and really likes it. He is suspicious of Lennox when he exhibits no symptoms of Post Traumatic Stress Disorder after his torture.
Jack Bristow: Jack is suspicious of Lennox.
Arvin Sloane: Sloane is now on Interpol's most-wanted list.
Intelligence: Lennox and Wallace were in deep cover for a few months investigating Renyo Markovic, who is touting something called 'Helix' to a number of terrorist organisations. Arden Jezek is Markovic's security chief. The CIA have no idea what Helix is and sent Lennox and Wallace in to investigate. Wallace posed as Markovic's driver and they discovered that he answered to someone else, but didn't find out who. They also know that Helix is ready for testing. In Poland, Sydney and Lennox discover that the device has been used twice. The first was Markovic, who made himself look like Lennox. It isn't made clear who the second is – but as Sydney learns there's another duplicate out there and we cut to 'Francie'. The CIA then get a phone call from Lennox. He says that he's the real Lennox and that the one with Sydney is the duplicate. The information about the ocular scan is disinformation.
Office Politics: Christine Phillips of the Clandestine Services Bureau arrives at the CIA. She is very badly shaken by the death of Wallace. James Lennox is one of the CIA's most decorated agents. He's based in LA. He and Wallace were secretly engaged. He is sent to a safehouse, where he passes the time trying to remember all Wallace's aliases and drinking heavily.

Home Front: Sydney introduces 'Francie' to Michael, but – for obvious reasons – 'Francie' doesn't acknowledge that this is the man Sydney said she had a crush on. While Sydney is in Poland, Francie places a camera in the television in her room. Later, she uses the hidden camera to watch Sydney and Vaughn making love.
Breaking the Code: Lennox is being kept in Room 47. Sydney uses her 'mountaineer' code; the CIA HQ is 'Boot Camp'. Location letters: O and O again.
Plot Devices: Emma Wallace is wrapped in C4, which is triggered by a remote detonator. Vaughn injects Jezek with a cardiotoxin that will induce a heart attack in an hour – he gets the antidote if he leads them to Markovic. Lennox is being tortured by having photoreactive acid dripped into his eyes. Project Helix is a gene resequencer that alters a patient's genetic code, making them an exact duplicate of someone else, down to their DNA. It would allow someone like Osama Bin Laden to adopt a new identity and allow someone to create decoys of themselves. It only works on people of a certain 'genetic disposition'. The person who adopts the new identity has to spend a couple of days in a coma. CIA intelligence suggests that there's one flaw – an ocular scan will reveal a slight flaw in the duplicate's iris. To get into the rail carriage containing the Helix device, Sydney uses a fibre-optic camera to locate the tumblers of the lock, then a tiny drill to open it. Sydney carries handcuffs. They have explosives to destroy the rail car. The CIA can send to just Sydney's earpiece and they send a message only to her, not to Lennox.
Action: Sydney fights her way out past some guards with a blind Lennox, who has to shoot a guard when Sydney's overpowered.
Undercover: Sydney wears a very small blue bikini, and lures Jezek into a changing room by making eyes at him and taking off her top. To get into Markovic's base, Sydney wears a light business suit and blond wig. In Poland she and Lennox wear black combat gear and beanie hats (which is handy, because it means the viewer can tell the two Lennoxes apart!).

Background Checks: Breaking through as a young actor in the likes of *Explorers*, Ethan Hawke has since gone on to great fame and acclaim, starring in *Hamlet* (in which he played the prince), *Training Day* and *Snow Falling On Cedars*. Olivia D'Abo appeared in *Wayne's World 2* and *Conan the Destroyer*.

Music: 'Pop goes the Weasel' (traditional), 'Moving in Stereo' by The Cars and, 'God Put a Smile Upon Your Face' by Coldplay.

Injuries: Lennox has acid dripped in his eyes. Yowch! He needs to keep bandages on his eyes at first or he'd go permanently blind. He makes a full recovery when Sydney treats him on the plane back.

The Big Picture: Sloane has had access to Helix and the plan to replace Francie with a duplicate makes sense. Is there a strategic reason to spy on Sydney at home? Does Sloane have wider-ranging plans to use Helix? The big mystery, though, is Markovic. He's a genetic scientist – why pick him to take Lennox's place? How can he fool Wallace, Lennox's fiancée, that he's the genuine article?

Debrief: 'It's nice to put a face with a name.' The series takes a breather, in an episode that could be an instalment of any spy show. Fans of the series complained at the time of release but, once again, it's sexy, action-packed and the guest stars really are stars. It's exactly what the show needs after the explosive events of episode **35**, 'Phase One'. With virtually none of the supporting cast (and those who are there, like Jack, given little to do), this is, on the surface, perhaps the first completely self-contained episode of the show. But Lennox and Wallace are clearly a warning for Sydney and Vaughn as they start up their relationship. Sloane's absence is also rather worrying – you wonder what he's up to when we're not looking! There's something very clever about transforming the 'moment we've all be waiting for' (Vaughn and Sydney getting together) into something sinister, with the unfeeling, voyeuristic Francie watching it along with us.

37
A Free Agent

Production: #E665

1st US Transmission: 9 February 2003
1st UK Transmission: 16 February 2003

Writers: Roberto Orci and Alex Kurtzman-Counter
Director: Alex Kurtzman-Counter
Guest Cast: Christian Slater (Neil Caplan), Terry O'Quinn (Kendall), Yvonne Farrow (Diane Dixon), Lindsey Ginter (Johnson), Tracy Middendorf (Elsa Caplan), Arthur Young (Aaron Caplan), William Dennis Hunt (Claude Shearer), Simon Gray (Peter Kuntz), Paul Michael (Tobias Dennet), Evan Arnold (David), Ahmed A Best (Seth)

Briefing: Sydney tells Vaughn she's going to quit the CIA, but Kendall refuses to accept the resignation. At an aquarium, scientist Neil Caplan and his family are abducted by Sark. Sloane phones Sydney at home to taunt her and then tells Caplan that he's to help him decipher a set of Rambaldi artefacts. Jack discovers the body of Gemler, the man who jammed Sloane's Alliance tracking device. From that, they trace Sloane first to an airport, then to Zurich. Sydney and Vaughn rescue Caplan's family. Sloane, meanwhile, is stealing Caplan's magnetometer from a bank. Sydney and Vaughn arrive as he's leaving, but he has rigged the building to explode. He's leaving – and Sydney's going with him.
OMG: Sloane phones Sydney!
Destinations: Los Angeles (US), Mojave (US), Zurich (Switzerland).
Mission: Sydney and Vaughn are sent to the Mojave airfield to recover the flight data recorder. Sydney is caught, but escapes and completes the mission.
Timescale: It's two weeks since the Alliance fell. Sydney says she has had 'two years of perspective' on the Alliance problem and later tells Dixon she's known the truth about SD-6 for two years (she hasn't, see **33,** 'A Higher Echelon' – set about a month ago, but it wasn't even a year since

she met Vaughn). Caplan's passport expires 07-14-04. Sloane bought a Tuscan villa for him and Emily six months ago. He's been on a 'thirty-year odyssey' after the Rambaldi secrets.

Transcripts: Jack (on Kendall): 'Legally he's right, ethically he's an ass.'

Vaughn: 'Welcome to the CIA.' Marshall: 'I've heard that one before.'

Sydney Bristow: Sydney and Vaughn wake up together and he is amused that she still calls him 'Vaughn', but she protests that she doesn't always. She tells him that she's graduating today. He's amazed she finds time to write papers, but she says that she doesn't intend to spend the rest of her life as a spy – completing her course was a demonstration of that. He correctly guesses that now SD-6 have been destroyed, she's going to quit the CIA. Kendall refuses to endorse her resignation – she's needed to find Sloane. She objects and Kendall says that if she quits she won't be allowed access to her mother. Sydney uses the opportunity to speak to Sloane honestly when he phones her, by saying that she used to fantasise about slashing his throat (although not stated explicitly here, that's how he had Danny killed). She realises when she attends a CIA briefing that her fight can't end until Sloane is beaten. She knows that 'agai' is a four-letter word meaning 'ice cream thickener', a clue in Will's crossword.

Irina Derevko: Irina knows that Sydney is graduating today. She tells her that, if she doesn't quit, she'll refuse to see her anyway. She thinks she is too forgiving.

Jack Bristow: Jack discovers Gemler's body.

Marcus Dixon: Sydney tells Dixon the CIA have cleared him of having any knowledge of SD-6's true purpose and that he's been offered a place with the CIA. He resents Sydney for not trusting him, only telling him the truth when it was convenient and says he never wants to see her again. Returning home, he tells everything to Diane, his wife, who leaves to stay at her sister's. The next day, she returns and he assures her that, while he's lied to her, his love for her and their children is true. He vows never to lie to her again.

Arvin Sloane: Sloane is now wanted in forty countries. He phones Sydney at home and expresses disappointment that she and Jack, the two people he trusted most in the world, were double agents. He tells her that he provided the intelligence that brought down the Alliance and that his involvement with them was simply a means to an end. He was 'with' the Army Corps of Engineers when they uncovered a 500-year-old Rambaldi manuscript that he studied. He's spent thirty years collecting Rambaldi manuscripts and prototypes. He phones Emily and lies to her, saying that he's looking around a Tuscan villa they can retire to, when he's really in a warehouse in Geneva. He tells Sark that he's already bought the villa.
Michael Vaughn: Vaughn can identify an M19-11 from the sound of it being cocked (Sydney says she'd have guessed it was a Beretta M9). He knows a Swiss headhunter for mercenaries who doesn't know he's CIA. Once again speaking French, he offers the man 500,000 (Euros?) for information, then breaks his nose, pours whisky on his head and threatens to set it alight when he refuses to say.
Marshall Flinkman: Marshall loves his new job at the CIA, ordering up some high-tech phone links to the National Security Agency, Department of Defense, FBI and the CIA. He doesn't get a hotline to the President. He still has the urge to weep openly from time to time. His first job is to recover data from Sloane's hard drive, which he previously wiped. He discovers the name Holden Gemler in Sloane's address book. Jack finds Gemler dead – with a creepy flashing eye. Marshall discovers it's an ocular implant with an internal memory. It shows Sloane killing Gemler, then arranging to hire a plane in the Mojave.
Mr Sark: Sark uses another Americanism: 'we'd like for you to'.
Intelligence: Security cameras at the aquarium show Sark kidnapping the Caplans. It's theorised that he is working with Sloane. Neil Caplan is a Cal Tech scientist who was working on knot theory, the study of how geometric objects can relate to each other. No Rambaldi artefacts were recovered from Alliance facilities. The CIA theorise

(correctly) that Sloane is building a Rambaldi weapon. Caplan discovers that each one of the artefacts Sloane has generates a unique magnetic signature. This determines how they fit together, but the variation is tiny and he needs the prototype magnetometer he designed to measure this. It's in the Amcor Bank vault in Geneva. Caplan is surprised when Sloane tells him that's two miles away, as he didn't realise he was in Switzerland. Tracking the flight data, the CIA discover that Sloane's plane stopped off at Bermuda before flying on to Geneva.

Office Politics: Kendall refuses to endorse Sydney's resignation.

Home Front: Neil Caplan has a wife called Elsa and a son, Aaron. They celebrate Aaron's birthday by visiting Long Beach Aquarium, but Neil is preoccupied with his current research which is two months from completion.

Breaking the Code: The magnetometer is stored in box 47-47 at the bank.

Plot Devices: Gemler has a cybernetic eye, a wetware ocular implant with a twelve-hour internal memory. Marshall writes a computer program that can lipread. He once detected a CIA tap because it interfered with an online game he was playing, causing his gnome to skip a frame when it swung its axe. Caplan has built a very sensitive magnetometer. Sloane wears a mask that's lined with carbon powder that allows it to fool an X-ray. Marshall tracks calls made to a mobile phone and traces Sloane from that.

Action: In a nod to *Raiders of the Lost Ark*, Sydney fights a man near a whirring propeller in the Mojave – and the man ends up sliced apart by the blades. Once again, Sydney jumps into a Ford Focus (an SVT) for a car chase, this time through Zurich.

Undercover: Sydney wears a gown and mortar board for her graduation. In the Mojave, Vaughn poses as an arms dealer, Mr Ludlow. Sydney is a maintenance technician in overalls. Sloane poses as an elderly man who wants to deposit $50 million at the Amcor bank.

Reality Checks: Sloane refers to the 'American war against terrorism'.

Background Checks: Christian Slater broke through in Michael Lehmann's deranged *Heathers*, but the peak of his movie fame is probably as a New York-accented Merry Man in *Robin Hood: Prince of Thieves*. Ahmed A Best isn't the same Ahmed Best who played Jar Jar Binks in the *Star Wars* prequels. Tracy Middendorf previously played victimised wives in *Angel* and the second season of *24*.
Trivia: The car chase is rather obviously filmed in LA – if the landscape doesn't give that away, the American numberplates and roadsigns do!
Music: 'My Sundown' by Jimmy Eat World, 'I Can't Forget' by Evan Olsen and 'Get Free' by The Vines.
Debrief: Another pared-down episode in a similar way to **36,** 'Double Agent', without too much of the convoluted double-bluffing. With a more anonymous actor playing Caplan, this might have been a bit dull – relatively, anyway. But Slater is fantastic, bringing real weight and pathos to the role. And this is, after all, the episode where Sloane and Sydney can finally just kick back and be enemies – that's well worth watching.

38
Firebomb

Production: #E666

1st US Transmission: 23 February 2003
1st UK Transmission: 23 June 2003

Writer: John Eisendrath
Director: Craig Zisk
Guest Cast: Terry O'Quinn (Kendall), Greg Grunberg (Agent Eric Weiss), Eli Danker (Kabir), Lina Patel (Alia Gizabi), Yvonne Farrow (Diane Dixon)

Briefing: Sloane forces Sydney to drive the getaway car. Vaughn jams the signal from the remote detonator, but Sark rescues Sloane and they get away from Sydney. Getting home, Vaughn and Sydney discover bugs in their apartment. Someone close to them is spying on them!

Sloane's latest Rambaldi device is ready: a neutron bomb. Sloane goes to see an Afghan warlord, Kabir, and offers to kill one of his enemies. Kabir picks his ex-wife – who Sydney and Vaughn are approaching to see if she has information on Kabir. Sydney rescues Kabir's ex-wife from the neutron-bomb attack which kills more than sixty people. Sydney goes to Afghanistan to secure the device, but is captured by Kabir.

Vaughn persuades Dixon to work with the CIA to save her. Kabir is killed and the neutron bomb secured, but Sloane escapes. Back in Geneva Sark can't understand Sloane's plan. Sloane reveals that Kabir had a missing Rambaldi manuscript, which Sloane now owns.

OMG: People in a church suddenly burst into flames – the Rambaldi device in action.

Mission: Sydney is sent to get information on Kabir's HQ from Dixon and fails. She and Vaughn go to Mexico City to get the information from Alia Gizabi. They extract her and Gizabi gives them the information. Sydney is then sent with a Delta Force team to Kabir's HQ. She's to secure the Rambaldi device before the special forces move in to take out Kabir. Sydney fails and she's captured. Dixon and Vaughn storm Kabir's base and rescue her.

Destinations: Zurich (Switzerland), Los Angeles (US), Kandahar (Afghanistan), Mexico City (Mexico), then back to Kandahar (Afghanistan).

Timescale: Rambaldi lived in the sixteenth century. Dixon foiled Kabir's plans 'last year' (which begs the question when – he's been pretty busy!).

Transcripts: Sydney (to Sloane): 'The CIA has a hit list. Thirty-five people worldwide its agents are allowed to kill . . . You're one of them. Which means when I kill you, I won't even be breaking the law.'

Sydney Bristow: Sydney can't contain her contempt for Sloane when they share a car, but couches it in terms of how much the CIA want him. Kendall accuses her of choosing not to kill Sloane when she had the chance, but she counters that he had satellite surveillance, unlike the CIA, which she doesn't think are doing everything they can. Later, though, she is reluctant to go to Dixon to ask about Kabir, wanting to respect his wish to have nothing more to do with intelligence work.

When Kabir's ex-wife, Alia Gizabi, refuses to go with Sydney, she knocks her out and carries her to the waiting van. This saves her life as the church is attacked with the Rambaldi device. When she sees the devastation, Gizabi agrees to tell them what she knows. However, her intelligence is out of date and Sydney is trapped in the building, captured by Kabir's men. Kabir tells her that if she admits she's CIA he might let her live. Some time passes – days? – before Kabir returns, threatening to cripple Sydney by taking a chisel to her kneecaps. As he places the chisel on her knee, Vaughn arrives and shoots him.

Sydney takes a bath and Vaughn brings her wine. She can't believe that every time they think they've seen the worst, something else comes along.

Sydney has never seen *Predator*, but seems sympathetic to Marshall's view that *Twins* isn't a good film.

Marcus Dixon: Sydney goes to see Dixon to ask him where Kabir's base is, but he won't help. She only wants a location, but he refuses. He's drawn the line.

When Sydney is captured, Vaughn goes round – the first time the two have been formally introduced – and persuades him to help Sydney. Dixon joins Vaughn in a mission to extract Sydney. He then takes up the offer from the CIA to work for them. He tells Sydney he can't judge her for not telling him the truth about SD-6. He's not sure what this means for his relationship with Diane.

Michael Vaughn: Sydney and Vaughn go to a baseball game. Vaughn gets a phone call from Weiss and it starts echoing and repeating itself. The apartment is bugged. He persuades Dixon to accompany him to Afghanistan to save Sydney – and it's Vaughn who shoots Kabir.

'Francie Calfo': 'Francie' watches Sydney exercising. She tells Sydney (who asks the direct question) that she hasn't slept with Will. Francie asks her why she's been acting oddly and Sydney is relieved – she thought Francie was. Francie tells her to talk to her more and, as soon as Sydney is in the shower, Francie calls Sark, telling him they found the bugs. Sark tells her to set someone up. She does so – murdering a plumber who came to the apartment and planting spare bugs in his locker.

Jack Bristow: When Jack asks Marshall to do something and he says 'a please would be nice', Jack just glares.

Will Tippin: Will makes a presentation to the Director of the CIA about Kabir. He feels a little out of his depth when he learns that two analysts from the Kennedy School at Harvard will be there too. But he runs rings round them and the CIA go with his suggestion.

Arvin Sloane: Having acquired the magnetometer, Sloane's Rambaldi artefact can be completed by Caplan. The artefact is so powerful that Sloane warns Sark not to let Caplan test it. Sark tests it himself, and is disconcerted by the result. The device is a powerful weapon. Sloane has another Rambaldi manuscript, one with a large hole in the centre of the top page. He goes to see Kabir, a Pashtun warlord, and is blindfolded so that he doesn't know where the base is. When Kabir says he doesn't do business with Americans, Sloane describes himself as a 'man with no country and few alliances' who believes the existing world order is corrupt. As a gesture of good faith, he gives Kabir an item (it could be a pen) that once belonged to Khushal Khan Khattak, a seventeenth-century warrior poet revered by Kabir. He admires a sixteenth-century carving of an ahrat – a destroyer of enemies. To prove himself, Sloane offers to destroy one of Kabir's enemies. Kabir picks his ex-wife in Mexico City and a (rather nervous) Sark is sent to demonstrate the device. When Gizabi is reported dead, Kabir agrees to wire Sloane $40 million, and gives him the ahrat – Sloane has destroyed his enemy. Sloane talks to Sydney after she's captured by Kabir saying he's always considered her his proudest achievement. He and Sark leave before her fate is sealed, though. Sark can't understand why Sloane has handed the neutron bomb to Kabir. Sark smashes open the ahrat and inside is a fragment of Rambaldi manuscript – one that matches the hole in the top page he already had.

Intelligence: There are 35 people in the world that CIA operatives are authorised to kill on sight and Sloane is one of them. Swiss banking laws mean that the CIA can't find out what Sloane stole (while they value discretion, you'd think that, as Sloane wasn't really a customer, one of their staff was killed and the building was rigged with explosives, they'd try harder to help). Sloane is spotted heading towards the Helmand Valley territory of Ahmad Kabir, a Pashtun warlord formerly associated with the Taliban, who controls an opium trade worth hundreds of millions of dollars. Last year, Marcus Dixon foiled Kabir's attempt to acquire Soviet surface-to-air missiles. When Dixon refuses to tell them where Kabir is based, the CIA need a new source of information. Two Harvard analysts suggest that Sharif Rabani, another warlord, hates Kabir and will sell them the information. Will counters this by saying that people like him haven't been much use. He suggests contacting Alia Gizabi, Kabir's ex-wife, who works at the Vatican Embassy in Mexico City. By coincidence, Kabir chooses his ex as the target of Sloane's weapon.

Weiss picks up an ECHELON intercept that Mexico City is targeting for an attack. Satellite surveillance picks up a hotspot in the church that disappears as quickly as it appeared. Sixty-two people are killed (or possibly 61 – Gizabi is listed as dead but survived). It's reported in the press as the result of a 'doomsday weapon'. Sark was spotted in Mexico City and tracked as far as Kabul before disappearing.

Office Politics: Vaughn apparently has operational control of the Swiss police – he can order them to stand down to let Sydney leave with Sloane. The CIA have 'cleaning crews' that sweep a room for bugs. Sydney doesn't believe that the CIA are doing enough to search for Sloane – they haven't got a satellite tasked for the mission.

Plot Devices: Sloane has a remote detonator. Marshall calculates that the Friedlin Model 42-C safe that the Amcor Bank has will block the radio signal and Vaughn puts the bomb in the safe. Sydney drives a blue Ford Focus ZX5 – as Sloane throws her the keys, this is his Focus, not the blue Ford Focus she drove up to the bank, see **37,** 'A

Free Agent'. Francie drives a blue Ford Focus SVT like Sydney's in **43,** 'Second Double'. Marshall states here that he's thinking of buying a Ford Focus. Yes, Ford receive a credit for supplying vehicles for the series.

Rambaldi designed and constructed the components of a suitcase neutron bomb in the sixteenth century. It has a capacity of 100 megawatts – it only needs 20 per cent of that for the Mexico City attack. If the device is so much as a microtesla out, there will be disastrous consequences. It's a directional weapon that acts like a microwave – all living matter in the area burns up, but it doesn't affect wood or cloth. It raises people's body temperature by 2,000 degrees, burning them up into fine ash. Identification is impossible afterwards. It works through walls, concrete and steel. There's no defence. It knocks out computer circuitry and, Marshall postulates, could be used to down aircraft. The device is retrieved from Kabir's base by the CIA. Sloane has a Rambaldi manuscript with a large hole in it. He fills it.

A bug is found in a light switch in Sydney's apartment. It was built by Marshall, who identifies it by his trademark Superman symbol he soldered into the circuitry (it's an M, not an S). It operates using an MD-14 data adapter, which cloaks the signal, making it undetectable by bug-killers and is a burst transmitter, meaning it saves up data then transmits it in one go, rather than sending a continuous stream of data. For her mission to Kandahar, Marshall gives Sydney the Cold Suit, a form-fitting outfit that makes her invisible to infrared cameras.

Action: Sloane jumps from the getaway car to Sark's van, which then rams the car, forcing it off the road. Sydney fights guards in Kandahar, is outnumbered by them and forced to surrender. When Dixon rescues her, he's in a vicious mood, wading through Kabir's men and even punching one of them off a balcony. They dodge fire from Kabir's men and escape in a truck.

Undercover: Sydney disguises herself as an elderly church-goer with a veil, walking stick and string of pearls, as well as a mask. In Kandahar she wears the Cold Suit (see **Plot Devices**).

Music: 'Freedom' by David Gray and 'On a High' by Duncan Sheik.
The Big Picture: Sloane needs money – and a lot of it. He already has the $100 million in bearer bonds he stole from SD-6 as part of the fake blackmail and now he has $40 million from Kabir. The attack in Mexico City is reported on television. The CIA quickly recover the Rambaldi device responsible. What, if anything, is reported about this success?
Debrief: The episode has an enormous coincidence at the heart of it: Sark testing the weapon on Kabir's wife the *exact moment* Sydney shows up to talk to her. Sloane's motives are also a little vague – he takes the $40 million from Kabir, but does he really just want the ahrat? If so, surely there's an easier way to acquire it, one that doesn't involve handing an Afghan warlord the rather useful neutron weapon he's spent two years building? But this is another great episode, one that covers a lot of ground, is a good showcase for Carl Lumbly's portrayal of Dixon and has a fantastic set-piece as the weapon is tested.

39
A Dark Turn

Production: #E667

1st US Transmission: 2 March 2003
1st UK Transmission: 30 June 2003

Writer: Jesse Alexander
Director: Ken Olin
Guest Cast: Terry O'Quinn (Kendall), Richard Lewis (Agent Mitchell Yaeger), Ravil Isyanov (Karpachev), Thomas Urb (Stuka), Michael Yavnieli (Techie), Yoshia Be (Chinese Captain), Michael Komurov (Russian Bodyguard), Jon Dixon (CIA Officer), Ryan O'Quinn (Local Driver)

Briefing: A lift car plummets over forty floors to the ground, killing a man and his two bodyguards. Sark reaches into the wreckage to steal the man's wallet. Irina explains that he's after Rambaldi's study of the human heart. She persuades Jack to let her join him on a field mission to find the document first and they go to Bangkok and Hong Kong, where they secure the manuscript.

Vaughn is under suspicion of espionage and Sydney realises he's up to something. She learns that he's been independently investigating Irina and concluded she's clean.

In Panama, Jack sets up a plan to capture Sloane using Irina as bait, but she double-crosses him. She meets up with Sloane and thanks him for extracting her.

OMG: Irina's let out and makes the most of it – first a lethal undercover mission, then her agenda becomes clear.

Mission: Irina and Jack are sent to recover Rambaldi's study of the human heart. The trail leads them to Bangkok and Hong Kong. The mission is a complete success. They are then sent, with two Delta Force guards, to Panama to capture Sloane. However, things don't go according to plan – Jack's plan, anyway.

Destinations: Russia (presumably), Bangkok (Thailand), Hong Kong (China), Los Angeles (USA), Panama.

Timescale: The CIA have known about Vaughn's covert activities for three months, but he says his investigation has lasted six.

Transcripts: Sydney: 'Weiss, have you seen Vaughn?' Weiss: 'That's all I am to you. Just a conduit to Vaughn.' Sydney: 'No, I'm just –' Weiss: 'Have you ever seen Vaughn and said, "Hey, where's Weiss?"'

Irina: 'I never understood how you managed to avoid getting caught up in it [the quest for Rambaldi].' Jack: 'I had something neither of you [Irina and Sloane] did.' Irina: 'Sydney.'

Irina: 'We should get to bed.' Jack: 'Yeah, we should.'

Sydney Bristow: Vaughn is trying to teach Sydney ice hockey at a local rink. She hasn't skated since she was five, when her mother took her. She says that sooner or later they're going to have to have a conversation, but Vaughn insists her mother isn't an issue for him. She's called into the CIA and made to sign a document. She's questioned by

Mitchell Yeager, a counterintelligence threat analyst, who is investigating Vaughn. She is asked whether she has an intimate relationship with Vaughn and refuses to answer, but he is unimpressed, asking her to choose between national security and her boyfriend. He asks her to scan Vaughn's laptop the next time she has access to it. Vaughn is surprised he wasn't consulted about Irina and Jack's mission to Bangkok. Sydney knows that it's because he's being investigated, but lies to him, saying it's no big deal. When he takes a shower, she turns on his laptop – but stops herself from scanning the hard disk. Later, she sees him pocket a piece of paper in the office and gets suspicious. When Vaughn explains, she goes back to Yaeger and hands him the scanning device – she trusts Vaughn.

Before Irina goes to Panama, she summons Sydney to her cell. She wants Sydney to know that whatever happens, she loves her.

Weiss tips off Sydney that Yaeger plans to formally charge Vaughn. She tracks Vaughn down to a bar.

Michael Vaughn: The CIA know Vaughn has been making unauthorised contact with Vladimir Pograski for the last three months. Vaughn has changed his cellphone a number of times, which is suspicious behaviour. It's believed he has downloaded illegal Xenon encryption software on to his laptop. When Sydney confronts him he says that when people question his loyalty it makes him insane. He was about to give her the key to his apartment (which is a little premature – she's not even been there, see **41,** 'Endgame'. For the last six months, Vaughn has been researching Irina. He's been horrified that he's had to work with his father's killer. He's paid for the investigation himself and this has involved unauthorised contact with FSB officers (see **35,** 'Phase One') and trips to Istanbul, Prague and Krakow. He downloaded Xenon to read KGB files. But, after all his investigations, he concludes that Irina is clean.

Jack Bristow: Jack, perhaps understandably, gets a little shirty when Kendall casually refers to Irina as his ex-wife, although he claims it doesn't bother him. When Irina asks why Jack hasn't persuaded Sydney to leave the CIA, he notes that their daughter can be stubborn. Jack says that he's had twenty years to reflect on Irina Derevko and he knows when she's lying. He believes she wants to help recover the manuscript. Kendall notes that he and Jack seem to have swapped over – Jack's usually the one who doesn't trust Irina – and is sceptical, but approves the operation. When Irina says Jack and Sloane were true friends, Jack notes that they shared an unsentimental patriotism and a devotion to their wives. He says Sloane changed and it was his obsession with Rambaldi that changed him.

Jack and Irina travel to Panama to catch Sloane, using the Rambaldi manuscript as bait. Although Kendall would have him courtmartialled for it, Jack cuts out Irina's subdermal tracking device. It will show up if she's scanned. Irina flatters Jack – he's smarter than Kendall. The two look into each other's eyes, then make love. Irina gets into Sark's car and the CIA track it via satellite. The satellite feed is cut and Jack has to admit to Kendall that he can't activate Irina's tracking device. Jack is left chasing a decoy car, as Irina meets Sloane. Kendall confirms that the Rambaldi manuscript has been stolen from CIA custody.

Irina Derevko: Irina knows Stuka, the last-known owner of the Rambaldi manuscript that Sloane is currently after. She says she could get it if she met Stuka face to face. She persuades Jack of the benefit – if it leads to Sloane's capture, then Sydney will be able to leave the CIA. She is injected with a miniature tracking beacon. She doesn't flinch when Marshall injects her and he's impressed how tough she is. Irina speaks Thai and Chinese. Irina goes on an operation, with Jack watching at the bar. She finds Stuka playing a game with a very young Thai woman, stabbing at the table between her splayed fingers and terrifying her. Irina takes the girl's place and doesn't react as Stuka plays the game. She grabs the knife, stabs his hand and asks him where the manuscript is. He tells her it's in Hong Kong and she slashes his throat anyway, stabs two more guards and escapes. She misses a fourth man – but Jack shoots him.

Yaeger met Irina when she was married to Jack and found her to be charming. She remembers meeting Sloane for the first time, when Sloane came round for dinner. Irina says that for years she was caught up in the same obsession for finding meaning in the Rambaldi manuscripts and artefacts as Sloane. Irina thanks Jack for raising Sydney.

In Hong Kong, Irina grabs the Rambaldi manuscript when she gets the chance. She's later seen eagerly making notes on the manuscipt, using a lot of Post-it notes.

In Panama, she meets Sark, and gets into his car with her guards. He shoots the guards and there's a chase with a Delta Force helicopter. Using a decoy car, Sark evades the CIA. He meets up with an ambulance – and Sloane. Irina thanks him for extracting her. Back in LA, Kendall finds the satchel Jack brought that should contain the Rambaldi manuscript is stuffed full of Post-it notes instead.

Will Tippin: Will tells Francie that Sydney's in the CIA, that he's seen her in action and that he's a CIA analyst – then he wakes up. He tells Vaughn about his dream and Vaughn assures him it's common and will pass.

'Francie Calfo': The fake Francie hypnotises Will into giving her the codes for the KH11 CIA satellite tasked to track Sloane. She tells him to forget her questions and to just remember having the best sex of his life. This intelligence is used to cut the CIA's surveillance of Sark's limousine once Irina is inside it.

Arvin Sloane: Sloane is low key this week – he receives the news that Irina has made contact and greets her when Sark extracts her.

Intelligence: Luri Karpachev was a Russian arms dealer who had contacts with SD-6 and with Irina. Irina thinks that Sloane killed him for a key card to his home safe. Sloane thought Karpachev had a Rambaldi manuscript, his study of the human heart. He acquired it in 1993, but sold it on to Ilya Stuka. Irina finds Stuka, who says he traded the manuscript to Chang in Hong Kong for opium rights (as Chang is the most common surname in the world and she seems to know who he's talking about, it's clearly an associate of theirs). Stuka thought Irina was dead. She is sure word will get back to Sloane that she was in Bangkok. She's right – Sark reports the sighting the next morning and contacts Irina via an email account, looking to purchase the Rambaldi manuscript. The KH11 satellite is now tasked with searching for Sloane.

Office Politics: Jack is given control of a Delta Force team to take down Sark and Sloane in Panama.

Breaking the Code: The lift at the beginning is heading for the 47th (and top) floor. Will gives the satellite codes as X8471-GY79863. However, the viewer sees the map he's remembering and it reads X8471-GY7983. Later, on Jack's display it's X48471-GY79863. Sloane's ambulance is number 027.

Plot Devices: There's a new Rambaldi manuscript in play – his study of the human heart, which comes wrapped in a leather satchel. It's part of Rambaldi's obsession with immortality. Jack and Irina recover it from Hong Kong. But Irina apparently steals it, then stuffs the satchel with Post-its. Irina is injected with a subdermal tracking device. In Hong Kong, they knock out a senior Chinese official by fitting him with a fake radio mike that sprays knockout gas. Jack has a pen that squirts acid that he uses to cut into a display case. Yaeger gives Sydney a tiny scanner that can read the hard disk of a laptop. All CIA cars have tracking devices fitted. Xenon is illegal encryption software.

Action: Irina fights her way out of Stuka's bar. In Panama, a Delta Force limousine chases Sark's car – and its decoy.

Undercover: Irina goes to Stuka's bar dressed in a tiny leopard-print dress and black leather choker.

Music: 'Freedom' by David Gray and 'On a High' by Duncan Sheik.

Injuries: Irina has a tracking device injected and then cut out, without apparently feeling any pain.

The Big Picture: Irina and Sloane are working together. But how long ago was this arranged? And, of course, what are they up to?

Debrief: 'A study of the human heart.' Seeing Irina in action is great fun, as she goes on a traditional Sydney-style mission, but *hacks* her way out of it. Sydney, for once, stays at home. Her 'plot' this week doesn't have the action and explosive revelations of the Jack and Irina story, but it's good grounding for her relationship with Vaughn. There are wonderful parallels between all the various characters – all the lovers and ex-lovers who can't trust each other, the demented family relationships. There's the great irony that just as Vaughn concludes that he's been torturing himself over nothing because Irina's on the level, Irina is smiling and joining Sloane.

40
Truth Takes Time

Production: #E668

1st US Transmission: 16 March 2003
1st UK Transmission: 7 July 2003

Writer: J R Orci
Director: Nelson McCormick
Guest Cast: Terry O'Quinn (Kendall), Amy Irving (Emily Sloane), Kevin Sutherland (CIA Agent), Christopher Curry (Heinz Bruckner)

Briefing: Sydney and Irina are in the middle of a shootout. Sydney shoots at her mother and her report states that a woman's been shot. Five days earlier, Jack was put in charge of a task force that's tracking down Irina and Sloane. Using a second tracking device he planted, the CIA track Irina to a biotech firm in Stuttgart. Sydney and Vaughn are sent to capture her, but Sark spots their team and the two escape, after blowing up the building. They have stolen an encrypted DNA database. They tip off Sloane, and he and Emily join them, to her horror.

Emily goes to the CIA office in Florence and asks to speak to Sydney. She agrees to trap Sloane and goes home wearing a wire. When it comes to it, though, she can't betray her husband. As the CIA tactical team storm their house, Sydney shoots Irina in the shoulder. Emily leaves with Sloane – and is shot by Dixon, who was aiming for her husband. Sloane and Irina escape by helicopter.

OMG: Emily is killed.
Mission: Sydney and Vaughn attempt to catch Irina in Stuttgart and prevent her from stealing the genetics database. They fail, rather spectacularly – their team is spotted by Sark (who beats up Vaughn); Irina gets away from under their noses, and the biotech building is blown up (presumably killing many people inside). In Tuscany, the mission is to capture Sloane and Irina. Again they fail, but Sydney does recover the genetic database. Emily is killed by Dixon.
Destinations: Tuscany (Italy), Stuttgart (Germany), Florence (Italy), Los Angeles (USA).
Timescale: Sloane tells Emily it's a couple of months since he learned Irina was alive.
Transcripts: Dixon: 'No one can be blamed for trusting their own mother.'

Irina (to Sloane): 'You may need to think of yourself as an honourable husband, a father figure. But I don't. I will never see that man in you, which frankly is why we have this agreement.'
Sydney Bristow: Jack tells Sydney that the operation in Panama didn't go according to plan and that Irina was colluding with Sloane. Sydney wants to believe that Sloane has set Irina up – but she took the Rambaldi manuscript with her. Sydney goes to her cell, where Dixon comforts her. Irina has left her earrings behind with a note saying she wants Sydney to have them (she already had them at the end of episode **27,** 'The Indicator', but presumably she gave them back to her mother when Irina was reprieved). Vaughn doesn't believe that Sydney should be part of the task force to catch Sloane and Irina, because she might hesitate if called on to shoot Irina, although Sydney assures him that she won't. In Stuttgart, Sydney goes after her mother when Irina calls her name. Jack later speculates that Irina was trying to save Sydney from the bomb, but Sydney doubts that. Sydney hasn't bought Vaughn a present since they started dating. Sydney is the only person that Emily wants to talk to. Sydney reaffirms what she said at Emily's funeral – she's the closest thing she has to a mother. She gets Emily to agree to wear a wire, return to

their villa and signal when Sloane is in place. Sydney will be ready with a tactical team. She leads the team and when the moment comes doesn't hesitate, shooting Irina in the shoulder (the left shoulder, just where Irina shot her, see **23,** 'The Enemy Walks In'). After returning home, Vaughn and Sydney go to bed, but she doesn't want to talk. Irina's earrings are on the bedside table and start signalling in morse – the message is 'truth takes time'.

Jack Bristow: Jack is now in operational command of the task force that's looking for Sloane and Irina. He planted a tracking device in Irina after removing the one she knew about. Marshall is baffled how he managed this. As Kendall points out later, planting a second tracking device means that Jack never trusted Irina, despite assuring Kendall he did. Jack counters that he's always objected to the way Kendall forced Sydney to confront Irina. Kendall can have his title of operational command back when Jack is sure Irina won't harm Sydney again.

Arvin Sloane: Sloane says Emily is in remission. He takes her to a Tuscan villa he said he bought the previous week (he's lying – or he lied to Sark, see **37,** 'A Free Agent'). Irina phones Sloane and Emily takes the call. Irina warns him that she's being tracked, and suggests Sloane leave his house in case he has been too. He quickly bundles Emily off to his private jet – which she knew nothing about – and a rendezvous with Irina, who Emily knows from when Jack was married to her, but thought was dead. Sloane says he is pursuing a truth, one that, among other things, will allow Emily to live cancer-free. Forever. Emily walks into the CIA office in Florence, saying she's the wife of Arvin Sloane, and that she'll only talk to Sydney. She tells her that Sloane was the only thing that gave her hope during her battle with cancer. He has told her his plan – which is to find out what Rambaldi was working on. He says he's doing it for them, but she can't have his crimes on her conscience. She'll lead them to Sloane, if the CIA promise not to execute him. He seems to consider quitting when Emily makes her objections clear. He asks Irina to buy him out – the contacts, the artefacts, the assets. He is serious, giving her the genetics database that's in his safe. He tells Emily that there is no point continuing if she is not with him and she reveals that she's wearing a wire, but she chooses to go with him. They make their way through a secret passage to Sark's waiting helicopter.

Marcus Dixon: Dixon doesn't blame Sydney for trusting her mother (see **Transcripts**). In Tuscany, Dixon has his crosshairs on Sloane's back, and fires – but (Sark's?) helicopter passes overhead and he moves ever so slightly. Emily is killed and Dixon is shocked by what he's done.

Irina Derevko: Irina infiltrates Brucker Biotech, but the tracking device Jack planted has tipped off the CIA. She downloads the encrypted genetic database and orders Sark to blow up the building. As she's leaving, she shouts to Sydney, prompting her daughter to chase her out of the building just before it's destroyed. When Sloane offers to sell Irina his part of their operation, Irina suspects either a trap or that she's underestimated his love for Emily. She and Sydney shoot at each other, neither apparently concerned if they hit the other. Sydney shoots Irina, who drops the genetic database disk.

'Francie Calfo': The fake Francie doesn't know the name of the quarterback she used to date in college – Sydney thinks it was either Frank or Hank. Francie has bought Vaughn a tie.

Will Tippin: Will goes to dinner with Francie, Sydney and Vaughn.

Michael Vaughn: Vaughn is debriefed by Yeager and his security clearance is downgraded. Jack keeps him in his task force and makes sure he keeps him field-graded. In Stuttgart, Vaughn is comprehensively out-fought by Sark, who kicks him down a stairwell then shoots him in the chest – and his bulletproof vest – and would have shot him in the head, if Sydney hadn't arrived.

Intelligence: The CIA believe that Irina somehow contacted Sloane while in custody. As Jack knows Irina, he's been given operational control of the effort to capture them. Irina says she still has loyal agents in St Petersburg, Madrid and Cairo. Sloane, Irina and Sark are after a genetic database. They target Brucker Biotech, the German equivalent of the human genome project, who have spent fifteen years developing high-resolution DNA maps. The database can be stored on one disk, is encrypted and (illegally) contains the DNA records of millions of private citizens. 'Genome', 'genetics' and related words are added to the ECHELON watch list.

Office Politics: Kendall refuses Emily's request to waive the death penalty for Sloane. Vaughn argues that they should agree and Jack – whose call it is – concurs.

Breaking the Code: The morse message that comes through Irina's earrings is a repeating pattern: kestimetruthta, which is when broken up, of course, 'truth takes time'.

Plot Devices: Jack planted a passive tracking device on – or in – Irina. It won't send out a signal until a designated time and is disabled with an electric shock from resuscitation gear. Sark has a powerful explosive charge he uses in Stuttgart. Marshall speculates that Sloane could be developing a DNA-specific weapon, one that could be introduced to a water supply to target just one individual. He could be developing a virus.

Action: A great, if one-sided, fight between Sark and Vaughn in Stuttgart, followed by a big explosion. The CIA storm Sloane's villa, blasting at guards, Sloane and Irina. They escape, to be rescued by Sark in a helicopter. Dixon, in a sniper's position, aims for Sloane, but hits Emily.

Undercover: Irina dons a severe business suit and puts her hair in a bun to play Scandinavian businesswoman Ms Hertzgar, who works for Schtat Pharmaceuticals. Sark is her assistant, Peter Garo.

Music: 'Amazing' by Josh Kelley and 'So Are You to Me' by eastmountainsouth.

Injuries: Vaughn is hit in the chest by a bullet, but is wearing a bulletproof vest.

Sydney shoots Irina in the left shoulder. It's the first time Irina registers any pain, so we can be sure she's in agony. Dixon shoots Emily in the back, killing her instantly.

The Big Picture: Sloane leaves Emily's body behind – clearly, from what he knows of Rambaldi, his immortality experiments prolong life, but they can't restore it. Sloane has been doing everything he does out of love for Emily. With her gone, what will he do now? Sydney wishes Irina was dead but keeps her mother's earrings close to her bed. **Debrief:** 'All that matters is this.' A trick beginning and a set-up early on that asks whether Sydney would be prepared to shoot her mother. Astute viewers know by now, though, that *Alias* is never as straightforward as that and can guess we're in for a twist. What we get instead of a simple moral dilemma is a sophisticated meditation on Sloane's motives – not only is he Emily's anchor, but she's what's spurring him on. Without her, he has no redeeming features, no moral compass. She's almost convinced him to quit (we never doubt that he means it) but, as she dies, so does any hope that he'll be redeemed, and we can see that. So can he, and that's his tragedy. It's a stroke of genius to have Emily killed by Dixon, the one man in the series who instinctively and unquestioningly understands the value of his wife's love and trust.

41
Endgame

Production: #E669

1st US Transmission: 30 March 2003
1st UK Transmission: 14 July 2003

Writer: Sean Gerace
Director: Perry Lang
Guest Cast: Greg Grunberg (Eric Weiss), Tracy Middendorf (Elsa Caplan)

Briefing: Emily's body is brought back to the US and Dixon reveals he's going to ask for a transfer. Sloane and Irina's trail has gone cold. Sydney decides to talk to Elsa Caplan again, but she's reluctant to help. Sydney discovers why – she's a Russian agent, sent to seduce Neil Caplan. She loves him and reveals that her Russian bosses have triggered a cyanide capsule. Sydney disobeys Jack and goes to Russia then Spain to find Caplan and rescues him.

Sloane gets satellite intelligence that shows that Dixon shot Emily. He gets the fake Francie to kill Dixon's wife, Diane, in a car bomb attack.

OMG: Sloane kills Dixon's wife.

Mission: Sydney isn't given a mission – she takes it upon herself to talk to Elsa Caplan, then follow that intelligence trail to Russia, then to Spain. Vaughn joins her and they rescue Caplan in the nick of time.

Destinations: Los Angeles (USA), Saria (Spain), Moscow (Russia).

Timescale: Sydney's encounter with the valley girls (see **Undercover**) takes place on a Tuesday. It's two months since Neil Caplan was kidnapped. Elsa says she met Neil seven years ago and he says he was recruited by the NSA six years ago – although he also implies he knew she was an agent all along.

Transcripts: Weiss: 'Do you know how spoiled you are? You know, a drawer! I wish I had a girlfriend to say, "Hey, do you want a drawer?"'

Sydney (on Elsa): 'She turned herself in.' Jack: 'She's not the first.'

Jack (to Vaughn): 'Just because you've gotten comfortable with my daughter doesn't mean you should be comfortable with me. If you don't report your next contact with Sydney immediately, I will take action that you will regret.'

Marcus Dixon: Dixon and Sydney escort Emily's coffin back to the US for repatriation. He confesses that he didn't have a clear shot. Sydney tells him she could have made the same mistake and his wife Diane insists that he's not responsible for Emily's death, Sloane is. Dixon has put in a request to be transferred to the Directorate of Intelligence – a desk job that might mean moving to Texas or Washington DC. By the end of the episode, Diane has told Dixon that he shouldn't transfer. They go out for a meal with Vaughn and Sydney. As she leaves, Diane's car is destroyed by a car bomb, killing her.

Sydney Bristow: Sydney goes to see Elsa Caplan and suggests that she undergoes hypnotic regression. Elsa takes offence, suggesting that Sydney was implying she wasn't doing enough. However Elsa's motives soon become clear – she's a Russian agent. Sydney takes her at her word, though, believing that she loves her husband. Elsa taps out the locator code for Neil's tracking device using morse code. Sydney then goes to a drugstore, knowing that a CIA team will be following her. She sends a message to Vaughn via Weiss's cellphone (see **Breaking the Code**) then creates a disguise (see **Undercover**) and gets past the CIA men.

She goes to Russia and meets an unnamed contact, who gives her the tracking device for $50,000. Sydney speaks Russian. She goes on to Spain, where she's joined by Vaughn, and they rescue Caplan, removing the cyanide pill seconds before it's about to be triggered.

Jack Bristow: Jack doesn't think there is a clear move to make in the hunt for Sloane and Irina. He endorses Sydney's efforts to talk to Elsa Caplan. When it's revealed that Elsa's a Russian agent, Jack clearly finds it difficult at first to see her as anything other than a second Irina – even going so far as to imprison her in Irina's old cell. Jack confronts her, saying he knows her and accuses her of prostituting herself for her country and speculates that she got pregnant by accident but felt it would redeem her. By the end, though, he's come to understand that Elsa isn't Irina and is genuinely motivated by love for her husband. He grants her defector status. He's furious with Vaughn for not keeping him informed about Sydney and snaps at him in a manner rather reminiscent of his comments to Danny in the first episode (see **Transcripts**). While he appreciates that Sydney and Vaughn succeeded in Spain, he warns her that he'll have her transferred if she goes behind his back again. Jack speaks fluent Russian and recognises that Elsa Caplan has a trace of a Ukrainian accent.

Michael Vaughn: Vaughn has a tattoo on his left bicep. Sydney still calls him 'Vaughn' in bed. Sydney says that he can use the middle drawer from now on, rather than bringing a backpack. This makes Weiss extremely jealous (see **Transcripts**). Sydney sends Vaughn a coded message and Jack is furious that he doesn't tell him about this. He orders him to keep him fully informed. When Vaughn keeps Jack in the dark about going to Spain, Weiss warns him that Jack is going to shoot him in the face. He takes the Caplans to Bambridge Island once Elsa has been granted defector status.

Irina Derevko: To demonstrate good will (!) Irina lets Caplan phone home. Elsa answers, but the phone is muted, so Neil can't talk to his wife (Irina neglects to mention that Sydney and Vaughn rescued Elsa and Aaron). Later, Caplan attacks her, choking her with his chain. Irina is caught out and, although she gets a kick in, she's probably only saved by Sloane, who shoots Caplan in the leg.

Arvin Sloane: Sloane is preoccupied with Emily's death. Irina is sympathetic, but practical – it's clear the CIA are on to them. Sloane isn't interested: he wants to see the satellite feeds from Tuscany and he wants to know who killed his wife. Irina tells him they are close to knowing what Rambaldi knew, but Sloane insists he wishes he'd never heard the man's name.

Sloane pushes a gun to Caplan's head and seems willing to pull the trigger. Irina reminds him that they need the code cracked and he says he doesn't care any more, but Irina manages to talk him down. He goes on to phone 'Francie', and asks her to use Will to get him the satellite feed from Tuscany. Sloane watches the footage and sees Dixon pull the trigger. He calls 'Francie' and tells her he needs something else. This, it transpires, is planting a car bomb under the Dixons' car.

Will Tippin: Will logs on to www.bouillabaisecentral.com using a CIA computer for 'Francie'. While he was in the shower – if *Alias* teaches us one thing, it's 'never have a shower at Sydney's place' – she placed a device in Will's phone to hack into any computer he's accessing.

Mr Sark: Caplan guesses that Sark is about 22 or 23. Sark says that he went to school in England at a very young age and became what he describes as prematurely ambitious. He says he wants what he never had.

Intelligence: When Sydney suggests Elsa is hypnotically regressed, she says she doesn't want the government snooping around her head. The Caplans received three calls, four months apart, always at the same time on Monday night, only lasting a minute. The CIA track this to Gregory Ivanov, an Itar-Tass journalist who's a known SVR (foreign intelligence) agent. They intercept a fax with one word: Razvyaska, which is the Russian for 'Endgame'. Elsa cries when she realises this – she's a Russian agent, sent seven years before to seduce Caplan. In 42 hours, Caplan will die when a cyanide capsule is released. Elsa knows that Sydney's mother was Irina Derevko (and speaks of her in the past tense). Presumably, 'Elsa' isn't her real name, but she's always referred to as such. Neil Caplan was recruited by the NSA six years before and has been keeping tabs on Elsa. Satellite surveillance of Sloane's base in Spain reveals five people inside. Downloading the genetic database should provide leads on Sloane and Irina. Marshall detects Sloane's accessing of 10Gb of satellite intelligence from Tuscany, after the event.

Office Politics: Marshall isn't happy with his parking place, which seems to be half a mile away from the office. The CIA have season tickets for the Lakers, four seats, twelve rows from the back.

Breaking the Code: The CIA agents following Sydney have the callsign 'Trailer', the CIA headquarters is 'Baseops'. Sydney sends Vaughn a coded message 'keep in mind I should use a slower roll'. Taking the first letters of the last six words, I-S-U-A-S-R and rearranging them, both Vaughn and Jack quickly determine that Sydney's going to Russia.

Plot Devices: Marshall has no idea how Irina's earrings picked up the morse signal, let alone where it was sent from. The genetic database has got ten million people's DNA information on it. It's encrypted with 8192 military-grade polymorphic encryption. Neil Caplan says he'll need a Cray supercomputer to crack the code. Caplan has a Russian pill in his left wrist that can be triggered to go off within 48 hours and release 15mg of cyanide (it's never explained why the Russians felt the need to build in a delay). It acts as a homing beacon, if you know its code and have the correct tracking device. Sydney has a watch that's got a built-in directional sound projector. This means she can send a message direct to Elsa when she's looking at the watch face and no one else can hear it. Francie has placed a device in Will's phone that means she can access a computer that he's accessing. She uses it to hack into the CIA network – but needs him to log on first. She uses a remote detonator to trigger the bomb in Diane's car – she's standing nearby.

Action: Sydney and Vaughn fight their way into Sloane's base in Spain, but Irina and Sloane aren't there. Vaughn goes after Sark, shooting at him.

Undercover: Sydney heads to a drugstore, buys Dalmatian-print wrapping paper, a blonde wig and tights and uses them to create a disguise based on the valley girls she passed on the way in. She claims to be a sigma gamma from West Virginia and joins them for their regular lunch date. In Russia she wears cartoonish cowgirl gear – a big black ten-gallon hat, waistcoat and breeches. She has long curly brown hair.

Trivia: The Caplans could be named after the Producer of the show, Sarah Caplan.

Music: 'Good Day' by Luce, 'Rain City' by Turin Brakes, 'Cannonball' by The Breeders and, 'Porushka-Paranya' by Baring Strait.

Injuries: Neil Caplan is shot in the leg, and needs a walking stick when he's reunited with his wife in Los Angeles.

The Big Picture: Sloane seems to have ordered the death of Dixon's wife, rather than Dixon himself. He says he no longer cares about the Rambaldi quest, but is that really the case?

Debrief: Neil Caplan's revelation that he's an NSA agent is perhaps a twist too far and is even more odd, because it's not necessary for the story. But Christian Slater puts in another great guest appearance in a role that really shouldn't be that memorable. The episode loses a little focus, starting out being about Dixon, then forgetting him until right at the end, but it's powerful stuff. Once again, *Alias* does its trademark: killing Diane Dixon is the most obvious course of revenge for Sloane to take, but it's genuinely shocking.

42
Countdown

Production: #E670

1st US Transmission: 27 April 2003
1st UK Transmission: 21 July 2003

Writer: Jeff Pinker (story by RP Gaborno)
Director: Lawrence Trilling
Guest Cast: Amanda Foreman (Carrie Bowman), Jonathan Banks (Brandon), Patricia Wettig (Barnett), Danny Trejo (Vargas), David Carradine (Conrad), Allen Evangelista (Jandu), James Carraway (Proteo Di Regno)

Briefing: Dixon holds a bomb over a man, and threatens to detonate it. He'll kill himself, but he has nothing to lose. Earlier, at Diane's funeral, Dixon is seen popping pills by Vaughn. A new Rambaldi prophecy has come to light – an apocalyptic event will happen in 48 hours. The CIA send Sydney and Dixon to follow the trail of a man named Di Regno, who is murdered and his heart stolen. It's not a real heart, it's just a Rambaldi device. Dixon gets increasingly violent as the mission progresses, worrying Sydney. They track the Di Regno heart to a shipyard in Colombia and storm it. They locate the device just as Rambaldi's apocalyptic deadline arrives – and nothing happens. Meanwhile, in Nepal, Sloane meets an old associate, Conrad, who hands him a new Rambaldi scroll that he promises will make his recent sacrifices worthwhile.
Mission: There's one overriding mission. Rambaldi has given a date that an unspecified apocalyptic event will occur – 48 hours after the CIA briefing. They are to prevent this event, whatever it might be. Although no one at the CIA realises it, they fail.

Sydney and Dixon are sent to investigate Di Regno. He'd already been identified by the CIA before he was murdered, so it's unclear if their mission was originally to make contact or whether they knew they'd be investigating the murder.

Having identified Vargas, they head to Guadalajara, his base of operations, and they get the information they need. This leads them to the Estrella shipyard. Sydney's mission is to secure one of the security posts to allow a Delta Force team in, then help them secure the Di Regno heart. If they fail, they're to destroy the shipyard. They secure the Di Regno heart and the apocalyptic event doesn't happen – apparently.

Destinations: Los Angeles (USA), Panama City (Panama), Guadlajara (Mexico), Nepal, Cartagena (Colombia).

Timescale: It's only a matter of days since Diane died and there are four days between her murder and Dixon going to Mexico. Rambaldi is from the fifteenth century.

Transcripts: Sloane: 'I'm taking leave. I want you to continue without me.' Sark: 'Sir, not to belittle your grief, but do not deny yourself the victory of a thirty-year pursuit.'

Dixon: 'If they find out I doctored my test I'll never work for the government again. How will I take care of my kids? Sydney, I don't know how to do this without Diane.'

Marcus Dixon: It is Diane's funeral, attended by Dixon's family (there are two young children, a boy and a girl who are both around ten), Sydney, Vaughn, Marshall and Jack. Dixon seems unfazed by seeing Di Regno's body with a hole where his heart should be. He does, however, apparently lose control when interrogating Vargas – so much so that Sydney shouts at him to stop. He goes to see Dr Barnett and insists it was a necessary level of force. He says he needs to be involved in the hunt for Sloane. He asks Sydney if she referred him to Barnett and believes her when she says she didn't.

He's worried about taking a drug test, as he has taken a painkiller, Vicodin. Although he's stopped now, it will show up in the test. When the test comes back, it's fine – Dixon has switched samples. Sydney goes to see him at home and he convinces her to cover for him. Once she has gone, he drives to a road bridge and climbs over the railing, clearly planning to kill himself.

In Colombia, his violent behaviour and his threat to detonate an explosive, killing himself and the suspect, leads Brandon (see **Office Politics**), Sydney and Vaughn to worry that he means it – but the countdown passes and it turns out Dixon deactivated the bomb. It was a tactic to get the information they needed.

Dixon later tells Sydney about climbing on to the bridge. He came down from it because he heard a baby crying – but it was only the branch of a tree. He realised then that he needed to be strong for his kids. He confesses to CIA personnel about switching the sample. Sydney admits she lied to Barnett and Vaughn, but she knows now she can rely on Dixon. It was Jack who recruited Dixon to SD-6.

Michael Vaughn: Vaughn sees Dixon popping pills at the funeral and tells Sydney. Although she isn't worried, he tells Dr Barnett. This angers Sydney, but he stands by his decision.

Sydney Bristow: Sydney sympathises with Dixon and doesn't find anything unusual about his desire to get back to work – it's what she did when Danny was killed. She is worried about Dixon's behaviour in Mexico, but she insists to Dr Barnett that she trusts him with her life and that he's one of the strongest people she knows. Sydney notices that Marshall is keen on Carrie Bowman (see **Office Politics**). Sydney speaks Spanish.

Jack Bristow: Jack does little except attend Diane's funeral and wait for Brandon's jurisdiction to expire.

Arvin Sloane: Sark has tracked down someone vital to Sloane and Irina's plan in Panama City. Sloane is distracted – he's killed the wrong person (Diane not Dixon). He tells Sark not to go in person, but to use someone else: Vargas. He then announces he's taking a leave of absence and he wishes Sark and Irina well. Sloane goes to Nepal. His sherpa (named in the credits, but not in dialogue, as Jandu) refuses to guide him over the north summit of the mountain, so he goes on alone and finds a monastery. He storms in, pushing his way past the monks to confront

Conrad, who sent him on the quest for Rambaldi artefacts. Conrad, somehow, knows that Emily has died. He takes out a scroll and says that thirty years ago he could only tell Sloane so much. He realises that Conrad knew then that Emily was going to die. Conrad says it was a necessary step on Sloane's journey and hands him the scroll – at precisely midnight, Eastern Standard Time. Sloane reads it and is shocked. Conrad tells him his journey has only just begun. Outside, there's a rumble of thunder. Sloane speaks Nepalese.

Irina Derevko: Irina is in Cyprus, inspecting a property they could use as a base now the Spanish facility has been lost. This is not shown.

Marshall Flinkman: It's love at first sight for Marshall, who falls for Carrie. He sees Carrie crying and offers her a handkerchief. It turns out she's crying at Joni Mitchell on her CD player, and she's a member of MENSA.

Marshall confesses that he's unnerved by the prophecy. He was brought up by 'inordinately empirical' agnostic parents, who forced him to wear a sweater when the temperature hit 52 degrees and taught him not to believe in Santa Claus or Tooth Fairies. But he's worried about the prophecy. Carrie checks he's not gay, then asks him out to sushi, if the world's still around in 36 hours.

Intelligence: Marshall copied the Rambaldi study of the human heart. He says it's as good as Da Vinci in his prime. However, there are mysterious squiggles on the page that, on closer inspection, are DNA sequences. Checking these against the genetic database they acquired, Marshall has discovered they are the DNA records of Proteo Di Regno, who lives in Panama City. Better than that, the DNA sequence is a code key that allows page 94 of the Rambaldi manuscript to be decoded. Page 94 lists times and dates of apocalyptic events: 7 September 1812 – Napoleon fights the Russians; 28 June 1914 – the assassination of Archduke Ferdinand; 6 August 1945 – Hiroshima. There's another date – 48 hours from now. Di Regno is murdered, his heart removed. He has the Rambaldi symbol < ○ > tattooed on his hand. A fingertip from a latex glove is discovered.

Marshall identifies the print on it as belonging to Emilio Vargas, a freelance assassin specialising in interrogation and 'wet work'. He's worked for the Russian mafia, the Triad and the Japanese Yakuza. Sydney and Dixon make contact, saying they were referred to him by Gurneyev, who was pleased with the work he did in Gdansk. Vargas tests them by saying the victim was Copertley, but Sydney corrects him – it was Janazik. Vargas revealed that he removed the man's eyes while keeping the optic nerve connected. Vargas reveals, under pressure, that Di Regno didn't have a heart, he had a 'machine'. Vargas has never heard of Sloane and was paid by wire transfer, but does know the Di Regno heart was heading for Colombia. CIA satellites track the truck moving the heart to the Estrella shipyard in Cartegena. Rambaldi said he had conquered tissue degeneration. As Marshall notes, there are two questions – what was keeping Di Regno alive and why does Sloane want it? Carrie Bowman notes that Di Regno was an art restorer and Hitler was a painter.

Office Politics: The National Security Agency have their own special section dealing with the Rambaldi issue. Two come to LA – Deputy Director Frederick Brandon and his associate Carrie Bowman, Special Projects. They take operational control of the LA operations centre until the time specified by the Rambaldi manuscript passes.

Breaking the Code: Page 94 of the Rambaldi manuscript is decoded: 94 is twice 47. In Colombia, the CIA use their regular Mountaineer/Basecamp/Boyscout callsigns. The Di Regno heart is in container 246 B.

Plot Devices: The Di Regno heart is apparently made of glass and filled with a glowing, golden liquid.

Action: Vargas is initially a match for both Sydney and Dixon when they fight. It's a brutal fight, with fists, knees and even swords flying. Sydney spins two small swords (the trademark move of Jennifer Garner's *Daredevil* character, Elektra), and breaks the handle of Vargas's sword. Then Dixon grabs him and hurts him so much even Vargas tells all. Sydney and Dixon are equally ruthless taking out security guards in Colombia.

Undercover: In Mexico, Sydney and Dixon pose as Triad members. Sydney wears a low-cut black dress with a pink petal print and Dixon wears a leather jacket.
Background Checks: Danny Trejo plays recurring characters in the *From Dusk Till Dawn* and *Spy Kids* franchises, and appeared in *xXx*. David Carradine was the star of 70s martial arts western series *Kung Fu*, and plays the eponymous character in Quentin Tarantino's *Kill Bill*.
Trivia: The wrestling club is called The Apocalypsis.
Music: 'Prayer' by Lizzie West, 'Mas' by Kinky and 'You're All I Need to Get By' by Aretha Franklin.
The Big Picture: What is the Di Regno heart and how does it fit into the larger Rambaldi mystery? What has Sloane learned and how will it lead to the apocalypse predicted by the prophecy?
Debrief: 'People that go there do not return the same.' Another balancing act, with a sensitive, realistic portrayal of grief in the Dixon plot and some almost absurd hi-jinks with Sloane and some Nepalese monks with prophecies of Armageddon. This is a great episode, one with over-the-top action but also genuine themes and parallels – both Dixon and Sloane have just lost their wives, and their reactions speak volumes about the sort of men they are.

43
Second Double

Production: #E671

1st US Transmission: 4 May 2003
1st UK Transmission: 28 July 2003

Writer: Crystal Nix Hines (story by Breen Frazier)
Director: Ken Olin
Guest Cast: Terry O'Quinn (Kendall), Michael Canavan (Special Agent McCain), Joel Swetow (Jens), Robert Joy (Hans Jurgens)

Briefing: Will is arrested by the CIA on suspicion of being the second Helix double. Sydney goes to Berlin to try to

clear his name and discover the true second double. Meanwhile, Will is transferred to Camp Harris, but Sark sends a team to extract him, to make him look guilty. Only Dixon and Will survive and Will escapes. Sydney is sent to a server farm in Marseilles to get conclusive proof Will is innocent, but Irina is waiting for her and wipes the database. 'Francie' picks up Will and whisks him away.
OMG: Sloane joins Jack for lunch.
Mission: Sydney and Vaughn are sent to Berlin to find out the identity of the second agent from Jurgens (see **Intelligence**), who doesn't know, but does know the information was on a server farm. They locate the server farm in Marseilles. Their mission is to secure the data. First of all, Sydney has to secure the kill switch that will wipe all the data. She fails – Irina is there and presses the switch.
Destinations: Los Angeles (USA), Berlin (Germany), Marseilles (France).
Timescale: It's a month since Jack manoeuvred Kendall out of operational control.
Transcripts: Jurgens: 'Please give me back my pants!'

Jack: 'You went behind my back.' Kendall: 'That's hardly unheard of in this office.'

Kendall: 'You know: we can help each other. We don't have to be adversaries.' Jack: 'I appreciate your magnanimity.' Kendall: 'Now you're just mocking me.' Jack: 'Yes.'
Will Tippin: Will's out jogging with Sydney when he's arrested by the CIA under suspicion of espionage in accordance with the Patriot Act (see **11,** 'The Confession'). He's arrested on Jack's authority and is suspected of being a Helix double. They knew that two people had been doubled. They know that two breaches of satellite security (in Panama and Tuscany) happened from Will's account and they found Provacillium in his car. He is given a medical scan to determine if he has the ocular scarring that Lennox reported, which he does. A digital recording of Sydney and Vaughn making love, see **36,** 'Double Agent' is found among his things. His fingerprint is found on a remote detonator. Sydney is sure that it's the genuine Will and he's being set up. She asks him about the night they

kissed but his hypnotic conditioning kicks in, and he's vague on the details. After Will escapes, he phones Sydney and is told he's on a CIA/FBI shoot-to-kill list. He tells her that he remembers research that Markovic had a 'farm' near Marseilles and speculates it's a server farm. He doesn't trust her ability to save him from the CIA, though. Instead he phones 'Francie', who picks him up.
Michael Vaughn: Vaughn and Sydney return from a debriefing feeling frisky – they spent the whole meeting thinking about each other. They mention the computer security breach. Vaughn didn't know Will and Sydney had kissed until she reminds Will of it.
'Francie Calfo': The bug in Vaughn's tie (**40,** 'Truth Takes Time') relays the conversation about the security breach to 'Francie', who contacts Sark. Irina orders him not to have Will killed. Instead she hypnotises Will to be evasive if he's asked personal questions. She also scars his eyeball, to make him look like a Helix double, see **36,** 'Double Agent'. When questioned by Sydney, Francie says that Will's not been himself since he went to see his parents in Chicago (**35,** 'Phase One'). Sydney tells her she works for the CIA. On Sark's order, Francie arranges a team to extract Will as he's being transferred to Camp Harris – then to kill him.
Sydney Bristow: At the sex club, Sydney ties up a grateful Jurgens – then Vaughn arrives and takes photos of the two of them together. They threaten to email Alba, Jurgens's wife, unless he reveals the identity of the second double. He doesn't know, but he does know that the data is stored in a server farm. The thing that would distress Sydney most if Will was a double is that it would mean the real Will would most probably be dead. Sydney speaks German.
Marcus Dixon: Whoever passed the satellite feed of Tuscany to Sloane caused Diane's death and this isn't lost on Dixon. He shows Will the pictures of Diane's charred corpse and explains that's why they couldn't have an open casket at the funeral. He hopes 'Will' faces the death penalty. When he protests his innocence, but can't remember when he first met Dixon, he grabs him by the throat.
Jack Bristow: Jack tells Sydney that she needs to question

Francie about Will's behaviour. He authorises her to tell her what she deems necessary. He discovers that the fingerprint was placed on the remote detonator – evidence that he has been framed, but not enough for the CIA. He authorises Sydney to go to the server farm in Marseilles. She notes that he'll get in trouble, but Jack tells her that he's not cut out for management. Jack goes to lunch and is rather surprised to be joined by . . .

Arvin Sloane: Sloane says he's missed Jack's poker face and confirms his suspicions that there are two snipers watching their every move. He says he forgives Jack for betraying him and asks when their friendship ended. Jack says that it was when he recruited Sydney to SD-6 without consulting him. Sloane says that if he'd known, he'd have done things differently, and asks Jack to come back to their partnership. He offers to tell him everything about Rambaldi, but Jack reminds him that he's not interested in Rambaldi. Sloane tells him that he no longer collects the artefacts as a window on the past and that he is one move away from proving it is more than that. Sydney won't be a pawn in the venture. Jack tells him that they won't work together again, but Sloane says they will, and sooner than he thinks. He leaves, warning Jack not to move or phone anyone for half-an-hour.

Irina Derevko: Irina has a contact who will tell her where the NSA store the Rambaldi artefacts. She gets the blueprints but, without a time-synchronised keycard, the plans are useless. Sark suggests that Sydney will give them the key in return for proof of Will's innocence. She's waiting for Sydney in Marseilles and makes the offer. She kills the head guard by slashing his throat, then throws the kill switch, wiping the data, but she's made a copy and will give Sydney a copy in return for a favour.

Intelligence: There is an NSA facility where they keep the Rambaldi artefacts. (These presumably include the ones recovered in the series so far. This isn't specified but, if so, it would include the neutron radiation weapon, see **38,** 'Firebomb', amongst other items.) Will was working on finding the second double and one lead is Hans Jurgens, head of Miracorp, the company that built the imaging software for Helix. He tells them, when coerced, that the information is on a server farm, but he doesn't know where. The CIA hunt for the server farm, finding it in Marseilles when Will suggests it to Sydney.

Office Politics: Will has passed the upper-level analyst test and as the person in that job, Roberts, is due for retirement, he may be in line for his job.

Kendall wants to send Will to Camp Harris for 'unrestricted interrogation' – Sydney calls it torture. The Department of Justice override Jack and agree to transfer Will to Camp Harris. Kendall assigns Dixon to escort him before he tells Jack. When Jack finds out, he speculates that Kendall is annoyed now he has his parking space.

Breaking the Code: The numberplate of Francie's car is 21BA333 (it's a blue Ford Focus). In Marseilles, Sydney and Vaughn use their 'Mountaineer' and 'Boyscout' callsigns.

Plot Devices: Provacillium is a medication taken by gene-therapy patients to keep the body from rejecting DNA mutations. The head guard at the server farm has a 'kill switch' on his wrist that, when pressed, wipes all the information on the servers. Sydney has a laser cutter to get past the fence of the server farm compound. She carries a crossbow which fires a grappling hook and her pistol has a silencer. Irina carries a cattle prod in Marseilles.

Action: Will's prison escort is attacked on Roosevelt Road, with a number of armoured vans forcing the prison van off the road and a sniper picking off agents who emerge. What follows is a bloodbath – five CIA agents and at least four mercenaries die, with Dixon killing the sniper and Will killing two mercenaries with a shotgun.

Undercover: Sydney goes to Berlin in a leather coat. When they infiltrate the sex club, Sydney changes to a red leather skirt and corset top. She wears a choker, carries a whip and has wild black hair. In Marseilles, Vaughn plays a drunk American tourist in an Hawaiian shirt soaked in champagne, who distracts the guards while Sydney gets past them. She wears full combat gear for the mission.

Reality Checks: The bug 'Francie' places in Vaughn's tie is problematic. For a start, it doesn't seem to listen in to the debriefing about the computer security breach, just when Sydney and Vaughn talk about it later. That's fair enough – perhaps it's only got a short range. It's odd that the CIA can't detect it – again, though, it may be specifically designed so they can't. It's not a particularly reliable place to put a bug – presumably Vaughn has quite a few ties. The main problem, though, is that, if it's ever found, it'll be blindingly obvious Francie planted it: she handed the tie to Vaughn, in full view of Sydney and Will.

Music: 'Speechless' by Macy Gray, 'I Wanna MMM' by The Lawyer and 'Corps a Corps' by Glendooz.

Trivia: In the USA, **43**, 'Second Double', was broadcast on the same night as **44**, 'The Telling', with the two episodes edited together with one set of opening credits.

Injuries: Sydney is attacked by Irina, who shocks her repeatedly with a cattleprod.

The Big Picture: Sydney owes Irina a favour, now, and she doesn't want Will to die. This can't be a good combination but the big question is Sloane. Last week he was nervous and wanting to quit – now he's read a new Rambaldi prophecy and he's supremely confident and sure Jack will join him. What on earth does he know?

Debrief: 'Syd . . . I swear it's me.' A number of plotlines start paying off in an episode that's a Kafkaesque nightmare for Will, but extremely amusing and entertaining for the audience. For once, instead of the rumour and misinformation, the evidence against Will is physical and right in front of everyone's eyes. Sydney trusts her friend, though. For the first time in a while, this episode is an ensemble piece, with everyone getting something signficant to do. Great stuff.

44
The Telling

Production: #E672

1st US Transmission: 4 May 2003
1st UK Transmission: 4 August 2003

Writer: JJ Abrams
Director: JJ Abrams
Guest Cast: Terry O'Quinn (Kendall), Amanda Foreman (Carrie), Jonathan Banks (Brandon), Greg Grunberg (Agent Eric Weiss)

Briefing: Irina gives the CIA vital information: she emails the DNA record of the second double to Marshall and she meets Sydney to tell her about Sloane's warehouse in Zurich and to explain what her plan has been all this time. Sydney leads a team to Zurich, but Sloane has already moved the artefacts. He captures Jack and the Di Regno heart and starts building the most powerful Rambaldi device yet, 'the Telling'. After capturing Sark in Sweden, the CIA home in on Sloane in Mexico City. They raid his base, an office block.

Sloane escapes with 'the Telling'. Irina also gets away. Returning home, Sydney confronts 'Francie', who has attacked Will. After a long and brutal fight, Sydney kills her, then collapses. She wakes up in Hong Kong, with no idea of how she got there. She contacts the CIA, who send Vaughn. He is wearing a wedding ring and tells Sydney she's been missing for almost two years.

OMG: Two years!

Mission: Sydney leads a team to Zurich to recover the Rambaldi artefacts, but Sloane is one step ahead of them. Sydney and Vaughn go to Stockholm to capture Sark and succeed. She leads another team to Mexico City. Jack is rescued, but Sloane gets away.

Destinations: Los Angeles (USA), Zurich (Switzerland), Stockholm (Sweden), Mexico City (Mexico).

Timescale: Sloane raided the NSA warehouse containing the Rambaldi artefacts one month after Irina signalled him in **33,** 'A Higher Echelon'. This would be the same week as episode **36,** 'Double Agent', which (by accident or design) didn't feature Sloane.

Transcripts: Marshall: 'We're verifying the data now, sir, but it looks legit. Legitimate.' Kendall: 'Yeah, I know what legit means.'

Sydney: 'How stupid are you to think I would ever believe you again?' Irina: 'Ultimately, you will do what you want. That's what free will's all about.'

Sydney: 'What are you talking about? Vaughn, why are you wearing that ring?' Vaughn: 'Syd, since that night . . . you were missing. You've been missing for almost two years.'

'Francie Calfo': Allison Doren was thought to have died in a bus crash her parents were told she had been burned beyond recognition. However, she's the second double. She and Sark kiss, and they seem fond of each other. Sark only now gets round to telling her that the Helix machine has been destroyed, when it happened months ago. He seems threatened by Will and the prospects that she's falling for him. She needs a regular supply of Provacillium or she gets feverish. She cries when she stabs Will, but has recovered shortly afterwards when Sydney returns. She accepts Sydney's offer of coffee ice cream, but the real Francie doesn't like coffee ice cream.

Will Tippin: Will and Francie are holed up in a motel and when 'Francie' mentions Jack, he gets suspicious, but she quickly assures him he'd mentioned him before. Francie goes into the bathroom to prepare some poison but before she can use it the CIA raid their room. Will is tested, but there's no Provacillium in his blood, so he's cleared. The CIA assign a therapist to help with the memory regression. He checks the bathroom cabinet for aspirin and finds Provacillium. He phones Sydney to warn her that Francie is the double, then 'Francie' attacks him, strangling, stabbing and (apparently) killing him.

Arvin Sloane: Sloane has all the pieces he needs to construct 'il dire', a particularly powerful Rambaldi artefact. He captures Jack, keeping him alive, he says, because they're friends. He believes that they are on the verge of great change and that he will instigate it.

Jack Bristow: Jack says he feels sorry for Sloane, who he thinks is using Rambaldi to fill a void in his life.

Marcus Dixon: Dixon is the agent who gets to Jack first and rescues him in Mexico City.

Michael Vaughn: Vaughn decides to go ahead and book a weekend in Santa Monica for him and Sydney.

Weiss: Harry Houdini was Eric Weiss's great-great-great-uncle. Weiss once thought about becoming a professional magician. He speaks German.

Marshall Flinkman: Carrie and Marshall went for their sushi date, but Marshall got very flustered and sweaty when he was going to kiss her. He asks Weiss, of all people, for help. Marshall goes to Zurich to assess the Rambaldi artefacts and persuades Jack to send Carrie along with him. Carrie hated Brandon, so feels particularly guilty when he's shot and killed in the ambush.

Irina Derevko: Irina is at the ice rink Sydney goes to. She wants a favour. She planned to betray the CIA, not Sydney. She now, apparently, wants to double-cross Sloane and let the CIA get the Rambaldi artefacts from Sloane's warehouse in Zurich. Irina then apologises and knocks Sydney out. This seems confusing. In the last episode, Irina wanted access to the NSA warehouse 'where they keep the Rambaldi artefacts'. Here, she knows that Sloane raided it months ago, and says the plan was to 'take down the Alliance and raid the CIA, *all at once*', so why did she need the blueprints last week? Has Sloane's abrupt departure, or the death of Emily, left her worried about his motives? It seems likely that she's been contacted by him since he returned from Nepal. He seems to have told her what he's planning (as he offered to tell Jack), and it's worried her. As ever, Irina's motives are unknown. Sydney speculates that it is a valid attempt to attack Sloane. Jack suggests she's feeling guilty and that they send a team to Zurich. Irina swears to Sydney that she didn't know that Sloane was going to move the artefacts in Zurich. He somehow knew she was going to double-cross him. Irina goes to Mexico City and is in Sloane's warehouse when the CIA team arrive. She's chased by Sydney on to the rooftop of the building, but jumps off, using a line and a grappling hook to get back into the building on the eighteenth or nineteenth floor. Weiss gives chase, but to no avail.

Sydney Bristow: Sydney has a busy couple of days – then a quiet couple of years. After her fight with Francie, she wakes up in an alley in Hong Kong with no memory of how she got there. She calls Kendall, who sends Vaughn to meet her. She's been missing for almost two years.

Intelligence: The CIA had 24 Rambaldi artefacts in an NSA facility in Nevada, Sloane has 23 in his warehouse at 266 Kroner Strasse in Zurich. Irina contacted Sloane, via Sark, in Japan, see **29,** 'The Counteragent' and proposed teaming up to take down the Alliance and raid the CIA's Rambaldi artefacts. Sloane has all 47 artefacts, following a raid on the NSA facility a month ago. Brandon didn't mention this to Kendall or Jack, to their astonishment.

Sloane doesn't have the Di Regno heart. Jack and Brandon agree to move it to Evans airforce base. Sydney and a team will go to Zurich to secure the artefacts in Sloane's possession and bring them back to Evans. In Zurich, though, they discover that the crates are full of ordinary domestic appliances – Sloane knew they were coming and has already moved the artefacts out. While that happens, Jack's convoy is attacked. Brandon is killed and Jack and the Di Regno heart are captured.

Irina tells Sydney that Sark will be at the Vel Smokander club in Stockholm the following night. Vaughn and Sydney apprehend him and Sark says he's happy to talk, as his loyalties are flexible.

Irina suggests that Sloane believes he's been chosen to realise the word of Rambaldi. She says that Sydney has also been chosen and that it's Sydney in the prophecy, not her. Only Sydney can stop Sloane.

Irina sends the CIA a DNA record of the second double. The CIA need to get Will in to check against it (it's surprising that they didn't take a DNA sample when they had him in custody before). The name on the DNA sample was AG Doren. Will remembers the name from somewhere. It was on the Project Christmas list. There were twenty people who attended the Project Christmas summer camp. As Will scrolls through the list, there are fifteen names: Douglas W Axtell, Matthew Wayne Brewer, Karen A Bartek, Diana Lynn Brown, Jennifer Beth Crary, Peter James Dacey, Ryan Robert Ferro, Chris Godfrey, Tricia Kay Goken, Harmony Leigh Gosbee, Allison Georgia Doren, Duane E Journey, Ross Frank Judd, Michael Allen Martinez, Mark A Rohmer and Benjamin Xavier Spek.

Office Politics: Kendall, perhaps predictably, wants to send Sark straight to Camp Harris.
Breaking the Code: Sloane has 24 Rambaldi artefacts, the American authorities have 23 (you do the maths!). This is 'classic Rambaldi'. The code for Sark's Mexico City base's security system is 11566. Sydney is officer 2300844 and her confirmation code is 'looking glass'.
Plot Devices: Sloane tells Jack that he is assembling a Rambaldi machine, 'il dire', which he translates as 'the Telling'. It has 47 pieces, including the Di Regno heart, and only takes a day or so to assemble. He doesn't explain what it actually *does*. There are power surges and rattles from the next room as it's tested. It's portable and, whatever it is, when the CIA tactical team arrive, Sloane prefers to leave with it, rather than use it.
Action: At the hockey rink, Sydney lunges for her mother with a hockey stick, but she easily parries and knocks her over. In Mexico City, there's a lengthy chase and gun battle as the CIA fight Sloane's men and Sydney goes after Irina. The best fight, though, is Sydney versus the fake Francie, in their apartment. This is a brutal business, as they work their way around, systematically breaking every piece of glass and using household items as weapons (the rubber chopping board makes a brief appearance – see **19,** 'Snowman' and **35,** 'Phase One'). After they've exhausted every knife, vase and window, Sydney grabs a gun and shoots Francie three times before collapsing.
Undercover: In Stockholm, Sydney wears a blonde wig and a very small black dress, which has a very short hemline and is low cut with halter top, so it's backless.
Reality Checks: Harry Houdini's real name was Erich Weiss.
Trivia: The working title of the episode was 'Inconnu'.
Music: 'Bleed to Love Her' by Fleetwood Mac. The incidental music as Francie and Sydney fight their way around – and smash up – their apartment is reminiscent of the music from the *Tom and Jerry* cartoons and may be a deliberate pastiche.
Injuries: Sydney is knocked out by Irina and has a big bruise on her forehead. Vaughn smashes Sark's face into a

table a couple of times, cutting him and giving him a nosebleed. Will is, apparently, killed. He's strangled then stabbed by Francie who dumps his body in the bathtub (why would she leave him alive?). However, two years later Vaughn says he's fine. Sydney and Francie punch, kick, stab and smash each other and both end up cut and bloodied. Sydney shoots Francie three times – in the arm, then once on each shoulder. The implication is that Francie's killed. When Sydney wakes up in Hong Kong, she has a mysterious, healed-over, scar on her stomach (she doesn't seem to get it in the fight with Francie).

The Big Picture: Why would Irina go to all the trouble of helping Sloane to get the Rambaldi artefacts only to turn on him? Why did she apparently not know about the raid on the NSA facility, when she proposed it in the first place? What on earth is 'the Telling'? The big question, of course, is is it really two years? And, if so, just what has happened in that time? Sloane reading the scroll was meant to herald an event as devastating as the First World War and the first atomic bombing. Is *Alias* now set in the aftermath of the apocalypse?

Debrief: 'There's a change coming, Jack. Something even I couldn't imagine'. As the great Keanu Reeves himself would put it: Whoa! An episode that pulls together all the plot threads of the series and demonstrates that the writers knew what they were doing all along (or are extremely good at winging it). This clears the decks for an apocalyptic finale – but the show's smarter than that. The final scenes are beautifully made – shot as if they're under water, with Sydney confused and disorientated. When Vaughn arrives, it's even more clear that something's gone very, very wrong. The revelation that we've just skipped two years is yet another breathtaking moment. The makers insist that it's not a trick – the third season takes place two years after the second. Either way, they're on a roll and taking the most risks any successful show has ever made.

Alias: The Future

At time of going to press, the first hints about the third season of *Alias* have been released. The season cliffhanger wasn't a trick – things really have moved on by two years and Vaughn really is married. Here are some of the rumours and reports:

The CIA are led to believe that **Sydney's** disappearance was masterminded by a mysterious new organisation, the Covenant. She gets an apartment with Weiss. During her two years away, of which she has no recollection, she had a relationship with an assassin played by Justin Theroux (from *Six Feet Under* as well as the movies *Charlie's Angels: Full Throttle* and *Mulholland Drive*). The scar she got is significant to the plot.

Vaughn married Lauren Reed, a British diplomat. Lauren is played by Australian actress Melissa George, who is best known as Angel in *Home and Away* and who's made small but memorable appearances in movies such as *Dark City* and *The Limey*. Sydney attacks Vaughn when she discovers the truth, but Lauren and Vaughn are going to stay married for the foreseeable future. In **44,** 'The Telling', Vaughn said he came 'back' to contact Sydney and, as the third season begins, he has left the CIA.

Jack Bristow is no longer with the CIA. If he believes Sydney to be dead, then what's motivated him for the last two years?

Sloane lives in Zurich and is now claiming to be one of the good guys. It's unclear whether Sark will return (he was in CIA custody the last we knew), or what the consequences of Sloane gaining control of Il Dire are.

Dixon, however, is the new director of the organisation. (Kendall still works there, though – his voice was heard in 'The Telling').

Irina will return, but it's unclear in how many episodes or in what capacity.

Both '**Francie**' and **Will** survived (Vaughn said Will survived, but not how, in 'The Telling') – but neither will be regular characters in the third season.
Marshall is going to become a dad!

The end of the first episode of the third season is meant to reveal another major change to the status quo. The promotional posters for the season ask us to 'Expect the Unexpected'. For most shows, that would be a cliché – for *Alias* fans, it's become a way of life. Whatever the third season brings, it's going to be a hell of a ride.

The Webgame

Most television shows these days set up an official website. *Alias* planned a 'web presence' in this way, but didn't have the money to design an elaborate site. Instead, in keeping with the covert nature of SD-6 and the show's version of the CIA, a number of sites were set up that linked to each other and that weren't publicised. This was designed, at first, by Eric Scott of the company Day for Night, with Technical Consultant Rick Orci and Jesse Alexander, one of the series supervising producers, helping with the content.

Season One
Sydney Bristow's email address was given on the character listings on the official ABC site. It was sydney.bristow@creditdauphine.com. From this, you could extrapolate that Credit Dauphine, the bank she tells the world she works for, has its own website. People who looked up *www.creditdauphine.com* found a small, if functional, website for the bank. There were a couple of links from this – one led to a search engine *www.find-whatever.com*, which led (if you entered the Rambaldi symbol < ○ >) to a site about Rambaldi, *www.followersoframbaldi.org*. There was also a site for Jennings Aerospace, *www.jenningsaerospace.com*. Elsewhere on the Credit Dauphine site was a fake message board where Anna Espinosa left a message. There was also the chance to apply for a loan or to contact a member of staff. If you did either, you started receiving emails from the bank and, depending on how you replied to them, you could get involved in an elaborate series of emails.

The beauty of the game was that the messages you received were often tangential or from new contacts. This meant that players found themselves wondering if every piece of spam they'd been sent was actually part of the game. Online fora sprang up to discuss the various clues and codes. Usually, a phrase or code from the most recent televised episode opened up a new section.

The reward for playing the game – apart from the satisfaction of working out the correct response from the clues given – were pieces of information about the fictional world of the show, including pages of Rambaldi manuscripts. It also introduced players to skills such as steganography (finding hidden images and files). It led to a final quiz, and perceptive – indeed, superhumanly perceptive – players had picked up the answers along the way. One answer required the complete run of highlighted letters from the location captions for the whole of series one: (sanidrnagoeslowdsaxioauvnvesrggeewteoogrle), giving some idea of the level of attention the creators of the puzzle were demanding.

The game proved popular, even if it wasn't always clear which sites were part of the game, and which weren't – there were plenty of red herrings.

Season Two

For the second season, a more straightforward – or at least more structured – game involving a 'chatbot' of CIA Agent Eric Weiss was set up. If you emailed Weiss saying 'I want to join the CIA', you would get a reply, and then you could correspond, with what he said depending on what you asked him.

Some of these replies were fun – if you typed in 'Star Trek', you'd get the reply 'You are a nerd'. But there was also a running game, one where you supplied some information, and got asked to supply some more. Planted messages started appearing on a couple of ABC message boards. Weiss would sometimes ask questions, and the game required you to find the codeword that led to the next stage – so, when he asked, 'What goes good with Bruschetta or makes a good salad dressing?', and you typed 'Vinegar', you were rewarded with a bit of news from the CIA. As you progressed through the game, you came nearer to your goal of being recruited by the CIA as an analyst. Once again, putting in names from the series –

anything from the basics, like 'Sydney' and 'Sloane' through to the names of more obscure characters would generate some kind of response.

At the time of writing, it's unclear if the second series game is over. But the webgame has become something of an *Alias* tradition, and no doubt there will be a new game in time for the third season.

The Prequel Novels

#1	*Recruited*	Lynn Mason
#2	*A Secret Life*	Laura Peyton Roberts
#3	*Disappeared*	Lynn Mason
#4	*Sister Spy*	Laura Peyton Roberts
#5	*The Pursuit*	Lizzie Skurnick
#6	*Close Quarters*	Emma Harrison
#7	*Father Figure*	Laura Peyton Roberts

Rather than take a conventional route of publishing spin-off novels set within the series' run, or simply novelising some of the episodes, publishers Random House have instead opted for a new tack. The *Alias* novels are prequels, short spy novels set several years before the events of episode **1**, 'Truth Be Told'. At the time of writing, only the first four are available, and follow Sydney through her recruitment, training and first few missions with SD-6. As such, the novels both fill in a great deal of background to Sydney's life, and weave themselves around the histories of the characters as explained on the show. *Recruited*, in particular, dances around the description of Sydney's recruitment, see **17**, 'Q and A'.

As prequels, the novels don't feature the full complement of characters. The CIA are obviously absent and Jack is still a distant figure, while Sydney has yet to meet most of her SD-6 colleagues. However, Sloane does appear briefly (albeit in a scene largely taken from episode **17**, 'Q and A'), while Sydney already has Francie as her college roommate. Most prominent of all is Noah Hicks, Sydney's fellow agent and one-time lover who she meets again, see **18**, 'Masquerade'. Hicks is exactly as portrayed by Peter Berg, and acts a heroic lead and influence on this younger, more naïve Sydney.

It's that naivety which marks the prequels as a separate entity to the TV series. This Sydney is younger, innocent to the point of idiocy. She drifts through these early adventures in a state of adolescent disarray, constantly gawping at the espionage world around her. She's impulsive, untested, and not really the same character as the Sydney Bristow we're introduced to in the show. The books reflect the relative innocence of this younger Sydney – they're straightforward spy adventures suitable for a young audience, the female lead constantly swooning over the dreamy Hicks. Adult readers may find these more teen-friendly adventures rather tiresome, although there's a wry amusement to be had from the various ironies of the format – the readers know what SD-6 *really* is, as well as the truth about Hicks, Jack and the late Laura Bristow.

Books #5 to #7, unpublished at the time of writing, seem to take a different tack. *The Pursuit* is a Vaughn novel and it's easy to see how *Alias*'s other straightforward hero will fit into these books. More Vaughn is a good thing, and the title for *Close Quarters*, along with the photo cover, implies parallel plot strands with both Vaughn and Sydney before they met. *Father Figure* is a far dodgier prospect, focusing as it does on Jack, who is one of the most enigmatic and fascinating characters in the series, and any kind of insight into his thinking could prove fatal to his mystique. Furthermore, it's hard to see how Jack – a character who tortures people with a blowtorch in the line of duty, a master manipulator fully aware of the corruption around him – will fit with the more naïve world of the prequel novels.

The books are an interesting oddity and currently the only fictional spin-offs from the television series. A comic book, scripted by JJ Abrams, was promised from Arcade Comics some time ago, while a computer game featuring the series cast and script by the writers is also in the works, but until then the prequel novels are the only option for the chronically *Alias* addicted.

Also available from Virgin:

THE BOND FILES

AN UNOFFICIAL GUIDE TO THE WORLD'S GREATEST SECRET AGENT

Andy Lane and Paul Simpson

- When did Bond discover R taking a shower?
- How long did it take before 001 finally showed up in Bond's universe?
- In which film was Oliver Reed originally intended to play James Bond?

James Bond is a global franchise and world-famous icon, not only on the silver screen, but on television, in comics, novels and even games. This completely revised and updated edition of the bestselling companion to the legendary 007 brings you the hidden facts – from the sublime to the ridiculous, from the best known to the most obscure.

'Leagues ahead of its rivals in that it's simply crammed with mouthwatering facts and trivia'

Film Review

'[The] ultimate guide'

DreamWatch

ISBN 0 7535 0712 9

CSI: THE FILES

AN UNOFFICIAL AND UNAUTHORISED GUIDE TO THE HIT CRIME SCENE INVESTIGATION SHOWS

Paul Simpson

CSI: Crime Scene Investigation and its spin-off show *CSI: Miami* combine the traditional cop show with technology and glossy production values to create two gripping series, based in Las Vegas and Miami, that have become worldwide hits. Only the Crime Scene Investigation team can answer the vital questions about a crime by studying the forensic clues left behind at the scene. What can maggots on a body tell us about the time of death? Does an earprint work in the same way as a fingerprint?

CSI: The Files encompasses every episode of the first three seasons of the original show and the first season of the spin-off, covering each episode in turn in accessible sections. It also covers the real-life cases and techniques on which the show is based.

ISBN 0 7535 0846 X

SLAYER

Keith Topping

With its literal representation of teenage horrors, *Buffy the Vampire Slayer* touches on a universal truth. In his bestselling unofficial guides to the surreal world of Sunnydale, Keith Topping analyses each episode of the show, presenting the highlights in categories such as: **A Little Learning is a Dangerous Thing**, **I Just *Love* Your Accent** and **Denial, Thy Name is Joyce**. He unearths pop culture references and soundtrack information and draws attention to the times logic flies out of the window, along with sections on the original feature film, the novels and the websites.

'Topping's terrific tome adopts the perfect attitude to this fizzing phenomenon . . . He rattles through each episode with focus on teen-angst metaphors, the brilliant feminist subtexts, and the dazzling use of "valley speak" . . . Colour me stunned'

Uncut

Seasons 1–5 **ISBN 0 7535 0631 9**
Season 6 **ISBN 0 7535 0738 2**

HOLLYWOOD VAMPIRE

AN EXPANDED AND UPDATED UNAUTHORISED AND UNOFFICIAL GUIDE TO *ANGEL*

Keith Topping

In order to atone for his sins, Angel now fights for humanity in the dark, seedy underworld of the superficially glamorous city of LA. In *Hollywood Vampire* Keith Topping explores the world of Angel, Cordelia, Wesley, Gunn, Fred and Lorne as they fight their own personal demons and the loneliness of the Big City in their search for redemption. This essential unofficial fan bible covers the show episode by episode, encompassing the highlights in categories such as: **Dreaming (As *Buffy* Often Proves) Is Free**; **The Charisma Show**; **There's a Ghost in My House** and **Sex and Drugs and Rock'n'Roll**. It also focuses on the shared history of *Angel* and *Buffy*, the novels and the websites, draws attention to logic flaws and points out numerous pop-culture references.

'The best episode guide there is . . . a must'
Fortean Times

ISBN 0 7535 0807 9

INSIDE BARTLET'S WHITE HOUSE

AN UNOFFICIAL AND UNAUTHORISED GUIDE TO *THE WEST WING*

Keith Topping

The West Wing has been one of the most talked-about and critically acclaimed series in the UK and in the US it is NBC's biggest hit drama show in years. *Inside Bartlet's White House* is an unofficial and essential guide to the show, diving deep into the world of American politics and searching for the truth and integrity behind the Bartlet administration.

Now updated to encompass Season Three and part of Season Four, covering the highlights of the episodes in categories such as **American History X, Sex and Drugs and Rock'n'Roll, A View from the Hill** and **Logic, Let Me Introduce You to This Window**, it is an essential look at the complex and fascinating world of the White House and the most powerful man in the world.

ISBN 0 7535 0828 1